Applied Econometrics Association Series

General Editors: **Jean H. P. Paelinck**, Emeritus Professor, Erasmus University, Rotterdam, and **Henri Serbat**, Chamber of Commerce, Paris

The vital importance of econometrics for understanding economic phenomena is increasingly recognised in every field of economics.

The discipline is based on 'scientific processes which aim to identify, explain and forecast economic phenomena using formalised tools to produce, measure, structure and model the information' (Gerard Duru and Henri Serbat, 1991).

The Applied Econometrics Association, established in 1974, seeks to develop the use of econometric tools by producing regular updates on the state of the art and the progress made in each specific field, and so to further the transformation of unconnected facts into pertinent information for use in analysis and decision-making.

The series was conceived to form a set of working references for advanced students and researchers in each specific field, as well as a guide to development across the discipline more broadly.

This exchange of knowledge will be continued permanently by the opening of a debate-site on the Internet [http://www.lyonl.fr/aea].

Titles include:

Françoise Bourdon and Jean Bourdon (*editors*)
WAGE ECONOMETRICS AND MODELLING

Fabrizio Carlevaro and Jean-Baptiste Lesourt (*editors*)
MEASURING AND ACCOUNTING ENVIRONMENTAL NUISANCES AND SERVICES

Arthur Getis, Jesús Mur and Henry G. Zoller (*editors*)
SPATIAL ECONOMETRICS AND SPATIAL STATISTICS

Siv S. Gustafsson and Danièle E. Meulders (*editors*)
GENDER AND THE LABOUR MARKET
Econometric Evidence of Obstacles to Achieve Gender Equality

Hans Heijke and Joan Muysken (*editors*)
EDUCATION AND TRAINING IN A KNOWLEDGE-BASED ECONOMY

Pavlos Karadeloglou (*editor*)
EXCHANGE-RATE POLICY IN EUROPE

Sandrine Lardic and Valérie Mignon (*editors*)
RECENT DEVELOPMENTS ON EXCHANGE RATES

Danièle Meulders, Robert Plasman and François Rycx (*editors*)
MINIMUM WAGES, LOW PAY AND UNEMPLOYMENT

Emile Quinet and Roger Vickerman (*editors*)
THE ECONOMETRICS OF MAJOR TRANSPORT INFRASTRUCTURES

Philippe Thalmann and Milad Zarin-Nejadan (*editors*)
CONSTRUCTION AND REAL ESTATE DYNAMICS

Applied Econometrics Association
Series Standing Order ISBN 0–333–71460–1
(*outside North America only*)

You can receive future titles in this series as they are published by placing a standing order. Please contact your bookseller or, in case of difficulty, write to us at the address below with your name and address, the title of the series and the ISBN quoted above.

Customer Services Department, Macmillan Distribution Ltd, Houndmills, Basingstoke, Hampshire RG21 6XS, England

Minimum Wages, Low Pay and Unemployment

Edited by

Danièle Meulders

Robert Plasman

and

François Rycx

palgrave
macmillan

First published 2004 by
PALGRAVE MACMILLAN
Houndmills, Basingstoke, Hampshire RG21 6XS and
175 Fifth Avenue, New York, N.Y. 10010
Companies and representatives throughout the world

PALGRAVE MACMILLAN is the global academic imprint of the Palgrave Macmillan division of St. Martin's Press, LLC and of Palgrave Macmillan Ltd. Macmillan® is a registered trademark in the United States, United Kingdom and other countries. Palgrave is a registered trademark in the European Union and other countries.

ISBN 1–4039–3642–0

This book is printed on paper suitable for recycling and made from fully managed and sustained forest sources.

A catalogue record for this book is available from the British Library.

Library of Congress Cataloging-in-Publication Data
Applied Econometrics Association. International Conference.
Minimum wages, low pay and unemployment / edited by Danièle Meulders, Robert Plasman and François Rycx.
p. cm. – (Applied Econometrics Association series)
Papers from the 79th Applied Econometrics Association Conference discussion on the "Econometrics of Wages".
Includes bibliographical references and index.
ISBN 1–4039–3642–0 (cloth)
1. Minimum wage – Europe – Econometric models – Congresses. 2. Wage differentials – Europe – Econometric models – Congresses. 3. Job satisfaction – Europe – Econometric models – Congresses. 4. Unemployment – Europe – Econometric models – Congresses. 5. Wages – Effect of wages on – Europe – Econometric models – Congresses. 6. Wages – Econometric models – Congresses. I. Meulders, Danièle. II. Plasman, Robert. III. Rycx, François, 1974– IV. Title. V. Series.

HD4920.5.A66 2004
331.2'2'015195—dc22 2003066148

10 9 8 7 6 5 4 3 2 1
13 12 11 10 09 08 07 06 05 04

Printed and bound in Great Britain by
Antony Rowe Ltd, Chippenham and Eastbourne

Contents

List of Tables

List of Figures and Graphs

Figures

Graphs

Introduction

Danièle Meulders, Robert Plasman and François Rycx

The 79th Applied Econometrics Association Conference was organised with the specific aim of stimulating discussion on the 'Econometrics of Wages'. Various sessions have in particular focused on *Minimum Wages, Low Pay and Unemployment.* The collection of papers in this book, originally presented at the Conference, provides some new insight into this topic. In what follows a short summary of these papers is presented.

Minimum wages, low pay and job satisfaction

Prior to April 2000 minimum wages in Ireland were set by number of industry-specific Joint Labour Committees. As a result the majority of Irish workers were not covered by these agreements. Furthermore for those that were covered the wages specified were often quite low and enforcement was weak. In April 2000 the Irish government introduced a national minimum wage of IR£4.40 (approx €5.60) an hour which covered almost all adult workers. In the opening chapter, Donal O'Neill (NUI Maynooth) uses Labour Force Survey data, along with data from a new survey of firms to describe the effect this legislation had on the labour market in Ireland. The author shows that firm's prior views on the likely impact of the minimum wage were not consistent with reported ex-ante outcomes. The evidence suggests that at the time it was introduced the minimum wage had little effect on most dimensions of business organisation in Ireland.

In Chapter 2, Lorenzo Cappellari (Università del Piemonte Orientale) use Italian panel data to analyse transition probabilities at the bottom of the earnings distribution during the 1990s. The analytical framework is characterised by the ability to account for endogeneity of initial conditions and earnings attrition. Results show that both are endogenous for the estimation of low pay transitions. In particular it is found that the low paid are more likely to exit from the earnings distribution compared to the higher paid, revealing higher employment instability. The data also reveal considerable state dependence, that is, the probability of experiencing low pay depends upon past low pay experiences rather than on personal attributes. Extensions of the model to longer term transitions suggest that state dependence effects are concentrated at the beginning of low pay spells, while subsequent low pay experiences contribute to a lesser extent.

In Chapter 3, Augustin De Coulon (Queen Mary, University of London and CEP, London School of Economics) and Boris A. Zürcher (Swiss State Secretariat for Economic Affairs) investigate whether the low-paid individual at one time tends to move to another state two years later. With the under-used Swiss Labour Force Survey, the authors construct three panels following individuals two years apart from 1992 until 1998. They observe on two transition matrices that the probability of being low paid is much higher for those low paid two years earlier than for those high paid two years earlier. In addition, they investigate this difference using a bivariate probit with endogenous selection into the initial state. Results on the determinants of the probability of remaining low paid and high paid are presented. The authors investigate whether the observed difference in low pay probabilities is due to individual heterogeneity or state dependence. Their results suggest that low-pay spells are both, transitory and persistent events. A sizeable portion of workers low-paid at some point in time succeeds to escape the low-pay segment within a two-year period. But between 69 and 81 per cent of the difference in low-pay probabilities is due to state dependence and this result provides further support to the view that time spent in low pay has a detrimental effect and tends to cause further spells of low pay.

Increasingly in the European Union low-paid employment and job quality have become important policy issues. Recently job satisfaction has been used as a proxy for job quality. In Chapter 4, Rannia M. Leontaridi (CELMR, University of Aberdeen and University of Stirling) and Peter J. Sloane (WELMERC, University of Wales Swansea and IZA) use the British Household Panel Study from 1991 to 1997 to explore further these issues. First they define low pay using the two-thirds of the median classification and examine the levels of overall job and pay satisfaction for the lower and higher paid groups by gender. Given the importance of comparative income measures in the literature their chapter focuses both on the actual level of pay and comparison pay, which is derived from a nationally representative sample in the New Earnings Survey. Second, they use a random-effects estimator to deal with problems of individual heterogeneity in the sample. Third, they explain changes in job satisfaction by changes in pay and other individual and industrial characteristics. Their chapter has particular relevance to current policy issues. For instance, if low-paid workers generally have high levels of job satisfaction this casts doubt on the suggestion that low-paid jobs are invariably of low quality. The results suggest surprisingly that there is no clear evidence that higher paid workers have higher job satisfaction than lower paid workers. This is particularly the case for women, which may be in accord with the compensating differentials theory as opposed to good jobs versus bad jobs view of the labour market. But it also emphasises that pay is not everything. This implication is reinforced when the authors consider mobility from low to higher paid jobs and vice versa. Overall, findings thus suggest that it is by no means always the case that moving from a lower paid to a higher paid job leads to increases in job satisfaction.

Low pay and unemployment

In Chapter 5, Anna Cristina D'Addio (CIM, University of Aarhus and HIVA, K.U. Leuven), Isabelle De Greef (IRES, Université Catholique de Louvain) and Michael Rosholm (University of Aarhus, IZA and CIM) investigate whether unemployment traps affect the transition into employment of Belgian individuals interviewed in the waves 3 to 7 of the Panel Study of Belgian Households. To compute replacement rates, the authors specify and estimate with maximum likelihood techniques a parametric random effects model on (unbalanced) samples of men and women. The estimates are subsequently used to predict wages for all individuals in the sample and to compute income ratios, that is, the ratios between income as employed and as unemployed. Further, to assess whether the amount of incomes in and out of work affects individuals' transition into employment, they have estimated a fixed effects logit model. Significant differences exist in the participation behaviour of men and women and the issue of sample selectivity seems more important for women. This suggests that their transition back into work is highly selective. Moreover, a high proportion of their transitions into work are associated with important financial losses. This problem also affects men, but to a lower extent. In addition, the authors notice that quite a high share of unemployed men and women that are unemployed over the whole survey period, are 'potentially trapped' financially in the unemployment state since their transition into work would be accompanied by a substantial reduction in their disposable income. This is particularly true for single women with and without young children. Finally the results of the fixed effects logit model suggest that women are particularly sensitive to the amount of income they are granted when out of work.

Against the background of the deteriorating fortunes of low-skilled workers in terms of their relative employment position, Ingo Geishecker (DIW Berlin) analyses in Chapter 6 how international outsourcing may affect the relative demand for low-skilled workers. In contrast to previous empirical work, the single elements of the input–output-matrix are used to disentangle international outsourcing and trade in final goods more accurately. The main finding is that, while in total manufacturing international outsourcing only has a negligible impact on the relative demand for low-skilled workers, there are however some industries, such as the electrical engineering, chemical, office machinery/computer and the paper industry, together accounting for about a quarter of total employment, where international outsourcing has been of high importance, explaining up to 47 per cent of the change in the relative demand for low-skilled labour between 1978 and 1993.

In the final chapter, Benoît Mahy and Isabelle Paindavoine (CRW, Université de Mons-Hainaut) analyse whether monopsonistic competition appears in the Belgian labour market situation, from a labour demand view. Belgian institutional facts tend to show that, though bargaining process appears to dominate wage determination, some firms could still pay wages that are lower than marginal productivities. These mark-ups or exploitation rates can be explained by monopsony, as it is shown by the theoretical model. The authors mention facts as some sectors that are dominated by few firms. Using a balanced panel of firms, they test for monopsonistic behaviour in two ways, testing for positive exploitation rates and for positive relationship between wages and employment among firms. They show that, even if they control for other potential explanations, tests are not conclusive. But they still support the monopsonistic assumption in 8.32 per cent of cases, a proportion that could further underestimate the reality for aggregation reasons. Considering other datasets, the authors also estimate that monopsony seems to dominate among firms occupying younger and lower skilled individuals. In policy terms, their results tend to show that deregulation could not necessarily serve to improve Belgian labour market shortage, while it probably worsens individual well-being.

Part I

Minimum Wages, Low Pay and Job Satisfaction

1
Low Pay and the Minimum Wage in Ireland

Donal O'Neill

1 Introduction

Prior to April 2000, minimum wages in Ireland were set by Joint Labour Committees (JLC). However, the wages specified in these agreements were often quite low and covered less than a quarter of the workforce. Furthermore the level of enforcement was quite weak, such that the specified wages had very little bite. In April 2000 the Irish government introduced a national minimum wage of IR£4.40[1] an hour, which would apply to most adult workers. When the rate was first suggested in 1997 it was envisioned that the full-time rate would correspond to approximately 56 per cent of median full-time adult pay. To put this in context, Table 1.1 summarises the relative bite of the minimum wage for a selection of other countries at this time. It is clear from this that the proposed Irish rate would have placed Ireland towards the top of this scale. As it turns out, when it was eventually introduced on the 1 April 2000, the relative bite of the minimum wage had fallen somewhat to about 44 per cent of the average wage.

The system used to implement the minimum wage laws also varies across countries. In countries such as France, Netherlands, Portugal, Spain and the United States the government sets a statutory minimum wage. In other countries such as Belgium, Denmark and Greece the minimum wage is set as part of National Collective Bargains, while in countries such as Austria, Germany and Italy sectoral minimum wages are set as part of collective agreements. The system adopted in Ireland involves a statutory rate, with the Minister for Enterprise, Trade and Employment having the discretion to decide on changes in the level specified for the minimum wage. There is no procedure or agreed policy with respect to indexation of that level as prices or earnings increase. The system

Table 1.1 International comparison of minimum wage rates

Country	Adult minimum wage relative to median full-time wages (1997)
Australia	54
Belgium	50
Canada	40
France	57
Ireland	56
Japan	31
Netherlands	49
Spain	32
United States	38
United Kingdom	44

Note: Data for all countries except Ireland are taken from Metcalf (1999).

adopted contains some age variation, with a separate rate, corresponding to 70 per cent of the adult rate, for employees under 18 years of age. Employers can also pay sub minimum rates for employees over 18 provided these individuals are either in structured training or in their first two years of employment. However, there is no scope for regional or sectoral variation in these rates. Since its introduction the adult rate was increased to IR£4.70 in July 2001 and is set to increase further to IR£5.00 on 1 October 2002. This chapter characterises those affected by the minimum wage legislation in Ireland and analyses the impact of the legislation thus far.

2 The characteristics of low-wage workers and firms

To examine the characteristics of the workers and firms most likely to be affected by the minimum wage we conducted a nationally representative survey of establishments to obtain detailed information on the employment and pay structure of these enterprises. In the first instance an owner or director of the firm was contacted in relation to the survey, which they in turn could forward to someone with direct responsibility for hiring in the establishment. All questionnaires were completed on a personally administered basis that involved the interviewer visiting each respondent and completing the survey on the premises. The first surveys took place in the last quarter of 1998, approximately 12–14 months prior to the introduction of the legislation. A total sample of 2330

Table 1.2 Classification of low paid by pay range, private sector employees

Pay range	**% of the population**	**% of all earning less than £4.50**
£4.00–£4.50	12.6	60.0
£3.00–£3.99	6.9	32.8
Less than £3.00 an hour	1.5	7.2

Table 1.3 Classification of private sector employees by gender

Gender	**% of all employees**	**% falling below £4.50**	**% of all those below £4.50**
Male	60.1	15.0	43.0
Female	39.9	30.4	57.0

enterprises was selected and 1064 surveys were successfully returned. In this section we use these responses to characterise both the workers and firms who were most likely to be affected by the adult minimum wage rate.[2] In particular, we look at the number of employees in the survey being paid IR£4.50 or less.

The first finding that emerges from the survey is that at the time the minimum wage was proposed 21 per cent of all private sector employees in the survey were earning £4.50 or less. Table 1.2 provides a more detailed breakdown of the incidence of low pay in the establishment survey. Here we classify the low paid into three wage ranges: those earning IR£4.00–IR£4.50, IR£3.00–IR£3.99 and less than IR£3.00 an hour. The first column indicates that approximately 13 per cent of private sector employees were being paid between IR£4.00 and IR£4.50 an hour, approximately 7 per cent received an hourly wage between IR£3.00 and IR£3.99, while only 1.5 per cent of private sector employees received an hourly wage of less than IR£3.00. The second column shows the composition of low paid by wage category. We see that 60 per cent of those earning less than IR£4.50 an hour had an hourly wage between IR£4.00 and IR£4.50. Almost one-third earned between IR£3.00 and IR£4.00 an hour, while only 7 per cent of low-paid workers earned less than IR£3.00 an hour.

Table 1.3 shows the risk and incidence of low pay by gender. From this we see that women faced a greater risk of being paid less than IR£4.50 than men are. The risk of being low paid was almost twice as high for women than men. The third column of the table also shows that women accounted for a disproportionately large percentage of the low paid.

Table 1.4 Age classification of private sector employees

Age group	**% of all employees**	**% falling below £4.50**	**% of all those below £4.50**
Aged 18 or less	4.8	80.4	18.3
Aged 19–25	29.1	34.2	47.3
Aged 26 or more	66.1	11.0	34.4

Table 1.5 Low pay by part-time/full-time status, private sector

Employment status	**% of those in population of employees**	**% falling below £4.50**	**% of all those below £4.50**
Part-time	14.6	64.4	45.0
Full-time	85.4	13.7	55.0

While female employees accounted for approximately 40 per cent of all private sector employees, they constituted 57 per cent of those paid less than IR£4.50 an hour.

Table 1.4 classifies workers into three age groups: those aged 18 or under, those aged between 18 and 25 and those aged 26 or more. It shows that the risk of being low paid is significantly higher for younger workers. Over 80 per cent of those workers aged 18 or less received an hourly wage rate of IR£4.50 or less. This compares to 11 per cent of workers aged 26 or more. The final columns shows that while younger workers were most at risk of being low paid they accounted for less than 20 per cent of all those who were low paid. Forty-seven per cent of those paid less than IR£4.50 an hour were aged between 19 and 25 while 34 per cent were 26 or older.

We have also looked at the breakdown of the sample by part-time versus full-time status where full-time is defined as working 30 hours or more a week. The results are presented in Table 1.5. Part-time workers faced a much greater risk of low pay than did those who worked full-time. Almost 65 per cent of part-time workers covered by the survey were working for less than IR£4.50 an hour, compared to only 13.7 per cent of full-time workers. However, the greater risk of being low paid does not mean that part-time workers constituted the majority of low-paid workers, since they accounted for less than 15 per cent of the total population. The results in the final column show that the majority of those being paid less than IR£4.50 an hour were full-time workers.

The survey of establishments not only provides information on the individuals affected by the minimum wage but is also a valuable source

Table 1.6 Occupational classification of private sector employees

Occupation	**% of all employees**	**% below £4.50**	**% of all those below £4.50**
Managers/Proprietors	15.7	4.5	3.3
Engineering/Science/ Computer/Other Professionals	6.2	0.6	0.1
Engineering/Science and Computer Technicians	3.8	1.1	0.2
Clerical/Secretarial	13.7	7.5	4.9
Skilled Maintenance/Skilled Production	10.1	14.6	7.0
Production Operatives	17.1	20.8	16.9
Transport and Communications	5.9	8.2	2.3
Sales	13.3	49.7	31.4
Personal Services	18.1	63.6	24.4
Labourers	6.1	32.5	9.4

of information concerning the characteristics of the occupations and establishments in which low-paid workers were found. Table 1.6 provides a breakdown of the low paid by occupational status. The first column shows that the distribution of employees across the occupations chosen is relatively uniform, the largest being production operatives who accounted for 17 per cent of all workers and the smallest being Science and Computer Technicians which accounted for 4 per cent of employees. However, much more significant differences emerge when we analyse the occupational classification of the low paid. The second column suggests that there were three occupations that were particularly vulnerable to low pay. These were Sales jobs, Personal Services and Labourers. In each of these occupations at least one-third of workers were being paid less than IR£4.50 an hour, with the figure being as high as two-thirds for those in the personal services. The first two of these occupations accounted for 56 per cent of all those who are low paid despite accounting for only 21 per cent of the total population. The other category which contributes significantly to the low paid are production operatives who accounted for 17 per cent of the low paid but they also account for 17 per cent of total employees.

Table 1.7 turns from an occupational breakdown of employees to a breakdown of low-paid workers by industry. Several important features emerge from this analysis. There were three sectors within which workers faced a relatively high probability of being low paid. Thirty-three per cent of all workers in the textiles and apparel industries were being paid

Table 1.7 Industry breakdown of private sector employees

Sector	% of all employees	% below £4.50	% of all those below £4.50
Building and Construction	7.7	9.1	3.3
Manufacture of Textiles and Apparel	2.0	33.2	3.3
Other Manufacturing and Production	25.8	9.7	11.8
Retail	17.0	38.8	31.3
Wholesale	5.1	22.5	5.5
Prop./Rent/Business Services	16.4	10.7	8.3
Hotels/Restaurants/Bars	11.1	49.3	26.0
Personal and Other Services	14.9	14.9	10.5

less than IR£4.50 an hour, almost 39 per cent of employees in the Retail sector received less than IR£4.50 an hour and almost 50 per cent of workers in the Hotel, Restaurant and Bar sectors received an hourly wage of less than IR£4.50. The final column of the table shows that it is the latter two of these sectors that accounted for the bulk of low-paid workers. Between them these two sectors accounted for 57 per cent of low-paid workers. Workers in the Textile and Apparel sector made up a relatively small proportion of those being paid less than IR£4.50 because they account for only 2 per cent of the total number of employees.

As well as describing the enterprises affected by the legislation we also asked firms to consider their likely responses to a situation in which the hourly wage of adult workers who were being paid less than IR£4.50 per hour were to rise to a minimum basic rate of IR£4.50. In particular, firms who had workers receiving IR£4.50 or less were asked for their views on how likely or otherwise each of 11 possible outcomes on business activities were as a result of introducing an hourly minimum rate of IR£4.50. The responses are summarised in Table 1.8 across sectors.

A total of 60 per cent of firms felt that it was likely that they would have to cut back on profit margins and 30 per cent felt it would be unlikely. In general, there was little variation by sector in this response, with the construction sector being least likely to reduce profit margins. Just under 62 per cent of firms indicated that they felt that the introduction of the minimum wage would improve staff morale, 20 per cent indicated that they felt it was unlikely to do so. Responses in the Retail; Hotel/Restaurant/Bar; and Personal and Other Service Sectors appear to be somewhat more optimistic than those in other sectors in terms of its effect on staff morale, with a substantially lower percentage

Table 1.8 Firms which have employees currently being paid less than £4.50 per hour classified according to their perceived responses to the hourly wage of adult employees (18 years and over) being raised to a minimum of £4.50 per hour (%)

Effect of raising adult hourly wage to £4.50	Sector								
	Build./ Constr.	Man./ Text./ Appar.	Other Man.	Retail	Wh. sale	Banking Finance	Hotel/ Res./ Bars	Pers. & Other Services	Total
Cut back profit margins									
Likely	47.8	78.7	58.1	61.5	61.5	61.2	58.7	60.5	59.7
Neither	1.7	4.6	8.9	7.2	7.8	1.3	16.4	13.9	9.8
Unlikely	50.5	16.7	33.0	31.3	30.7	37.5	24.9	25.6	30.5
Total	100.0	100.0	100.0	100.0	100.0	100.0	100.0	100.0	100.0
Improve staff morale									
Likely	50.2	41.7	54.7	66.8	52.1	62.5	56.9	71.9	61.8
Neither	12.5	25.0	19.7	13.7	13.0	2.6	26.4	26.1	17.9
Unlikely	37.3	33.3	25.6	19.5	35.0	34.9	16.7	2.1	20.3
Total	100.0	100.0	100.0	100.0	100.0	100.0	100.0	100.0	100.0
Substitute labour with capital									
Likely	1.0	21.4	25.3	4.8	8.8	2.0	8.5	15.1	7.7
Neither	1.7	13.6	9.5	13.5	5.1	7.9	17.6	14.6	13.1
Unlikely	97.2	65.0	65.2	81.7	86.0	90.1	73.9	70.3	79.2
Total	100.0	100.0	100.0	100.0	100.0	100.0	100.0	100.0	100.0

Table 1.8 Continued

Effect of raising adult hourly wage to £4.50	Sector								
	Build./ Constr.	Man./ Text./ Appar.	Other Man.	Retail	Wh. sale	Banking Finance	Hotel/ Res./ Bars	Pers. & Other Services	Total
Increase productivity									
Likely	23.0	25.1	23.0	18.5	11.9	26.3	25.2	25.2	22.0
Neither	4.2	28.4	13.8	22.9	13.4	25.7	29.0	26.1	23.3
Unlikely	72.8	46.4	63.2	58.6	74.7	48.0	45.7	48.7	54.7
Total	100.0	100.0	100.0	100.0	100.0	100.0	100.0	100.0	100.0
Result in going out of business									
Likely	1.4	37.0	13.0	14.2	13.6	10.5	24.6	18.7	16.7
Neither	11.9	9.7	10.0	7.6	6.8	11.2	17.3	20.4	12.3
Unlikely	86.7	53.2	77.0	78.2	79.6	78.3	58.1	61.0	71.0
Total	100.0	100.0	100.0	100.0	100.0	100.0	100.0	100.0	100.0
Retrain staff									
Likely	12.3	36.6	32.6	32.5	28.6	3.9	29.3	27.6	27.4
Neither	13.7	18.1	20.0	21.0	14.0	26.3	27.9	29.5	23.5
Unlikely	74.0	45.4	47.4	46.5	57.4	69.7	42.8	42.9	49.1
Total	100.0	100.0	100.0	100.0	100.0	100.0	100.0	100.0	100.0
Increase subcontracting									
Likely	3.1	30.8	15.4	5.7	6.6	1.5	2.1	8.1	5.1
Neither	1.4	7.6	11.8	7.8	9.5	20.1	17.5	14.9	12.3

Unlikely	95.4	61.6	72.8	86.6	83.9	78.4	80.4	77.0	82.6
Total	100.0	100.0	100.0	100.0	100.0	100.0	100.0	100.0	100.0
No effect on business									
Likely	69.7	34.3	32.6	41.1	32.3	42.8	36.7	33.8	40.1
Neither	1.4	9.7	14.7	15.9	16.7	8.5	32.8	28.9	20.5
Unlikely	28.9	56.0	52.7	43.0	51.0	48.7	30.5	37.3	39.4
Total	100.0	100.0	100.0	100.0	100.0	100.0	100.0	100.0	100.0
Reduce non-wage costs									
Likely	2.1	22.3	12.6	19.7	9.9	10.5	12.0	22.5	15.1
Neither	11.5	24.2	9.6	14.6	4.1	1.3	40.1	27.2	21.2
Unlikely	86.4	53.5	77.8	65.7	86.0	88.2	47.8	50.3	63.7
Total	100.0	100.0	100.0	100.0	100.0	100.0	100.0	100.0	100.0
Improve IR									
Likely	26.1	29.0	33.9	38.5	38.3	65.0	30.5	56.0	38.9
Neither	24.1	30.0	19.9	14.6	11.9	11.4	36.1	21.8	22.1
Unlikely	49.8	41.0	46.3	46.9	49.9	23.6	33.4	22.1	39.0
Total	100.0	100.0	100.0	100.0	100.0	100.0	100.0	100.0	100.0
Reduce staff turnover									
Likely	25.1	36.1	24.8	26.8	24.7	38.2	24.1	41.4	28.2
Neither	12.9	34.7	23.0	23.4	19.3	26.3	40.4	23.2	27.8
Unlikely	62.0	29.2	52.2	49.8	55.9	35.5	35.5	35.4	44.0
Total	100.0	100.0	100.0	100.0	100.0	100.0	100.0	100.0	100.0

of respondents in all three sectors indicating that they felt the increase in wage level would be unlikely to improve staff morale. An important finding in this analysis is that only 8 per cent of firms in aggregate felt that the substitution of labour with capital would result from the introduction of the minimum wage while just under 80 per cent felt that this was unlikely to be the outcome. As one might expect, a much higher percentage of firms in the two manufacturing sectors indicated that it was 'likely' that substitution of labour with capital would be a result of minimum wage legislation. This implies that for many of the sectors analysed here any potential job losses as a result of the legislation will reflect scale rather than substitution effects.

Of the other effects analysed we notice that about one-quarter of firms thought that productivity increases were likely to arise from the legislation and that this was evenly spread over sectors, while 17 per cent of firms noted that it was likely that the introduction of the minimum wage would result in them going out of business. This was particularly high in the Manufacture of Textile and Apparel and also in the Hotel/Restaurant/Bar sectors. In contrast, a total of 40 per cent of firms said that that the legislation was unlikely to have any effect on its operations. In the next section we analyse labour market outcomes after the introduction of the legislation. In doing so we also compare firms' a-priori expectations with their ex-post actions.

3 The labour market consequences of the minimum wage legislation

Changes in the wage structure after the legislation

To analyse the consequences of the legislation we conducted a follow-up survey of these firms in the late 2000/early 2001, approximately six months after the legislation was enacted. Attempts were made to contact each firm in the original survey. In addition a large number of additional firms were contacted. In total, information was collected on 1045 firms, 587 of which were interviewed in the first survey. In addition we identified 50 firms who had gone out of business by the time of the second sweep and a further 106 likely went out of business. This brings the total matched between the two surveys up to 743.[3]

Table 1.9 compares employment structure by pay range across the two surveys. As noted earlier 21 per cent of all persons employed in 1999 were paid a basic hourly rate of IR£4.50 or less. By 2001 this figure had fallen to just over 4 per cent of all workers. Details on comparable percentages for full-time and part-time workers are also given in the

Table 1.9 Persons engaged classified according to broad pay scale and full-time/part-time status for 1999 and 2001

	£4.50/hr or less		£4.51–£5.51		£5.51–£6.50		£6.51 or over		Total *N*	
	1999	2001	1999	2001	1999	2001	1999	2001	1999	2001
Full-time	13.7	2.2	15.8	10.6	17.6	16.1	52.9	71.1	741 000	1 048 100
Part-time	64.4	16.9	17.8	36.1	10.4	16.6	7.4	30.4	126 700	174 500
All persons	21.1	4.3	16.1	14.2	16.5	16.2	46.3	65.3	867 700	1 222 600

table. For example, in 1999 a total of 14 per cent of full-time workers were paid IR£4.50 or less per hour. By 2001 this percentage had fallen to a little over 2 per cent. Similarly, in 1999 a total of 64 per cent of part-time workers were paid less than IR£4.50 per hour. This figure was reduced to 17 per cent by 2001. By any standards chosen these changes would appear to represent very substantial reductions in the 'risk' of falling into the lowest pay grade outlined in the table. The 4.3 per cent of persons engaged who currently receive IR£4.50 or less represents approximately 52 600 persons, 23 000 of whom are employed on a full-time basis.

One can also see from the table that the percentage of full-time workers in the basic pay scale IR£4.51–IR£5.50 also fell over the period in question – from 16 per cent to 11 per cent. In contrast, the percentage of part-time workers in this pay scale increased from 18 per cent to 36 per cent. Furthermore, the percentage of part-time workers being paid IR£6.51 or more also increased substantially – from 7 per cent in 1999 to 30 per cent in 2001.

A detailed sectoral breakdown of the pay structure in both years is provided in Table 1.10. The bottom panel of this table provides the breakdown for all workers. This shows that the 'risk' of falling into the low wage group in 1999 was highest in the Hotel/Restaurant/Bar sector (49 per cent). This was followed by the Retail sector (39 per cent) and Manufacture of Textiles and Apparel (33 per cent). These three sectors stood out in the earlier survey as having particularly high rates of low-paid employees. It is clear from the table that by 2001 the situation has improved dramatically across all sectors. However, the 'risk' of low pay in the Hotel/Restaurant/Bar sector (14 per cent) and also the Retail sector (10 per cent) is still substantially above that in all other sectors. This means, for example, that the 'risk' or probability of being paid

Table 1.10 Persons engaged classified according to broad pay scale, sector of employment and full-time/part-time status for 1999 and 2001

	£4.50/hr or less		£4.51–£5.51		£5.51–£6.50		£6.51 or over	
	1999	2001	1999	2001	1999	2001	1999	2001
Full-time								
Build./Construction	9.0	2.3	10.9	3.2	20.4	9.2	59.7	85.4
Man. Textiles/Appar.	32.2	2.9	23.0	23.0	14.9	40.6	29.9	33.5
Other Manuf.	8.9	1.9	17.6	10.6	20.2	22.8	53.3	64.8
Retail	24.0	3.5	23.6	20.0	20.8	22.6	31.7	53.8
Wholesale	14.2	0.8	19.7	9.2	19.0	19.0	47.1	70.9
Banking/Fin./Bus.	5.9	0.8	7.6	5.2	10.9	11.3	75.6	82.7
Hotel/Res./Bar	31.3	8.5	27.1	39.2	15.2	24.2	26.3	28.1
Pers. & Other	11.9	1.3	8.8	4.0	16.8	6.8	62.5	88.0
All Sectors	13.7	2.2	15.8	10.6	17.6	16.1	52.9	71.1
Part-time								
Build./Construction	12.2	2.2	3.0	7.2	40.9	9.3	43.9	81.4
Man. Textiles/Appar.	42.6	6.2	34.7	26.0	16.5	57.0	6.2	10.7
Other Manuf.	22.1	6.0	24.2	26.8	45.0	31.5	8.7	35.7
Retail	80.8	22.4	13.3	36.3	3.0	14.2	2.9	27.1
Wholesale	67.2	28.7	21.2	35.2	4.6	9.7	6.9	26.4
Banking/Fin./Bus.	57.8	11.9	17.6	24.1	10.4	14.0	14.1	50.1
Hotel/Res./Bar	79.0	23.0	16.7	63.7	4.1	10.8	0.2	2.6
Pers. & Other	38.0	5.3	25.5	12.8	12.3	24.4	24.2	57.5
All Sectors	64.4	16.9	17.8	36.1	10.4	16.6	7.4	30.4
All persons								
Build./Construction	9.1	2.3	10.6	3.3	21.2	9.2	59.1	85.2
Man. Textiles/Appar.	33.2	3.3	24.1	23.3	15.0	42.6	27.7	30.8
Other Manuf.	9.7	2.1	18.0	11.5	21.6	23.2	50.7	63.2
Retail	38.8	9.9	20.9	25.1	16.2	19.8	24.2	44.8
Wholesale	22.5	3.4	19.9	11.6	16.7	18.2	40.8	66.8
Banking/Fin./Bus.	10.7	1.6	8.5	6.7	10.8	11.5	69.9	80.3
Hotel/Res./Bar	49.3	13.8	23.2	48.1	11.0	19.3	16.5	18.8
Pers. & Other	14.9	1.8	10.8	5.1	16.3	9.0	58.0	84.1
All Sectors	21.1	4.3	16.1	14.2	16.5	16.2	46.3	65.3

IR£4.50 or less per hour in the Retail sector is 2.3 times the aggregate average probability for all sectors combined. The chances that persons engaged in the Hotel/Restaurant/Bar sector are paid IR£4.50 or less per hour is 3.2 times the average for all workers. At the same time there was a significant fall in the absolute number of persons paid at IR£4.50 per hour or less in both sectors. The figure in retailing fell from an estimated 57000 in 1999 to 19000 in 2001. Comparable figures for the Hotel/Restaurant/Bar sector are 47500 persons in 1999 to 15000 in

Table 1.11 Firms classified according to the percentage of their staff whom they recorded as having received an increase in hourly rate as a direct result of the introduction of the minimum wage

	Percentage of persons receiving an increase in hourly rate as a direct result of minimum wage					
	None	**Less than 10%**	**10% to less than 20%**	**20% to less than 50%**	**50% or more**	**Total**
Sector						
Building and Contract	98.8	0.4	0.2	0.2	0.4	100.0
Manufacture Textiles and Apparel	66.1	10.3	5.2	5.2	13.3	100.0
Other Manufacture	77.2	6.3	4.5	6.9	5.1	100.0
Retail	76.5	0.9	2.2	10.3	10.1	100.0
Wholesale	86.9	2.5	1.9	5.1	3.6	100.0
Banking/Finance/ Business	89.8	0.4	3.7	2.0	4.1	100.0
Hotels/Restaurants/ Bars	76.3	2.0	1.4	17.8	2.5	100.0
Personnel and Other Services	86.4	0.3	2.6	4.4	6.3	100.0
All firms	84.5	1.2	2.2	6.8	5.3	100.0

2001. To greater or lesser degrees the same overall trends in regard to the Retail and Hotel/Restaurant/Bar sectors are apparent among both part-time and full-time staff. Although part-time workers in the Wholesale sector appear to be relatively disadvantaged it should be pointed out that part-time workers in this sector account only for an estimated total of 4800 persons. This means that the 28.7 per cent of part-time workers in the sector who are paid IR£4.50 or less represent in the order of 1400 persons.

In the second survey we also asked firms to indicate the percentage of their staff whom they recorded as having received an increase in their hourly pay as a direct result of the introduction of the minimum wage. Table 1.11 provides a sectoral breakdown of the responses. We see that about 85 per cent of respondents said that no one in their company had received an increase as a direct result of the introduction of the minimum wage. This reached almost 100 per cent in Building and Construction. The three sectors which were most affected were the Manufacturing of Textiles and Apparel, the Retail sector and the Hotel/ Restaurant/Bar sector. These results are consistent with the ex-ante results presented in Table 1.7.

When asked about the reduced minimum wage rates for young and inexperienced workers, 18 per cent of respondents said they had never heard of these sub minimum rates, and a further 76 per cent said they had never used them. While only 6 per cent overall said they had used these lower rates the figure was higher in certain sectors, such as the Retail and Hotel sectors. Nevertheless, even in these sectors the percentage was below 15 per cent.

Changes in employment after the legislation

It is clear from these tables that the wage structure changed substantially between 1999 and 2001. Part of this change reflects the introduction of the minimum wage over this period, though part also reflects general wage growth in the economy. In this section we look at the likely impact of the legislation on employment in Ireland. The traditional competitive model of the labour market predicts that minimum wages reduce employment due to higher wage costs (see Allen, 1938 or Hicks, 1963 for comprehensive discussions about labour demand responses to wage changes in a competitive labour market). However, this model has been challenged recently, largely as a result of findings that seem to indicate that the employment effects of minimum wages are small and in some cases may even be positive (Card and Krueger, 1995). This has resulted in a renewed interest in monopsony models of the labour market and in particular dynamic monopsony models (see e.g. Dickens *et al.*, 1999). In these models frictions in the labour market can result in a situation where increases in the wage rate carry not only a cost but also an associated benefit in the form of greater labour supply. This can arise due to reductions in staff-turnover or an increased ability to fill vacancies among other reasons. This does not arise in the competitive model as it is assumed that firms can hire all the labour they require at the going wage rate. The upward sloping firm's labour supply curve is the key feature of monopsony type models and can lead to a situation where modest increases in the minimum wage can increase employment.[4]

In a recent paper O'Neill, Nolan and Williams (2002) use the matched sample of firms in the two surveys to assess the impact of the minimum wage on employment in Ireland. They use variation in labour market outcomes across firms over time to identify the minimum wage effect. In particular firms who reported having low-wage workers in the first sweep were used as the treatment group; that is, those most likely to be affected by the legislation. Almost 50 per cent of firms in the first sweep are recorded as having had at least one worker receiving less than IR£4.50 in 1999 and on average 45 per cent of workers in these firms received less than IR£4.50. Changes in labour market outcomes over time for this group were compared with those firms who had no minimum wage workers in 1999. This specification suggests that the minimum wage had very little impact on employment over this period. Average employment growth for the affected enterprises was 17.6 per cent over this period, compared to 18.8 per cent for firms that had no workers in the low wage category in 1999. The *p*-value on the estimated difference in growth rates was 0.84. This finding is robust to a number of specification checks and strongly supports the view that employment growth among firms with low wage workers prior to the legislation was not significantly different to that for firms not affected by the legislation.

We can also use published national employment data to examine the employment effects of the minimum wage. The Quarterly National Household Survey is carried out each quarter by the Central Statistics Office. The purpose of the survey is the production of quarterly labour force estimates. Information is collected continuously throughout the year, with 3000 households surveyed each week to give approximately 39 000 households in each quarter. This sample is used to produce quarterly employment figures for the Irish economy which can be dissaggregated by gender, industry and region. Of interest in this study is the sectoral data. As noted earlier two sectors; the Retail sector and the Hotel, Restaurant and Bar sector together accounted for 57 per cent of low-paid workers and these sectors also reported a relatively large proportion of their workers affected by the legislation. To the extent that the minimum wage had a significant impact on employment we would expect most of the action to occur in these two sectors. To examine this we analyse quarterly employment growth figures in these two sectors between 1997 and 2002. In particular, we estimate the following equation

$$\%\Delta E_t^j = \alpha + \beta_1 \mathrm{MW}_{t-1} + \beta_2 \mathrm{MW}_t + \beta_3 \mathrm{MW}_{t+1} + \sum_{i=1}^{3} \delta_i \mathrm{SDUM}_i + \gamma \%\Delta E_t^{\mathrm{indus}}$$

where

$\%\Delta E_t^j$ denotes the quarterly employment growth at time t in sector j, where j = Retail sector or the Hotel/Restaurant/Bar sector.

MW_t is a dummy variable denoting a quarter in which the minimum wage was introduced or increased.

MW_{t-1} is a dummy variable denoting a quarter preceding an increase in the minimum wage.

MW_{t+1} is a dummy variable denoting a quarter following an increase in the minimum wage.

$SDUM_i$ is a series of quarterly dummies.
$\%\Delta E_t^{\text{indus}}$ denotes the quarterly employment growth in the entire industrial sector at time *t*.

The strategy in this specification is to use time variation in the employment growth rate in the most affected sectors to identify the minimum wage effect. The employment growth in the entire industrial sector at time *t* is used to control for national employment trends, while the seasonal dummies control for industry-specific seasonal effects. The minimum wage is allowed to affect employment growth, not only in the quarter it is introduced but also in the preceding quarter (a lead effect) and the following quarter (a lag effect).[5] Although the number of observations available for this analysis is limited, it does have an advantage over the earlier approach in that it uses information on the second minimum wage hike in July 2001, which was not used in the earlier analysis.

The results are presented in Table 1.12, where the first column refers to the Wholesale and Retail sector and the second column refers to the

Table 1.12 The impact of minimum wage changes in the Wholesale and Retail sector and the Hotel/Restaurant/Bar sector (*t*-stats in parenthesis)

Variable	**Wholesale/Retail**	**Hotel/Restaurant/Bar**
Constant	1.95*	−1.26
	(3.47)	(−1.02)
MW_{t-1}	−1.18	1.56
	(−1.24)	(0.74)
MW_t	1.73	0.38
	(1.73)	(0.17)
MW_{t+1}	−0.09	1.6
	(−0.09)	(0.74)
$SDUM_1$	−1.66*	2.02
	(−2.12)	(1.17)
$SDUM_2$	0.897	6.7*
	(0.55)	(1.87)
$SDUM_3$	−5.2*	−5.4*
	(−5.9)	(−2.78)
$\%\Delta E^{\text{indus}}$	0.54	1.09
	(1.78)	(1.65)
R^2	0.93	0.92
N	18	18

Note: * Significant at 5% level.

Hotel/Restaurant and Bar sector. Looking at the seasonal dummies we see, as expected, high employment growth in the Hotel sector during the summer months. Employment growth is also significantly less in both sectors during the autumn period (the omitted dummy corresponds to the winter months). The overall industry employment growth is positively related to sectoral employment growth but is on the margin of statistical significance. However, of more interest to us are the minimum wage variables. In neither sector is employment growth significantly different in the months surrounding the minimum wage relative to other months. The sum of the minimum wage coefficients and their standard errors are 0.46 (1.92) and 3.5 (4.25) in the Wholesale/Retail sector and the Hotel/Bar/Restaurant sector. There is no evidence of a negative minimum wage effect and none of the coefficients, either individually or combined are statistically different from zero. While we must be careful in drawing too much from these estimates, since identification is based on just two minimum wage changes, the results are consistent with the earlier findings based on the more detailed firm surveys. Using information on wage changes resulting from the legislation Nolan *et al.* (2002) suggest that −0.5 may be an upper bound for the elasticity of labour demand among firms included in our survey. Our finding that the minimum wage appears to have had a relatively small impact on employment is consistent with recent work on the UK national minimum wage, which was introduced one year before the Irish legislation (see e.g. Stewart, 2001).

Changes in other outcomes after the legislation

As noted earlier the establishment surveys that we carried out contain not only information on employment structure but also information on the potential effects of the minimum legislation on a number of other outcomes. In the first survey we asked firms the likely impact of a hypothetical increase in the wage rate to the level specified in the legislation. The responses to these questions were discussed in Section 2. In the second survey we asked firms to state what effect the legislation actually had on these same outcomes. Tables 1.13 and 1.14 summarise the responses by sector. We see in Table 1.13 that very few respondents felt that the minimum wage had a significant effect on their operations in terms of the way work is organised, working hours, use of less experienced staff, increased prices for their products, profit levels, reducing expenditure on training and development of employees, monitoring of employees, increasing spending on training, use of technology or machinery and improving the quality of service. About 4 per cent did

Table 1.13 Firms classified according to their perceptions of the impact of the minimum wage on a series of operational and related aspects of their business

Perceived effect of minimum wage	Build. and Cons.	Man./ Text./ Appar.	Other Man.	Retail	Whole sale	Bank/ Fin./ Bus.	Hotel/ Res./ Bars	Pers./ Other Servs.	Total
Changed pay and benefits structure									
Significant	0.8	5.2	4.9	5.0	3.3	2.0	7.8	2.9	3.7
Slight	0.6	17.0	10.3	9.5	8.5	11.9	27.3	13.7	11.7
None	98.6	77.9	84.8	85.6	88.2	86.0	64.9	83.4	84.6
Changed work organisation									
Significant	0.2	3.3	18.0	2.1	1.0		2.0	0.3	1.0
Slight	0.6	8.5	3.2	6.7	7.5	9.5	17.5	6.4	7.7
None	99.2	88.2	94.9	91.2	91.5	90.5	80.6	93.2	91.3
Reduction of working hours									
Significant	0.2		0.5	1.2			0.6	0.3	0.5
Slight	0.4	3.3	2.7	7.6	3.6	6.0	30.2	6.1	8.4
None	99.4	96.7	96.8	91.2	96.4	94.0	69.3	93.6	91.1
More inexperienced staff									
Significant	0.2		0.9	1.4			0.8	0.3	0.6
Slight	0.8	5.2	4.3	5.3	7.5	6.3	30.6	10.0	9.1
None	99.0	94.8	94.7	93.3	92.5	93.7	68.5	89.7	90.3
Increased prices									
Significant	0.4	6.7	3.2	1.4	1.7	0.4	2.2	4.5	1.8
Slight	1.6	15.2	10.6	15.2	13.6	8.0	46.2	10.3	14.9
None	98.0	78.1	86.1	83.4	84.8	91.6	51.5	85.2	83.2
Reduced profits									
Significant	0.4	5.2	3.9	3.8	1.8	0.2	2.2	2.2	2.1
Slight	2.2	21.8	12.8	19.3	12.7	12.1	41.0	11.5	16.3
None	97.4	73.0	83.3	76.9	85.5	87.7	56.8	86.3	81.6
Reduced expend on training									
Significant			0.5	2.0			0.6		0.6
Slight	0.6	6.7	3.4	2.9	4.3	6.1	14.7	6.2	5.4
None	99.4	93.3	96.0	95.1	95.7	93.9	84.7	93.8	94.0
Tightened control on labour									
Significant	0.2	6.7	4.7	4.1	2.6	0.4	3.4	0.9	2.2
Slight	1.0	13.6	7.4	9.6	8.5	6.3	18.6	8.5	8.6
None	98.8	79.7	87.9	86.3	88.9	93.3	78.0	90.6	89.2
Increased training and development									
Significant	0.4		2.2	0.4	2.5	0.4	2.0	2.3	1.2
Slight	0.2	6.7	5.4	6.3	5.1	6.1	25.4	6.5	7.8
None	99.4	93.3	92.4	93.3	92.5	93.5	72.7	91.2	91.0

Table 1.13 Continued

Perceived effect of minimum wage	Build. and Cons.	Man./ Text./ Appar.	Other Man.	Retail	Whole sale	Bank/ Fin./ Bus.	Hotel/ Res./ Bars	Pers./ Other Servs.	Total
Increase in technology/ machinery									
Significant	0.4	5.2	3.8	0.5	1.7	0.6	0.6	2.0	1.0
Slight	0.6	11.8	5.3	6.5	5.9	6.7	15.8	6.2	6.8
None	99.0	83.0	91.0	93.0	92.5	92.7	83.6	91.8	92.2
Quality of service/ product									
Significant	0.4		0.5	1.9	0.8	0.2	0.8	1.4	1.0
Slight	0.6	13.6	7.0	7.8	6.7	6.9	17.5	6.8	7.7
None	99.0	86.4	92.4	90.2	92.5	92.9	81.7	91.8	91.3

Table 1.14 Firms classified according to their perceptions on the direction of effect of the minimum wage on a number of areas of business, by sector

	Effect of minimum wage on								
	Build. and Cons.	Man./ Text./ Appar.	Other Man.	Retail	Wh. sale	Prop./ Rent/ Bus.	Hotels Res./ Bar	Pers. & Other Servs.	Total
Staff morale									
Decrease	0.4	1.8	0.9	2.0	1.6			0.5	0.8
No effect	96.1	81.0	88.2	82.4	87.6	97.0	72.1	89.4	87.4
Increase	3.5	17.2	10.9	15.6	10.7	3.0	27.9	10.1	11.8
Productivity									
Decrease	0.4		1.6	0.9	0.8		0.3	0.3	0.5
No effect	95.9	83.0	92.0	88.2	94.3	97.8	88.6	94.7	92.8
Increase	3.7	17.0	6.3	10.8	4.9	2.2	11.1	5.0	6.7
Staff retraining/ upgrading									
Decrease	0.2			0.9	1.6	0.2	0.6	0.3	0.6
No effect	99.6	93.3	93.1	92.7	92.5	97.8	94.1	96.2	95.3
Increase	0.2	6.7	6.9	6.3	5.8	2.1	5.3	3.5	4.1
Subcontracting									
Decrease	0.4		0.7		0.8		0.3	1.0	0.4
No effect	99.0	93.1	95.6	95.5	96.6	97.5	97.5	99.0	97.3
Increase	0.6	6.9	3.6	4.5	2.6	2.5	2.2		2.4
Staff turnover									
Decrease	3.1		1.3	1.7	1.6		16.3	1.0	3.4
No effect	96.3	86.4	92.7	92.9	92.5	97.0	73.7	95.8	92.0
Increase	0.6	13.6	6.0	5.4	5.8	3.0	10.0	3.2	4.7
Industrial relations									
Decrease	3.1	5.1	1.1	0.9	0.8		0.6	0.3	0.9
No effect	96.5	87.9	95.1	95.2	94.2	97.9	97.2	97.4	96.3
Increase	0.4	6.9	3.8	3.9	5.0	2.1	2.2	2.3	2.7

say that there was a significant impact on workers' pay and benefits structures, for example, overtime or pay supplements. A considerably larger percentage said that the minimum wage had a slight effect across these various dimensions, with the highest proportions giving that response tending to be in the Textiles and Clothing and particularly in the Hotel/Restaurant/Bar sectors.

Firms were then asked about the impact of the minimum wage on aspects of their business such as morale, productivity, retraining, subcontracting, turnover and industrial relations. We see from Table 1.14 that most firms in each instance said that the minimum wage had no effect in any of these areas. Among the minority who said there was some effect, most felt that morale had improved, productivity had increased and industrial relations had improved. The most even divide was in the case of staff turnover, where only 8 per cent felt the minimum wage had an impact but 3 per cent then said it had decreased and 5 per cent that it had increased. As noted earlier reductions in staff turnover are sometimes cited as justification for monopsony type models of the labour market, which in can turn can generate positive employment effects for minimum wages. Interestingly in this respect 16 per cent of firms in the Hotel sector report that the minimum wage decreased staff-turnover. The average across all sectors was 3.4 per cent. However this must be balanced by the fact that 10 per cent of firms in this sector said that turnover actually increased – the average here was 4.7 per cent. This sector is also more likely to report having increased prices and seen their profits fall as a result of the legislation.

Finally, it is interesting to compare the ex-ante responses to the likely impact of minimum wages provided in the first survey with the ex-post reactions given in the second survey. We begin by looking at the firms who went out of business. We noted in Table 1.8 that almost 17 per cent of firms in the first survey reported that the minimum wage would likely see them go out of business. In contrast, as noted earlier, we identified 50 firms or 4.7 per cent of the original sample that had certainly gone out of business between 1999 and 2001. A further 106 firms could not be contacted at the original address, so they had either moved or had gone out of business but we could not clearly establish which was the case. Almost half of these 156 firms had no minimum wage workers in the first survey. For firms that did have minimum wage workers we can cross tabulate their ex-ante perceptions with their ex-post actions in order to determine the ex-post accuracy of their perceptions. The results are

Table 1.15 Cross-tabulation of perceived consequences of the minimum wage on likelihood of closure and actual ex-post business status

Business status in 2001 after the introduction of the	**As of 1999 how likely do you think it is that a minimum wage of £4.50 will result in your firm going out of business (%)**			
	Likely	**Neither likely nor unlikely**	**Unlikely**	**Total**
In business 2001	0.13	0.11	0.56	0.80
Out of business 2001	0.03	0.03	0.14	0.20
Total	0.16	0.14	0.70	1.00

given in Table 1.15. Looking first at the 16 per cent of firms who initially stated that the proposed minimum wage would likely lead to them going out of business we see that only 19 per cent (0.03/0.16) of these firms actually did go out of business. Furthermore, this is not very different to the 20 per cent of firms who did not feel the minimum wage would lead them to go out of business but nevertheless had gone out of business by the time of the second survey. There seems to be little relationship between a firm's ex-ante belief about closing down and the ex-post likelihood of having gone out of business.

Table 1.16 correlates firms' ex-ante and ex-post reactions to the minimum wage along a number of other dimensions – namely its effect on profits, substitution of capital for labour, reduced turnover and increased productivity. Again these results suggest that firms' initial perceptions are only weakly related to ex-ante outcomes. For instance although 21 per cent of firms initially thought that the minimum wage would reduce staff-turnover, 95 per cent of these firms subsequently reported that the minimum wage had no effect on staff turnover. Likewise although 17 per cent of firms initially felt that the minimum wage would increase productivity, 82 per cent of these subsequently reported that it had no effect on productivity. Indeed, as noted earlier, the picture that emerges from the final column in each of these panels is that not only does the introduction of the minimum wage appear to have had no effect on Irish employment, it also appears to have had little effect on most dimensions of business organisation at the time it was introduced.

Table 1.16 Cross-tabulation of perceived consequences of the minimum wage on likelihood of closure and actual ex-post business status

Did the introduction of the minimum wage lead to a reduction of profits in your firm	As of 1999 how likely do you think it is that a minimum wage of £4.50 will result in cutting back on profit margins (%)			
	Likely	**Neither likely nor unlikely**	**Unlikely**	**Total**
Significant effect	0.04	0.00	0.02	0.06
Slight effect	0.26	0.00	0.07	0.34
No effect	0.35	0.03	0.23	0.60
Total	0.65	0.03	0.32	1.00
Did the introduction of the minimum wage lead to an increased use of technology	**As of 1999 how likely do you think it is that a minimum wage of £4.50 will result in the substitution of low wage workers with machines**			
	Likely	**Neither likely nor unlikely**	**Unlikely**	**Total**
Significant effect	0.00	0.00	0.01	0.01
Slight effect	0.02	0.02	0.14	0.18
No effect	0.03	0.09	0.69	0.81
Total	0.05	0.11	0.84	1.00
Did the introduction of the minimum wage lead to a reduction in staff turnover	**As of 1999 how likely do you think it is that a minimum wage of £4.50 will reduce staff turnover**			
	Likely	**Neither likely nor unlikely**	**Unlikely**	**Total**
Significant decrease	0.00	0.00	0.00	0.00
Slight decrease	0.01	0.00	0.06	0.07
No effect/increased	0.20	0.29	0.44	0.93
Total	0.21	0.29	0.50	1.00
Did the introduction of the minimum wage lead to a increase in staff productivity	**As of 1999 how likely do you think it is that a minimum wage of £4.50 will increase productivity**			
	Likely	**Neither likely nor unlikely**	**Unlikely**	**Total**
Significant increase	0.00	0.00	0.00	0.00
Slight increase	0.03	0.02	0.09	0.14
No effect/decreased	0.14	0.24	0.48	0.86
Total	0.17	0.26	0.57	

4 Conclusion

A national minimum wage was introduced in Ireland on 1 April 2000. This chapter draws on a number of sources to describe the characteristics of those firms and workers most likely affected by the legislation. It also analyses the likely consequences of the legislation for these workers and firms. Not surprisingly women and younger workers faced a greater risk of being affected by the legislation, as did workers in the Retail sector and the Hotel/Restaurant and Bar sector. While there were relatively large changes in the pay structures within firms over this period, our analysis shows that these changes appear to have had little impact on employment or other features of the firm's organisation. However, one must be careful in drawing inferences from these results. In many respects the introduction of the minimum wage in Ireland may have been relatively smooth primarily because it took place at a time when the economy was growing rapidly and wages were increasing. These results need not generalise to an economy that is in decline. However, as noted earlier, the responsiveness of labour demand to wage changes seems to be relatively small – the elasticity is approximately −0.5 for the very small number of firms who were most adversely affected by the legislation. Thus while the general response to the introduction of a national minimum wage has been positive, the challenge for policy makers is to ensure that future alterations to the minimum wage are implemented in a smooth fashion so that it has the desired effects at minimum cost.

Acknowledgements

I would like to thank Brian Nolan and James Williams for their contribution to earlier joint research on the impact of the minimum wage in Ireland.

Notes

1. IR£1 is approximately 1.27 Euro.
2. This part of the analysis draws heavily on work by Nolan *et al.* (1999).
3. Although sample attrition between the two surveys may be a potential problem we have carried out a number of checks which suggest that attrition was random with respect to the pay structure of the firm.
4. For a summary of these models and recent empirical analysis related to the minimum wage see Brown (1999).
5. A similar specification was used by Aaronson (2001) to look at the price pass-through effects of the minimum wage.

References

Aaronson, D. (2001) 'Price Pass-Through and the Minimum Wage', *Review of Economics and Statistics*, LXXXIII(1), pp. 158–69.

Allen, R.G.D. (1938) *Mathematical Analysis for Economists*, London: Macmillan.

Brown, C. (1999) 'Minimum Wages, Employment and the Distribution of Income', in *The Handbook of Labor Economics*, volume 3, Elsevier Science.

Card, D. and Krueger, A. (1995) *Myth and Measurement: The New Economics of the Minimum Wage*, Princeton, NJ: Princeton University Press.

Dickens, R., Machin, S. and Manning, A. (1999) 'The Effects of Minimum Wages on Employment: Theory and Evidence from Britain', *Journal of Labor Economics*, 17, pp. 1–22.

Hicks, J. (1963) *The Theory of Wages*, New York: Macmillan.

Metcalf, D. (1999) 'The British National Minimum Wage', Centre for Economic Performance Working Paper, March.

Nolan, B., O'Neill, D. and Williams, J. (1999) 'New Firm-Level Data', chapter 7 in *The Impact of the Minimum Wage in Ireland,* Published by Department of Enterprise, Trade and Employment, Dublin, Ireland (ISBN 0–7076–6787–9).

O'Neill, D., Nolan, B. and Williams, J. (2002) 'Evaluating the Impact of a National Minimum Wage: Evidence from a New Survey of Irish Firms', NUI Maynooth Working Paper.

Stewart, M. (2001) 'The Impact of the Introduction of the UK Minimum Wage on the Employment Probabilities of Low Wage Workers', University of Warwick, mimeo.

2
Mobility at the Bottom of the Italian Earnings Distribution

Lorenzo Cappellari

1 Introduction

The issue of low-paid employment has received considerable attention from researchers and policy makers in recent years (see OECD, 1993, 1996). The rise of earnings inequality occurred in many industrialised economies has placed a growing proportion of the employed labour force below pre-determined 'decency thresholds' in the earnings distribution, raising equity concerns and revitalising interest in redistributive tools such as minimum wages (see Freeman, 1996). Authors have also stressed that the diffusion of low-paid employment might lead to efficiency losses if it is concentrated in industries with monopsonistic labour markets in which rising inequality translates into a widening gap between equilibrium wages and their perfectly competitive level (Lucifora, 1998).

Recent research on low-paid employment underlines the need of a longitudinal analysis of the phenomenon (Stewart and Swaffield, 1999; Dickens, 2000). Evidence on the degree of mobility across the low pay threshold from one period to another can reveal to what extent low pay is a transitory or prolonged episode of earnings careers, yielding insights into the urgency of income support policies for the low paid. Stewart and Swaffield (1999) have also shown for Britain that low pay might be state dependent, that is, low pay in one period raises the *coeteris paribus* probability of low pay in the future, a fact which should be taken into account when defining target groups for policy.

The present chapter addresses these issues using Italian panel data on individual earnings in the 1990s. The econometric framework allows for initial conditions endogeneity along the lines set out by Stewart and Swaffield (1999). As shown in their paper, analysing low pay mobility requires current low pay probabilities to be conditioned on their lagged values, which is endogenous as long as there is some serially correlated unobserved earnings component. In addition I also control for endogenous earnings attrition. Mobility within the classes of the earnings distribution over time can be observed only for employees with valid earnings at each point in time, while individuals who exit from the sample of earnings recipients due to either panel attrition or movement out of the employment will not contribute to estimation. If these individuals have unobserved characteristics which are correlated with their propensity to move across the low pay threshold (say because they have weaker labour market attachment), estimating low pay dynamics on the balanced earnings panel will yield biased estimates. Bingley *et al.* (1995) found that attrition is not ignorable when estimating mobility on Danish data. Finally, I investigate longer term mobility by extending the set-up above to account for earnings transitions over three consecutive panel waves, thus analysing higher order dynamics.

The analytical framework relies on estimation of multivariate probability models with which low pay transition probabilities equations can be estimated while controlling for the probability of lagged low pay and the probability of having valid earnings. Simulated maximum likelihood (SML) techniques are used to estimate multidimensional integrals.

Results indicate that the exogeneity hypothesis can be rejected for both initial conditions and attrition. In particular, earnings attrition probabilities and low pay probabilities at the beginning of the transition are positively associated, suggesting that low paid jobs are more unstable compared to higher pay. Moreover, I find that while observed attributes have some impact in shifting the probability of crossing the low pay threshold, a relevant share of earnings persistence is accounted for by state dependence effects, suggesting that policies targeted on 'problem groups' among the low paid might have a limited impact, as low pay experiences affect, by themselves, earnings progressions, irrespective of personal attributes. Endogeneity of initial conditions and attrition appear to be relevant also in the case of higher order dynamics. Results from this latter model suggest that state dependence effects are concentrated at the beginning of a low pay spell, while subsequent low pay experiences contribute to a lesser extent.

2 The SHIW data

The data used in this study originate from the panel component of the Survey on Households Income and Wealth (SHIW), administered by the

Bank of Italy since 1977. Interviews have been carried out on an annual basis until 1987 and biannually afterwards until 1995, while the latest wave refers to 1998. The sampling unit is the household; however, detailed information is available also at the individual level. Although originally designed as a repeated cross-sections sample, the survey includes a panel sub-sample since 1989. While initially fairly small, the proportion of panel households (i.e. households sampled in at least two consecutive waves) has increased in recent waves, being approximately 40 per cent since 1993.[1]

This study utilises the last three waves of the survey, that is, 1993, 1995 and 1998. Apart from the aforementioned limited size of the panel sub-sample before 1993, data limitations prevented us from extending the analysis to earlier waves. In particular, information on individuals' parental background (education and occupation) for the head of household and the spouse has been introduced in the survey only since 1993. As we will see below, these variables play a crucial role in the econometric analysis, implying that the model cannot be estimated on waves preceding 1993. In addition, the structure of the questionnaire changed over time, in particular for what concerns labour market variables, and the selected waves provide good degree of homogeneity in the available information.

For the purposes of this analysis I select full-time employees aged 18–58 if female and 18–60 if male who were members of panel households. Table 2.1 provides a description of the SHIW sample in 1993 and 1995, the two years in which the starting point of an earnings transition can be observed. Column 1 reports the composition of the selected sample with respect to a set of personal and job characteristics.[2] Reported figures show that SHIW data reproduce the characteristics of the whole population of Italian employees. Column 2 reports the same statistics as column 1 but computed on the whole SHIW cross-sectional sample, that is, it also includes employees who are members on non-panel households. A comparison between the two columns shows that there are no relevant differences in sample structure between the cross-sectional sample and the sub-group of employees from panel households. Column 3 of the table restricts the attention to employees from panel households with valid earnings in two consecutive waves, that is, the balanced sample of earnings recipients; it is only for this sub-sample that transitions across the low pay threshold can be observed. Comparisons with columns 1 and 2 reveal that employees in the balanced sample tend to be more educated, more likely to hold non-manual jobs, to work for large employers and to be affiliated to the

Table 2.1 Sample means (cols 1–3) and probability of being in the balanced panel (col. 4)

	(1)	(2)	(3)	(4)
Female	0.36	0.36	0.35	0.66
Male	0.64	0.64	0.65	0.68
Potential labour market experience	19.31	19.11	19.23	0.67[(a)] 0.57[(a)]
Education < High school	0.46	0.48	0.43	0.63
Education ≥ High school	0.54	0.52	0.57	0.70
Blue collar	0.43	0.45	0.40	0.62
White collar (low level) – Teacher	0.48	0.46	0.50	0.71
White collar (high level) – Manager – Magistrate – Professor	0.10	0.09	0.10	0.71
Manufacturing	0.28	0.30	0.28	0.66
Agriculture	0.02	0.03	0.02	0.51
Construction	0.05	0.06	0.05	0.57
Retail trade	0.09	0.09	0.08	0.59
Transport and communication	0.03	0.03	0.03	0.61
Financial and related services	0.07	0.06	0.06	0.65
Personal and household services	0.03	0.03	0.02	0.56
Public sector	0.42	0.39	0.46	0.73
Firm size ≤ 19[(b)]	0.39	0.41	0.35	0.57
20 ≤ Firm size ≤ 99	0.23	0.24	0.23	0.64
100 ≤ Firm size ≤ 499	0.15	0.15	0.17	0.71
Firm size ≥ 500	0.22	0.21	0.24	0.70
North-west	0.23	0.25	0.22	0.65
North-east	0.23	0.22	0.24	0.68
Centre	0.20	0.22	0.20	0.69
South and islands	0.34	0.31	0.34	0.66
1993	0.49	0.51	0.59	0.81
1995	0.51	0.49	0.41	0.54
Number of observations	5 581	11 282	3 730	5 581

Notes: Pooled SHIW data for 1993 and 1995.
Full time employees aged 18–58 if female and 18–60 if male.

Column (1) considers only employees from panel households.
Column (2) considers the whole SHIW sample (employees in both panel and non-panel households).
Column (3) considers only employees from panel households and with valid earnings in two consecutive waves (balanced panel).
Column (4) provides the proportion of observations in the balanced panel conditional on the indicated personal characteristic.

(a) Figures computed on the samples with less than 20 years and more than 30 years of experience.
(b) Estimates by firm size are conditional on being a private sector employee.

public sector when compared to the cross-sectional sample, all features which may indicate a strong labour market attachment.[3] Column 4 investigates the features of the balanced panel by a different perspective, that is, by reporting the probability of being in the balanced sample conditional on observed characteristics. First, we can observe that such a probability is lower for the more experienced group of workers, who leave the earnings distribution to enter retirement. Also, column 4 confirms that the probability of being in the balanced panel is higher for more educated individuals, those in non-manual occupations, in the public sector and in larger firms. The table also reveals that the rate of exit from the earnings distribution is larger between 1995 and 1998 than it is for the 1993–95 transition. This can be explained by the longer width of the former observation window, implying a larger chance of leaving the sample of wage earners, and by the fact that both sample size and the proportion of panel households were slightly lower in 1998 compared to the previous waves (see D'Alessio and Faiella, 2000).

3 Low pay definitions and aggregate transition probabilities

Several definitions of low pay threshold have been proposed by previous studies, with alternatives ranging from some legally set minimum pay (Smith and Varvricheck, 1992) to fixed proportions of median or mean earnings (Stewart and Swaffield, 1999) or to relative definitions based upon quantiles (Gregory and Elias, 1994; OECD, 1996). In this study I follow this latter approach. In particular, in order to assess the sensitivity of results to the use of different thresholds, two low pay cut-offs have been analysed in parallel, namely the bottom quintile and the third decile of the distribution of hourly net earnings for full-time employees aged 18–58 if female and 18–60 if male.[4] The use of order statistics guarantees that thresholds are robust to outliers and can be easily updated over time. Moreover, it should be stressed that low-pay cut-off points have been computed from the whole SHIW cross-sectional sample (i.e. employees from panel and non-panel households) but have then been applied to analyse transition probabilities of a sub-sample, namely employees from panel households in the balanced panel of earnings recipients. Hence an individual moving out of – say – the poorest fifth does not need to be replaced by another individual moving into low pay, as would be the case if low pay thresholds were computed from the balanced sample of earnings recipients. In this sense, the thresholds utilised in this study combine the absolute and relative approaches.

Table 2.2 Descriptive statistics of the distribution of nominal hourly earnings

	1993	1995	1998
p10	6.73	7.05	7.97
p20	8.01	8.55	9.44
p30	8.93	9.62	10.58
p50	10.81	11.54	12.50
p90	19.42	20.03	21.88
2/3 median	7.21	7.69	8.33
Mean	12.32	12.83	14.22
Std. Dev.	7.53	6.69	8.29
Log(p75/p25)	0.22	0.22	0.22
Log(p90/p10)	0.46	0.45	0.44
Log(p99/p1)	1.04	0.99	1.00
CPI (1993 = 100)[(a)]	—	108.70	116.90
Number of observations	5 686	5 554	4 934

Notes: SHIW cross-sections – Full time employees aged 18–58 if female and 18–60 if male. Thousands of lire.
(a) source ISTAT.

Table 2.2 reports summary statistics of the distribution of nominal hourly earnings in the three SHIW waves. It can be observed that mean earnings exceed the 50th percentile of the distribution, a symptom of distribution (positive) skewness. Also, it can be observed that nominal mean earnings grew rather slowly between 1993 and 1995 (approximately 2 percentage points per year), and faster afterwards (an average increase of 3.5 percentage points per year between 1995 and 1998). If contrasted with the evolution of the Consumer Price Index (CPI) (also reported) these figures show that real earnings have been declining between 1993 and 1995 and recovering afterwards, so that by the end of the 1990 decade the growth of nominal earnings is almost in line with that of consumer prices.[5] The table also reports some measures of earnings dispersion in the three years, namely the standard deviation of earnings levels and the log-ratio between selected percentiles; estimates suggest that the earnings distribution has been stable during this period.

Low pay transition rates are reported in Table 2.3. The first two rows in the table report the transition matrix of hourly earnings for the 1993–95 and 1995–98 transitions respectively. The probability of persisting in low pay is 56.2 per cent between 1993 and 1995, while the corresponding figure for the 1995–98 transition is slightly higher at 57.9 per cent. Since we should expect three year persistence rates to be lower than two year ones – the chance of moving out of low pay being larger over wider time

Table 2.3 Low pay transition probabilities

Sample and low pay definition	Destination state / Origin state	High pay	Low pay	Out of the earnings distribution of full time employees								No. of obs.
				Part-time	Self-empl.	Unempl.	House-wife	Retired	Student	Other	Attrited	
(1) transition 1993–95	high pay	93.80	6.20	—	—	—	—	—	—	—	—	1 871
1st quintile	low pay	43.79	56.21	—	—	—	—	—	—	—	—	338
(2) transition 1995–98	high pay	93.12	6.88	—	—	—	—	—	—	—	—	1 293
1st quintile	low pay	42.11	57.89	—	—	—	—	—	—	—	—	228
(3) pooled transitions	high pay	93.52	6.48	—	—	—	—	—	—	—	—	3 164
1st quintile	low pay	43.11	56.89	—	—	—	—	—	—	—	—	566
(4) pooled transitions	high pay	90.93	9.07	—	—	—	—	—	—	—	—	2 834
3rd decile	low pay	32.25	67.75	—	—	—	—	—	—	—	—	896
(5) pooled transitions	high pay	65.31	4.52	—	—	—	30.17	—	—	—	—	4 531
1st quintile	low pay	23.67	31.23	—	—	—	45.10	—	—	—	—	1 031
(6) pooled transitions	high pay	65.31	4.52	1.32	1.77	1.88	0.35	5.32	0.09	0.35	19.09	4 531
1st quintile	low pay	23.67	31.23	3.49	3.01	8.63	1.94	2.13	0.19	0.97	24.73	1 031

Notes: SHIW data – Full time employees from panel households aged 18–58 if female and 18–60 if male.
Rows (1) to (4) consider balanced panels.
Row (5) includes employees with valid earnings in the starting year but not in the arrival one.
Row (6) distinguishes between exits from the earnings distribution and attritors.

windows – the estimates suggest that the earnings rigidity at the bottom end of the distribution increased in the second half of the 1990s. On the other hand the probability of falling into low pay from higher pay was 6.2 per cent and 6.9 per cent for the two and three year transition, respectively.

The model of low pay transition probabilities will be estimated pooling data from the two transitions following the approach of Stewart and Swaffield (1999). The third and fourth rows of Table 2.3 provide aggregate transition rates for the two low pay thresholds obtained after pooling transitions. Raw low pay persistence is estimated to be 56.9 per cent when the threshold is the bottom quintile and 67.7 per cent when the third decile is used. On the other hand, the probability of falling into low pay is 6.5 per cent and 9 per cent, respectively. These figures show that the conditional low pay probability varies considerably according to the conditioning starting state, that is, the probability of experiencing low pay is characterised by state dependence. Using the difference $\text{prob}(L_t | L_{t-s}) - \text{prob}(L_t | H_{t-s})$ (with L_t and H_t indicating low and high pay in year *t*, respectively) as a measure of raw state dependence, Table 2.3 indicates that conditional low pay probabilities rise by 50 per cent points when the starting state changes from high pay to low pay and low pay is set at the bottom quintile of the distribution; the corresponding figure for the third decile is 59 per cent.

State dependence in aggregate transition rates could arise from individual *heterogeneity* or *genuine state dependence* (GSD).[6] In the first case, the larger conditional low pay probability characterising the initially low paid is due to observed and unobserved persistent factors which affect low pay propensities and differ between workers above and below the low pay threshold. In this case, policies targeted according to the factors causing persistence can reduce entrapment into low paid jobs. In the case of GSD, on the other hand, it is the experience of low pay which, by itself, modifies individual tastes and constraints, increasing the probability of future low pay experiences.[7] This implies that policies targeted on 'problem groups' might be misplaced and the whole pool of low-paid employees should form the focus for intervention. The model of the next section will test for and measure the extent of GSD in low pay transition probabilities.

Row 5 of Table 2.3 enlarges the sample for the analysis of transition probabilities by including also those employees who exit from the earnings distribution during the transition. As can be seen, the impact of this inclusion is substantive: 30 per cent of those who earn above the low pay threshold in the starting year leave the distribution during the transition, and the figure rises to 45 per cent when the initially low paid are taken into account. Including these exits consequently changes conditional low pay probabilities in the arrival year, which are now remarkably lower. Overall, the average (over transitions and starting states) rate of exits from the distribution of earnings is approximately 33 per cent.[8] Additional insights on patterns of attrition from the earnings distribution are provided in row 6 of Table 2.3, where destination states of those who exits from the earnings distribution are specified. The estimates indicate that employees who start from low pay and exit the distribution are more likely to end up in part-time or self-employment, unemployment or to exit from the SHIW sample, when compared to workers initially high paid. These figures seem to suggest that low pay jobs are characterised by larger instability compared to high pay jobs. In particular, the evidence about entry rates into unemployment is consistent with the presence of cycles of low pay and unemployment as singled out by Stewart (1999). On the other hand, higher entry rates into retirement from high pay compared to low pay may reflect the life cycle of earnings.

4 A model of low pay transition probabilities

The estimation of an econometric model for low earnings mobility requires researchers to tackle two potential sources of endogenous sample selection inherent to this kind of problem; this section lays out an analytical framework that enables us to analyse earnings mobility while controlling for both of them.

A first source of endogeneity arises from the so-called *initial conditions problem* (see Heckman, 1981b and Stewart and Swaffield, 1999, for the case of low pay transitions). The problem is one of endogeneity of the lagged dependent variable in a dynamic panel data model. Estimating conditional low pay probabilities requires conditioning current low pay on past low pay. Unobservability of the initial conditions of the earnings process and serial correlation of earnings unobservables (due to unobserved heterogeneity and/or shocks persistence) imply that a common component – the initial condition – will be present in unobervables at each time period, causing past low pay to be endogenous with respect to current low pay. Stewart and Swaffield (1999) show that the problem can be handled as an endogenous selectivity one, in which transition probabilities and the probability of selection into the initial state are simultaneously estimated.

The second source of endogenous selection is due to non-random attrition from the earnings distribution. As long as individuals exiting from the sample of earnings recipients have unobservable characteristics which are correlated with their propensity to move across the low pay threshold, estimating the model of earnings transition on the balanced sample will produce a sample selection bias. Again, the problem can be solved by modelling the probability of selection into the balanced sample and earnings transition probabilities simultaneously. This kind of approach has been applied by Bingley *et al.* (1995) to model wage mobility in Denmark.

The present chapter adopts a three-variate probit set-up to simultaneously model the probability of selection into the balanced panel, the probability of selection into the initial pay state and the probability of transition across the low pay threshold. The model extends the one of Stewart and Swaffield (1999) by adding an attrition equation and will be estimated pooling transitions from the SHIW.[9] Let us assume that at the start of a transition (period $t-s$) earnings can be observed for a random sample of N employees and can be written as

$$g(y_{it-s}) = \boldsymbol{\delta}'\mathbf{x}_{it-s} + u_{it-s}, \quad i = 1,\ldots,N \tag{1}$$

where in the SHIW sample s is either equal to 2 or 3, y_{it-s} is a measure of earnings for individual i in period $t-s$, $\mathbf{x}$ is a column vector including a constant term and observed attributes, $\boldsymbol{\delta}$ is an associated parameter vector and u_{it-s} is an error term. Moreover, following Stewart and Swaffield (1999), I assume that there exists a monotone transformation $g(.)$ such that the unobserved earnings component is standard normal distributed. Let λ_{t-s} be the low pay threshold in period $t-s$ and L_{it-s} be an indicator variable for the low pay event, $L_{it-s} = I(y_{it-s} \leq \lambda_{t-s})$, where $I(A)$ equals 1 whenever A is true and 0 otherwise. The probability that an individual will be low paid in period $t-s$ is

$$\begin{aligned}\text{prob}(L_{it-s} = 1) &= \text{prob}(y_{it-s} \leq \lambda_{t-s}) = \text{prob}(g(y_{it-s}) \leq g(\lambda_{t-s})) \\ &= \Phi(g(\lambda_{t-s}) - \boldsymbol{\delta}'\mathbf{x}_{it-s}) = \Phi(\boldsymbol{\beta}'\mathbf{x}_{it-s}),\end{aligned} \tag{2}$$

where $\Phi(.)$ is the standard normal cumulative density function (c.d.f.), the new constant term in $\boldsymbol{\beta}$ subsumes the difference between $g(\lambda_{t-s})$ and the old constant in $\boldsymbol{\delta}$ and the coefficients associated with individual characteristics in $\boldsymbol{\beta}$ are the same as in $\boldsymbol{\delta}$, but with opposite sign. It has to be stressed that the use of the specification in (1) does not require any distributional assumption on wages or log-wages. Moreover, the non-linear treatment of the wage variable implicit in (1) corresponds to the idea that the wage process is not continuous, but some break occurs in correspondence of the low pay threshold. In this way the effect of workers attributes on low pay probabilities can be estimated directly; to obtain similar effects from usual (log-) wage regressions, distributional assumptions would be needed (see Lillard and Willis, 1978).

Next let r^*_{it} be some latent propensity of retention into the earnings distribution between periods $t - s$ and t:

$$r^*_{it} = \boldsymbol{\psi}'\mathbf{w}_{it-s} + \nu_{it}, \tag{3}$$

where the error term ν_{it} is distributed as in (1) and $\boldsymbol{\psi}$ and $\mathbf{w}$ are column vectors. If r^*_{it} is lower than some threshold (which can be set to 0 without loss of generality) individuals exit from the earnings distribution between $t - s$ and t; otherwise they remain into the distribution so that their transition can be observed. Let R_{it} be a dummy indicator of the retention outcome: $R_{it} = I(r^*_{it} > 0)$.

Finally, let us specify the earnings distribution of year t conditionally on the outcomes of both initial low pay and retention:

$$h(y_{it}) = \begin{cases} \boldsymbol{\gamma}_1'\mathbf{z}_{it-s} + \varepsilon_{it} & \text{if } L_{it-s} = 1 \text{ and } R_{it} = 1, \\ \boldsymbol{\gamma}_2'\mathbf{z}_{it-s} + \varepsilon_{it} & \text{if } L_{it-s} = 0 \text{ and } R_{it} = 1, \end{cases} \tag{4}$$

where the $\boldsymbol{\gamma}$s and $\mathbf{z}_{it-s}$ are column vectors and $h(.)$ is a monotonic unspecified transformation such that the error term ε_{it} is standard normally distributed.[10] The parameter vector in (4) switches according to the outcomes of initial low pay, that is, the $\boldsymbol{\gamma}$s parameterise earnings transitions. Also, period t earnings distribution can not be observed if individuals exit from the sample of earnings recipients during the transition, that is, when $R_{it} = 0$. By applying a transformation similar to the one used in (2) for period $t - s$ earnings, period t low pay probabilities may be written as follows:

$$\text{prob}(L_t) = \begin{cases} \Phi(\boldsymbol{\eta}_1'\mathbf{z}_{it-s}) & \text{if } L_{it-s} = 1 \text{ and } R_{it} = 1, \\ \Phi(\boldsymbol{\eta}_2'\mathbf{z}_{it-s}) & \text{if } L_{it-s} = 0 \text{ and } R_{it} = 1. \end{cases} \tag{5}$$

In order to derive the likelihood function of the model some assumption on the joint distribution of the errors of (1), (3) and (4) is needed. Here I allow them to be jointly distributed as a three-variate normal (denoted by N_3) with zero means, unit variances and free correlation:

$$(u_{it-s}\ \nu_{it}\ \varepsilon_{it}) \sim N_3[0\ 0\ 0;\ 1\ 1\ 1;\ \rho_1\ \rho_2\ \rho_3]. \tag{6}$$

Correlation across equations allows for individual specific unobserved heterogeneity. Testing the statistical significance of the correlation coefficients in (6) provides a test for the exogeneity of the two selection mechanisms. In particular, ρ_1 measures correlation in unobservables between initial low pay and retention, indicating whether the initially poor are more or less likely to be in the balanced sample compared to those initially highly paid. ρ_2 measures correlation of unobservables between initial low pay and conditional low pay, showing whether the initially poor are more or less likely to persist or fall into low pay compared to the initially highly paid. Finally, ρ_3 measures correlation in unobservables between retention propensities and low pay transitions, indicating whether those in the balanced sample are more or less likely to persist in low pay or to fall into it compared to those exiting the distribution.

To summarise, the model consists of a low pay probit equation for period t with endogenous switching on the outcomes of period $t-s$ low pay probit and endogenous partial observability depending upon the outcomes of the retention probit. Note that multiple selectivity (into initial low pay and into the balanced panel) takes place simultaneously, that is, no assumption has been made about nesting sequences between the two selection equations. Moreover neither selection equation is conditioned on the other, a feature whose relevance will be clearer later on.

The likelihood contribution of individual i can be written as

$$\begin{aligned} l_i = {} & \Phi_3(k_i\boldsymbol{\eta}_1'\mathbf{z}_{it-s},\ m_i\boldsymbol{\psi}'\mathbf{w}_{it-s},\ q_i\boldsymbol{\beta}'\mathbf{x}_{it-s};\ k_im_i\rho_3,\ k_iq_i\rho_2,\ m_iq_i\rho_1)^{L_{it-s}R_{it}} \\ & \times \Phi_3(k_i\boldsymbol{\eta}_2'\mathbf{z}_{it-s},\ m_i\boldsymbol{\psi}'\mathbf{w}_{it-s},\ q_i\boldsymbol{\beta}'\mathbf{x}_{it-s};\ k_im_i\rho_3,\ k_iq_i\rho_2,\ m_iq_i\rho_1)^{(1-L_{it-s})R_{it}} \\ & \times \Phi_2(m_i\boldsymbol{\psi}'\mathbf{w}_{it-s},\ q_i\boldsymbol{\beta}'\mathbf{x}_{it-s};\ m_iq_i\rho_1)^{(1-R_{it})} \qquad (7) \\ k_i = {} & 2L_{it}-1;\ m_i = 2R_{it}-1;\ q_i = 2L_{it-s}-1, \end{aligned}$$

where $\Phi_j(.)$ is the j-variate normal c.d.f. To solve the computational problem posed by the presence of three-variate normal integrals I utilise SML estimation, so that in estimation $\Phi_3(.)$ is replaced by its simulated counterpart $\tilde{\Phi}_3(.)$. In particular, I adopt the so-called *GHK simulator*.[11]

Note that although the $\boldsymbol{\eta}$ vectors in (7) are estimated conditioning on initial low pay, the whole expression refers to the joint probability of the data. Transition probabilities can be computed as

$$\begin{aligned} \hat{\text{prob}}(L_{it}=1 \mid L_{it-s}=1, R_{it}=1) &= \frac{\tilde{\Phi}_3(\hat{\boldsymbol{\eta}}_1'\mathbf{z}_{it-s},\ \hat{\boldsymbol{\psi}}'\mathbf{w}_{it-s},\ \hat{\boldsymbol{\beta}}'\mathbf{x}_{it-s};\ \hat{\rho}_3, \hat{\rho}_2, \hat{\rho}_1)}{\Phi_2(\hat{\boldsymbol{\psi}}'\mathbf{w}_{it-s},\ \hat{\boldsymbol{\beta}}'\mathbf{x}_{it-s};\ \hat{\rho}_1)} \\ \hat{\text{prob}}(L_{it}=1 \mid L_{it-s}=0, R_{it}=1) &= \frac{\tilde{\Phi}_3(\hat{\boldsymbol{\eta}}_2'\mathbf{z}_{it-s},\ \hat{\boldsymbol{\psi}}'\mathbf{w}_{it-s},\ -\hat{\boldsymbol{\beta}}'\mathbf{x}_{it-s};\ \hat{\rho}_3, -\hat{\rho}_2, -\hat{\rho}_1)}{\Phi_2(\hat{\boldsymbol{\psi}}'\mathbf{w}_{it-s},\ -\hat{\boldsymbol{\beta}}'\mathbf{x}_{it-s};\ -\hat{\rho}_1)} \qquad (8) \end{aligned}$$

where hats denote estimates.

In order identify the model, exclusion restrictions are needed in terms of variables entering the **x** or **w** vectors but not the **z** one, that is, variables affecting either initial low pay or retention but, conditional on these, with no effect on low pay transition.[12] Heckman (1981b) suggests that initial conditions can be instrumented by using information prior to labour market entry. Stewart and Swaffield (1999) use indicators of parental education and occupation. Since 1993 the SHIW has included questions on occupation and education of the household head's and spouse's parents.[13] A set of 10 dummies for manual occupation, non employment, education equal to or greater than high school and missing information on education or occupation was derived for each parent and has been used as instrument. In addition, as pointed out by Stewart and Swaffield (1999), a quadratic term in experience (which enters the equation for initial low pay) can be excluded from the equation for low pay transition given its interpretation of wage change equation. Based on this assumption, the equation for initial low pay is over-identified and the validity of parental background as instruments can be tested. Identification of the retention equation requires variables affecting employment probabilities plus information on participation into the survey, the implementation of interviews and personal characteristic of the interviewer (e.g. Zabel, 1998). While there is no clear a priori on variables of the first kind that can be excluded from the transition equation, information of the second kind is not available in the SHIW. However, as pointed out above, neither of the two selection equations is conditional on the other, implying that the retention equation can be identified using the same set of instruments used for initial conditions.

The endogenous switching structure of the model allows us to investigate the issue of state dependence. First of all, a measure of aggregate state dependence (ASD) can be computed from estimated parameters as the difference in average conditional low pay probabilities, with averages taken over the samples of the initially low paid and high paid in the balanced sample:

$$\begin{aligned} \text{ASD} = & \left\{ \sum\nolimits_{\{i:L_{it-s}=1,\,R_{it}=1\}} \hat{\text{prob}}(L_{it}=1|L_{it-s}=1, R_{it}=1) \Big/ \sum\nolimits_{\{i:L_{it-s}=1,\,R_{it}=1\}} L_{it-s} \right\} \\ & - \left\{ \sum\nolimits_{\{i:L_{it-s}=0,\,R_{it}=1\}} \hat{\text{prob}}(L_{it}=1|L_{it-s}=0, R_{it}=1) \Big/ \sum\nolimits_{\{i:L_{it-s}=0,\,R_{it}=1\}} (1-L_{it-s}) \right\}. \end{aligned} \tag{9}$$

Second the hypothesis of absence of GSD can be formulated as $H_0: \eta_1 = \eta_2$, that is, the impact of personal attributes on conditional low pay probabilities does not depend upon past low pay experiences.[14]

Finally, an indicator of GSD may be defined as the difference in conditional low pay probabilities an average individual would have experienced had she started the transition from below or above the low pay threshold, the average being taken over the balanced sample of earnings recipients:

$$\text{GSD} = \left(\sum_i R_{it}\right)^{-1} \sum_{i:R_{it=1}} \left\{ \frac{\tilde{\Phi}_3(\boldsymbol{\eta}_1'\mathbf{z}_{it-s}, \hat{\boldsymbol{\psi}}'\mathbf{w}_{it-s}, \hat{\boldsymbol{\beta}}'\mathbf{x}_{it-s}; \hat{\rho}_3, \hat{\rho}_2, \hat{\rho}_1)}{\Phi_2(\hat{\boldsymbol{\psi}}'\mathbf{w}_{it-s}, \hat{\boldsymbol{\beta}}'\mathbf{x}_{it-s}; \hat{\rho}_1)} - \frac{\tilde{\Phi}_3(\eta_2'\mathbf{z}_{it-s}, \hat{\boldsymbol{\psi}}'\mathbf{w}_{it-s}, -\hat{\boldsymbol{\beta}}'\mathbf{x}_{it-s}; \hat{\rho}_3, -\hat{\rho}_2, -\hat{\rho}_1)}{\Phi_2(\hat{\boldsymbol{\psi}}'\mathbf{w}_{it-s}, -\hat{\boldsymbol{\beta}}'\mathbf{x}_{it-s}; -\hat{\rho}_1)} \right\}. \tag{10}$$

5 Results

Results obtained by estimating the simulated three-variate probit of the last section on the pooled transitions sample are presented in Table 2.4.[15] Explanatory variables for the transition equation included in the **z** vector are a gender dummy, potential labour market experience, an education dummy, occupational dummies, dummies for industrial affiliation, employer size dummies, regional dummies and a dummy for the 1995–98 transition. The **x** vector includes all variables in the **z** vector plus a quadratic in potential labour market experience and the set of parental background dummies. Finally, following the discussion about identification of the retention equation in the previous section, the **w** vector is set equal to **x**; I will refer to a unique **x** vector from now onwards.

Results are presented in terms of 'marginal effects' of explanatory variables on the conditional low pay probabilities given by (8). A change in an element of **z** also implies a change in the corresponding element of the **x** vector, thus changing not only the conditional probability, but also the conditioning ones. In order to hold conditioning events constant when computing marginal effects on transition probabilities I proceed as follows.[16] I compute predicted probabilities for the two conditioning events (using estimated parameters from the three-variate probit, the **x** vector and univariate normal c.d.f.'s) and average them over the relevant samples, that is, observations in the balanced sample for the retention probability and observations in the balanced sample and below or above initial low pay for the probabilities of initial low or high pay. I next compute the arguments of these average predicted

Table 2.4 Results[a] from SML estimation[b] of trivariate probit models for conditional low pay probabilities

Low pay threshold	**First quintile**				**Third decile**			
Initial pay state	**Low pay**		**High pay**		**Low pay**		**High pay**	
Average prediction	0.57		0.06		0.68		0.09	
Base category[c]	0.74		0.17		0.81		0.21	
Deviations from base category								
Female	0.07	(1.67)	0.08	(3.06)	0.05	(1.74)	0.08	(2.97)
30 years of potential labour market experience	−0.02	(1.05)	−0.02	(2.12)	−0.03	(2.15)	−0.01	(1.00)
Education ≥ High school	−0.14	(2.37)	−0.06	(2.64)	−0.08	(1.92)	−0.06	(2.26)
White collar (low level) – Teacher	−0.05	(0.83)	−0.09	(3.74)	−0.06	(1.18)	−0.10	(3.89)
White collar (high level) – Manager – Magistrate – Professor	0.04	(0.29)	−0.08	(2.20)	0.05	(0.52)	−0.15	(4.01)
Public sector	0.04	(0.52)	−0.11	(4.20)	−0.15	(2.11)	−0.11	(3.34)
Agriculture	−0.10	(1.01)	0.03	(0.52)	−0.13	(1.77)	0.0002	(0.002)
Construction	0.09	(1.47)	0.00	(0.10)	0.01	(0.11)	0.05	(1.00)
Retail trade	−0.06	(1.03)	0.05	(1.26)	0.02	(0.52)	0.05	(1.16)
Transport and communication	0.02	(0.14)	−0.08	(1.37)	−0.07	(0.81)	−0.03	(0.45)
Financial and related services	0.06	(0.69)	0.00	(0.02)	0.08	(1.33)	−0.07	(1.28)
Personal and household services	−0.11	(1.14)	0.04	(0.58)	−0.02	(0.30)	−0.05	(0.69)
20 ≤ Firm size ≤ 99	−0.10	(1.68)	−0.06	(2.20)	−0.07	(1.83)	−0.05	(1.51)
100 ≤ Firm size ≤ 499	−0.17	(1.75)	−0.06	(1.83)	−0.08	(1.55)	−0.06	(1.73)
Firm size ≥ 500	0.02	(0.24)	−0.10	(3.75)	−0.03	(0.50)	−0.11	(3.22)
North-west	−0.22	(3.17)	−0.03	(1.12)	−0.11	(2.43)	0.01	(0.32)

Table 2.4 Continued

Low pay threshold Initial pay state	First quintile				Third decile			
	Low pay		High pay		Low pay		High pay	
North-east	−0.16	(2.69)	−0.04	(1.47)	−0.04	(0.99)	−0.02	(0.70)
Centre	−0.10	(1.64)	0.01	(0.32)	0.02	(0.65)	0.03	(1.03)
transition 1995–98	−0.04	(0.83)	0.003	(0.12)	−0.10	(2.43)	0.0001	(0.002)
$\rho 1$ (initial conditions-retention)	−0.069	—	(2.18)	—	−0.092	—	(3.17)	
$\rho 2$ (initial conditions-transition)	−0.427	—	(3.32)	—	−0.351	—	(2.81)	
$\rho 3$ (retention–transition)	0.299	—	(1.88)	—	0.343	—	(2.16)	
test1 ($df = 20$)(d)	20.75	—	0.4119	—	19.15	—	0.5122	
test2 ($df = 20$)(e)	82.95	—	0.0000	—	91.18	—	0.0000	
test3 ($df = 20$)(f)	62.65	—	0.0000	—	82.73	—	0.0000	
State dependence(g)	0.50	—	0.26	—	0.59	—	0.32	
Model $\chi^2(df = 98)$	2 182.86	—	0.0000	—	2 541.48	—	0.0000	
Log likelihood	—	−5 696.67	—	—	—	−6 350.99	—	
Number of observations	—	5 535	—	—	—	5 535	—	

Notes: SHIW data, pooled transitions 1993–95 and 1995–98 – Full time employees aged 18–58 if female and 18–60 if male.

(a) Marginal effects, see text for computation. Absolute t-ratios in parentheses refer to SML coefficients.
(b) GHK simulator with 75 random draws.
(c) Male, 20 years of potential experience, blue collar worker, manufacturing, firm size < 20, lives in the South or Islands, 1993–95 transition.
(d) LR test of exclusion of parental background dummies from conditional low pay equations, *p*-value in Italic.
(e) Wald test of exclusion of parental background dummies from selection equations, *p*-value in Italic.
(f) Wald test of equality of coefficients in conditional low pay equations, *p*-value in Italic.
(g) Aggregate state dependence (left) and genuine state dependence (right), see text for computation.

probabilities and use them into the multivariate normal c.d.f.'s of (8), thus holding the probabilities of the conditioning events fixed. Finally, each marginal effect is calculated as the change in the conditional probabilities of (8) induced by a change in an element of **z** with respect to a base category. The base category is given by an employee with 20 years of potential labour market experience and a value of 0 in all the dummy variables in **z**. For dummy variables the effect is the change in transition probabilities with respect to the base category when the dummy changes from 0 to 1. For potential labour market experience the effect is the one determined by a change of the variable to 30 years.

It is instructive to begin our discussion of results by considering the estimated covariance matrix of error terms. The three correlation coefficients are statistically significant at usual confidence levels: thus both initial conditions and retention are endogenous for the estimation of low pay transitions and should not be ignored. The correlation between unobservables of initial low pay and retention is negative reflecting the higher propensity to exit from the balanced panel of the low paid compared to the higher paid. Correlation of unobservables between initial conditions and conditional low pay probabilities is also negative, meaning that those who begin the transition below the low pay threshold are less likely to experience a small earning change – and thence to be low paid at the end of the transition – compared to the higher paid, a finding reflecting Galtonian regression towards the mean. Finally, correlation in unobservables between sample retention and conditional low pay probability is positive. Individuals in the balanced earnings sample have a higher probability to either persist in low pay (if they are low paid at the start of the transition) or to fall into it (if they are initially high paid). This last finding combines evidence from the two other correlation coefficients. Given that the low paid have a lower retention probability ($\rho_1 < 0$) and a lower conditional low pay probability ($\rho_2 < 0$) compared to the higher paid, then the conditional low pay probability will be higher in the balanced sample compared to what it would had been in the absence of earnings attrition.

The bottom panel of Table 2.4 also reports results from tests for the validity of parental background variables as instruments. While these variables do not appear to be significant in the equations for conditional low pay probabilities, their simultaneous exclusion from the two selection equations is rejected. These results support the use of parental background variables as instruments for the multiple selectivity equations.

The average (over the balanced earnings sample) predicted conditional low pay probability is reported at the top of the table. The model replicates the aggregate transition rates of Table 2.3. The stylised individual used as a reference for the computation of marginal effects has low pay persistence and entry rates higher then the sample average ones. Comparing the reference individual with a female employee with otherwise similar characteristics shows that the latter experiences larger conditional low pay probabilities, between 5 and 8 percentage points depending upon the case considered, while the underlying estimated coefficient for the female dummy is statistically significant at usual confidence levels. Increasing labour market experience from 20 to 30 years, on the other hand, reduces conditional low pay probabilities by a lesser extent and the underlying coefficients do not always appear to be precisely estimated. Holding a high school degree reduces the probability of persistence below the lowest threshold by 14 percentage points, while the effect is smaller in size, but with underlying coefficients still precisely estimated, when the higher cut-off point or drops into low pay are taken into account. Marginal effects for occupation reveal an asymmetric impact on conditional low pay probabilities: while for the initially high paid in non-manual jobs the probability of falling into low pay is some 8 to 13 percentage points lower compared to high paid manual workers, for employees below the low pay threshold no statistically significant association can be detected. For high-level non-manual workers this finding might reflect a small cell size problem. For low-level non-manual workers and teachers, on the other hand, this result suggests that factors which keep employees out of low pay may lose their effectiveness once low pay has been experienced. The public sector dummy displays the same kind of asymmetric effect noted above for occupation dummies, but only for the lowest threshold. Marginal effects for private sector industrial affiliation, on the other hand, do not reveal any clear pattern. Conditional low pay probabilities are significantly lower for employees in medium sized private sector firms compared to small firms. Conversely, when large sized firm are taken into account, the kind of asymmetric impact characterising occupation dummies applies. An asymmetric impact of observed factors on conditional low pay probabilities applies also for regional dummies, but this time in the opposite direction. For example, north-western employees have a probability of low pay persistence that is 10 to 22 percentage points lower than that of workers from the South or Islands, while no significant differential characterises the probability of falling into low pay from higher pay. Finally, we can see that conditional low pay probabilities do not vary significantly over transitions. Since the latter transition occurs over a wider interval, this evidence points towards increasing distributional rigidity in the second half of the 1990s.

Results about differences in the impact of personal attributes on conditional low pay probabilities between workers above and below the low pay threshold are consistent with the existence of GSD effects. A formal test for the absence of GSD (formulated as equality of parameter vectors in the two conditional low pay equations) is reported at the bottom of Table 2.3. For both low pay thresholds the null hypothesis $H_0 : \eta_1 = \eta_2$ is overwhelmingly rejected. Measures of ASD and GSD computed according to (9) and (10) are also reported. GSD constitutes a substantial share of aggregate figures, the ratio GSD/ASD being approximately 53 per cent for both thresholds. These figures are in line with the ones reported by Stewart and Swaffield (1999) for Britain. The test and measures of state dependence thence indicate that a relevant share of low pay persistence may be ascribed to past low pay experiences, which modify individual tastes or constraints and make more difficult for an individual to move onto the higher part of the distribution, irrespective of personal attributes.

6 Taking a longer run view

Results presented so far refer to low pay probabilities conditional on both retention and one period lagged low pay states. This section proposes an extension of the analytical framework aimed at assessing the features of longer term low pay persistence. In particular, I will look at the three SHIW waves simultaneously and will estimate 1998 low pay probabilities conditional on earnings attrition and pay states in 1993 and 1995. The model presented in this section has never been applied before to the analysis of earnings mobility – at least to my knowledge – and represents an intermediate analytical perspective between models of first order transitions like the one of Section 4 and low income spells analyses like the ones discussed in Jenkins (2000). As such, it allows studying the covariates of low pay persistence distinguishing between different sequences of previous low pay while controlling for the endogeneity issues outlined in Section 4. In addition, parameter estimates can be used to assess state dependence over the longer run.

Table 2.5 provides an illustration of transition patterns considering the three available waves simultaneously and using the first quintile as low pay threshold, with the relevant sample now being given by 1993 employees with valid earnings. The first row of the table shows that a different treatment of earnings attrition is needed when modelling the three-years transition compared to the two-years case. The latent retention propensity needs now to cross two thresholds in order for employees to be in balanced panel of earnings recipients, that is, being in

Table 2.5 Retention and low pay conditional probabilities – three years transition

Observed in	**1993 only**	**1993 and 1995**	**1993,1995 and 1998**	**No. of obs.**
(1) 1993 pay state				
High pay	16.17	37.54	46.28	2 232
Low pay	30.88	40.70	28.43	489
(2) 1998 pay state	High pay	Low pay		
1993 pay state				
High pay	93.22	6.78	—	1 033
Low pay	49.64	50.36	—	139
(3) 1998 pay state	High pay	Low pay		
1993 and 1995 pay states				
L93, L95	32.43	67.57	—	74
H93, L95	55.36	44.64	—	56
L93, H95	69.23	30.77	—	65
H93, H95	95.39	4.61	—	977

Notes: SHIW data, 1993–98 transition – Full-time employees from panel households aged 18–58 if female and 18–60 if male. Low pay defined as first quintile of the hourly earnings distribution. L_t = low pay in year *t*; H_t = high pay in year *t*.

sample between 1993 and 1995 and between 1995 and 1998. Treating retention as binary, that is, distinguishing only between balanced panel versus non-balanced panel observations would imply a loss of information in estimating the 1995 earnings distribution. The Table also show that the probability of being in the balanced sample is much larger for those who start the transition from above rather than below the low pay threshold, again pointing towards the importance of jointly modelling earnings attrition and transitions. The second row of the Table looks at the 1993–98 balanced sample and reports earnings transition probabilities from 1993 to 1998. It can observed that while the probability of falling into low pay from higher pay is approximately the same as for the shorter term transitions of Table 2.3, the probability of low pay persistence is some 6 to 8 percentage points lower, as can be expected by the fact that a wider time windows is taken into account. Finally, the bottom line of the Table provides the probabilities of 1998 pay states conditional on 1993 and 1995 pay states. Employees who have been low paid in both 1993 and 1995 face a probability of being low paid in 1998 in the order of 68 per cent, larger than the ones characterising two years transitions. Having entered low pay after an initial high pay experience is also associated with considerable low pay persistence, in the order of

45 per cent; comparing this figure with the one for employee who have always been low paid suggests the existence of positive duration dependence at the aggregate level. Climbing out of low pay and falling back into it is a less likely but still relevant phenomenon, with an associated probability of 31 per cent. Finally those who have never been low paid before 1998 have conditional low pay probability below 5 per cent.

Modelling earnings mobility and attrition over three waves

Since it is no longer appropriate to treat retention into the earnings distribution as binary, I model retention outcome as a multiple response discrete ordered variable:

$$r^*_{it} = \boldsymbol{\psi}'\mathbf{w}_{it-5} + \nu_{it}; \quad R_{it} = t(r^*_{it})$$

$$t(r^*_{it}) = \begin{cases} -1 & \text{if} \quad r^*_{it} \in (-\infty, \tau], \\ 0 & \text{if} \quad r^*_{it} \in (\tau, \ 0], \\ 1 & \text{if} \quad r^*_{it} \in (0, +\infty) \end{cases} \tag{11}$$

$$i = 1, \ldots, N_{93}; \quad \tau < 0.$$

Expression in (11) uses the same notation as in (3), but there are differences to be stressed. First of all, the sample is restricted to 1993 employees with valid earnings since we are now studying a single three-year transition. Second, there is now an additional intermediate outcome of the earnings attrition process, that is, having valid earnings in the first two years of the transition but not in the third.[17] Accordingly, I introduce an additional threshold in the support of r^*_{it}, τ, while holding the threshold for being a (three-year) balanced panel member normalised to 0. The mapping $t(.)$ transforms r^*_{it} into a discrete ordered variable R_{it}. Explanatory variables are measured at the beginning of the transition.

The 1993 earnings distribution is specified analogously to equation (1), the analogy being that 1993 is the starting year of the transition, with the dummy variable L_{it-5} indicating the occurrence of low earnings at the start of the transition. The 1995 earnings distribution, on the other hand, can only be observed conditionally on staying in the sample of earnings recipients:

$$g_{t-3}(y_{it-3}) = \begin{cases} \boldsymbol{\omega}'\mathbf{x}_{it-5} + e_{it-3} & \text{if} \quad R_{it} \geq 0, \\ \text{unobserved} & \quad \text{otherwise} \end{cases} \tag{12}$$

$$L_{it-3} = I(y_{it-3} \leq \lambda_{t-3}).$$

Finally, I study 1998 earnings conditionally on past pay states and retention:

$$h(y_{it}) = \begin{cases} \gamma_1' \mathbf{z}_{it-5} + \varepsilon_{it} & \text{if} \quad L_{it-5} = 1 \quad \text{and} \quad L_{it-3} = 1 \quad \text{and} \quad R_{it}=1, \\ \gamma_2' \mathbf{z}_{it-5} + \varepsilon_{it} & \text{if} \quad L_{it-5} = 0 \quad \text{and} \quad L_{it-3} = 1 \quad \text{and} \quad R_{it}=1, \\ \gamma_3' \mathbf{z}_{it-5} + \varepsilon_{it} & \text{if} \quad L_{it-5} = 1 \quad \text{and} \quad L_{it-3} = 0 \quad \text{and} \quad R_{it}=1, \\ \gamma_4' \mathbf{z}_{it-5} + \varepsilon_{it} & \text{if} \quad L_{it-5} = 0 \quad \text{and} \quad L_{it-3} = 0 \quad \text{and} \quad R_{it}=1, \end{cases}$$

$$L_{it} = I(y_{it} \leq \lambda_t). \tag{13}$$

Equations (1) (applied to the unique starting year, 1993), (11), (12) and (13) provide a framework for the analysis of three-years transition controlling for multiple responses in attrition. As before, errors are assumed to be jointly normally distributed:

$$(u_{it-5}\ v_{it}\ e_{it-3}\ \varepsilon_{it}) \sim \mathrm{N}_4[\mathbf{0}, \boldsymbol{\Omega}], \tag{14}$$

where $\mathbf{0}$ is a row vector of zeros and the $\boldsymbol{\Omega}$ matrix has diagonal elements equal to unity and extra-diagonal elements equal to cross-equations correlation coefficients, while N_4 is the four-variate normal density. After applying a change in parameters similar to the one applied in the case of the two-year transition to equations (12) and (13) we obtain vectors κ and η_1 to η_4, respectively, which index the probability of having earnings below the low pay threshold. Likelihood contributions for this model are given in the Appendix.

Additional identifying restrictions would be required for this model compared to the one in Section 4. In fact, the 1995 earnings distribution is observed conditionally on $R_{it} > -1$, that is, if individuals survive in the sample of income recipients after 1993. In turn, 1995 pay states enter the conditioning set for 1998 low pay probabilities. Thence, assuming, as we did in Section 4, that parental background variables (plus the square of experience) enter earnings levels but not earnings changes, we would need to include these variables into the 1995 earnings equations, implying that additional instruments should be included into the retention equation. However, as pointed out earlier, there are no variables in the SHIW that could be used for this purpose. Thence, I base identification of the relationship between retention and 1995 earnings levels on functional form, and the vector of regressors will be the same in all the three conditioning equations.

Results

Results from simulated estimation of the four-variate probit model are reported in Table 2.6. The level of aggregation of explanatory variables is higher compared to the two-year model of Section 4 since, as seen in

Table 2.6 Results[a] from estimation of four-variate probit model for 1998 conditional low-pay probabilities (absolute t ratios, *p*-values)

1993 and 1995 pay states	L93 L95		H93 L95		L93 H95		H93 H95	
Female	0.410	(1.07)	0.202	(0.54)	0.241	(0.63)	0.368	(2.17)
Potential labour market experience/10	−0.006	(0.04)	−0.010	(0.05)	0.194	(1.11)	0.048	(0.55)
Education ≥ High school	0.958	(1.35)	−0.332	(0.51)	−0.308	(0.71)	−0.345	(1.67)
Non-manual occupation	−1.342	(1.91)	0.504	(0.79)	−0.542	(0.95)	−0.283	(1.39)
Other manufacturing, retail trade, financial and other services	0.263	(0.75)	0.006	(0.02)	0.178	(0.50)	0.169	(0.86)
Public sector	0.553	(0.93)	0.174	(0.34)	0.446	(0.70)	−0.332	(1.65)
North	−0.484	(1.50)	−0.485	(1.41)	0.126	(0.38)	−0.167	(1.08)
Constant	0.401	(0.71)	−0.516	(0.99)	−0.568	(1.08)	−1.695	(5.70)
τ	—	−1.156	—	—	—	(37.32)	—	—
ρ_1(initial conditions 1993–retention)	—	−0.110	—	—	—	(3.02)	—	—
ρ_2(initial conditions 1993–95)	—	0.589	—	—	—	(14.39)	—	—
ρ_3(initial conditions 1993–transition)	—	−0.413	—	—	—	(1.65)	—	—
ρ_4(initial conditions 1995–retention)	—	−0.071	—	—	—	(1.16)	—	—
ρ_5(retention–transition)	—	0.359	—	—	—	(1.57)	—	—
ρ_6(initial conditions 1995–transition)	—	−0.154	—	—	—	(0.56)	—	—
Average prediction		0.68	— —	0.44	—	0.3 —	0.04	—
Aggregate State Dependence[b]	—	—		0.24	—	0.38 —	0.64	—
Test(df = 24, H$_0$: $\eta_1 = \eta_2 = \eta_3 = \eta_4$)	—	26.11	—	—	—	(0.3475)	—	—
Genuine State Dependence[b]	—	—		0.06	—	0.26 —	0.43	—
Log likelihood	—	—	—		−4351.957	—	— —	—
$\chi^2(df = 82)$	—	—	—		1 074.94 (0.0000)	—	— —	—
Number of observations	—	—	—		2703	—	— —	—

Notes: SHIW data, transition 1993–98 – Full-time employees aged 18–58 if female and 18–60 if male. Reference category for dummy variables: male, blue collar worker, manufacturing lives in the Centre, South or Islands. L_t = low pay year t; H_t = high pay year t. Low pay defined as first quintile of hourly earnings.

(a) SML coefficients. GHK simulator with 50 random draws

(b) Deviations of 1998 conditional low pay probabilities from the L93 L95 case.

Table 2.5, cell size is now tiny. By first considering the estimates of the cross-equations correlation coefficients reported at the bottom of the table, it can be observed that all the patterns emerged from the two-year model are confirmed. Those who earn below the low pay threshold of a given year are more likely to drop out of the earnings distribution during the transition compared to the higher paid, as indicated by the negative estimates of ρ_1 and ρ_4, although in the second case the estimate precision is lower. The coefficient ρ_2 measures reduced form correlation between low pay probabilities in 1993 and 1995 and it is positive and precisely estimated. The correlation between initial conditions and low pay transition measured by ρ_3 and ρ_6 is negative (as it was in the case of the two-year model), indicating the presence of Galtonian regression effects. The correlation between unobservables of low pay transition and 1995 low pay probabilities is not precisely estimated: it may well be that this effect is absorbed by the simultaneous control for correlation between 1993 initial conditions and transition and reduced form low pay correlation (i.e. ρ_3 and ρ_2, respectively). Finally, the correlation between retention and transition probabilities measured by ρ_5 is positive and precisely estimated. Comments analogous to those made when the result was found for the two years case also apply now.

Among those who experienced low pay in 1993 and 1995, the probability of experiencing low pay in 1998 is lower for non-manual workers compared to employees in blue collar occupations, as well as for northern workers compared to workers living in the rest of the country.[18] This latter effect can also be observed among those who entered low pay in 1995 after having been in the high pay area of the distribution in 1993, whereas the remaining coefficients estimated for this group are not statistically significative at usual confidence levels. For the groups of employees who climb out of low pay in 1995 and fall back into it in 1998, no clear association can be detected between 1998 conditional low pay probabilities and personal attributes. Finally, for employees who did not experience low pay in 1993 and 1995, estimated coefficients indicate quite clearly that the probability of falling into low pay in 1998 is higher for female workers, less educated employees, blue collar workers and workers in the public sector.

Estimated coefficients from the four-variate probit can be used to investigate the extent of GSD in longer term transition in a fashion similar to the one adopted in Sections 4 and 5. The bottom panel of the table reports 1998 conditional low pay probabilities estimated for each of the four sequences of past low pay; again, we can note how model predictions replicate the aggregate figures of table 2.5. The table also reports measures of ASD and in particular, the 1998 conditional low pay probability of those who have always been low paid is contrasted with the ones from the other sequences of past low pay. The next row in the table reports a test for GSD, the null hypothesis given by the equality of coefficients vectors across the four low pay sequences (H_0: $\eta_1 = \eta_2 = \eta_3 = \eta_4$). The null hypothesis is clearly not rejected, an outcome which is opposite to the findings of the previous section. However, it might be that the test is biased by the tiny cell size, which drives estimated coefficients towards zero and thence towards equality across low pay sequences. Finally, measures of GSD analogous to those of the previous section are reported. For each balanced panel observation 1998 conditional low pay probabilities have been computed for each sequence of past low pay. Next the differences between the probability conditional on having always been low paid and each of the three other sequences have been computed. Reported figures are the average of these differences over the balanced sample. Again, we should expect tiny cell size to bias the measurement of GSD downward, a *caveat* to bear in mind when interpreting results. What emerges from these calculations is that the ratio GSD/ASD is approximately 25 per cent when columns (1) and (2) are compared. Thence, when comparing conditional low pay probabilities between employees who entered low pay in the previous period and those who had always been observed in low pay, the incidence of GSD is much lower than the one emerged in the two years model. This finding suggests that whatever the causes of GSD, they produce their effect as soon as individuals are touched by low pay, while subsequent low pay experiences contribute to a lesser extent. The GSD/ASD ratio is instead higher at approximately 68 per cent for the two other sequences of past low pay. Interestingly, the low pay experience in the first year of observation does not seem to matter here, that is, the relevance of GSD is the same for individuals who have never been low paid and for those who managed to escape from low pay during the 1993–95 transition.

7 Concluding remarks

This study has used data from the SHIW to analyse the earnings mobility of low paid Italians. In particular models of low pay transition probabilities have been estimated while controlling for endogenous initial conditions and endogenous attrition from the earnings distribution. With this aim, SML techniques have been used.

Results from models of wave-to-wave transitions indicate that both initial conditions and attrition are endogenous and should be properly controlled for. In particular, results on earnings attrition suggest that employees below the low pay threshold of a given year are less likely to survive into the earnings distribution of the next observation period compared to higher paid individual, a symptom of higher instability of low paid employment. The analysis of the relationship between personal attributes and low pay transition probabilities has shown that employees with low educational qualifications, female employees and southern workers have higher risks of being trapped into low pay. The probability of dropping into low pay, on the other hand, appears to be associated with manual jobs and with jobs in the metal-manufacturing industry and in small firms.

The analysis also indicates that state dependence effects play a relevant role in creating low pay traps: it is the experience of low pay which modifies the economic environment faced by individuals, increasing the probability of future low pay experiences irrespective of personal attributes. While the chapter does not investigate the causes of these effects, these results points towards the need of policies targeted on the whole pool of low paid employees, rather than on specific 'problem groups' within it.

I also studied transition probabilities allowing for second order dynamics. Results show that longer term low pay traps tend to occur among manual and southern workers. On the other hand, female employees and employees with low educational attainment are more likely than otherwise similar individuals to drop into low pay after having stayed out of it in the two periods prior to observation. Investigation of state dependence effects show that the bulk of it occurs at the beginning of a low pay spell, while the contribution of subsequent low pay experiences is less pronounced. Caution has to be exerted when considering results from this latter model due to tiny sample sizes which prompts for future applications on richer data.

Acknowledgements

Thanks go to W. Arulampalam, C. Dell'Aringa, S. Jenkins, C. Lucifora and M. Stewart for helpful comments. Data availability from the Bank of Italy and financial support from the Catholic University of Milan and the Nuffield Foundation under the New Career Development Scheme are gratefully acknowledged. Usual disclaimers apply.

Appendix: likelihood contributions for the three-year transition model

This Appendix reports likelihood contributions for the model of Section 6.

If $R_{it} = 1$, that is, for employees with valid earnings in 1993, 1995 and 1998, likelihood contributions are given by:

$$l_i = \Phi_4\,(k_i \boldsymbol{\eta}_\theta{}'\mathbf{z}_{it-5}, p_i \boldsymbol{\kappa}'\mathbf{x}_{it-5}, \boldsymbol{\psi}'\mathbf{w}_{it-5}, q_i \boldsymbol{\beta}'\mathbf{x}_{it-5}; \\ k_i p_i \rho_6, k_i \rho_5, p_i \rho_4, k_i q_i \rho_3, p_i q_i \rho_2, q_i \rho_1)$$

$$k_i = 2L_{it} - 1;\ p_i = 2L_{it-3} - 1;\ q_i = 2L_{it-5} - 1 \tag{A.1}$$

with $\theta = 1$ if $L_{it-3} = L_{it-5} = 1$, $\theta = 2$ if $L_{it-3} = 1$ and $L_{it-5} = 0$, $\theta = 3$ if $L_{it-3} = 0$ and $L_{it-5} = 1$ and $\theta = 4$ if $L_{it-3} = L_{it-5} = 1$. If $R_{it} = 0$, that is, when individuals exit from the earnings distribution in 1995, likelihood contributions are given by:

$$\begin{aligned} l_i = {} & \Phi_3(p_i\boldsymbol{\kappa}'\mathbf{x}_{it-5}, -\boldsymbol{\psi}'\mathbf{w}_{it-5}, q_i\boldsymbol{\beta}'\mathbf{x}_{it-5}; -p_i\rho_4, p_iq_i\rho_2, -q_i\rho_1) \\ & - \Phi_3(p_i\boldsymbol{\kappa}'\mathbf{x}_{it-5}, \tau - \boldsymbol{\psi}'\mathbf{w}_{it-5}, q_i\boldsymbol{\beta}'\mathbf{x}_{it-5}; -p_i\rho_4, p_iq_i\rho_2, -q_i\rho_1). \end{aligned} \tag{A.2}$$

Finally, if R_{it} = -1, that is, for observations with valid earnings only at the start of the transition, likelihood contributions take the following form:

$$l_i = \Phi_2(-\boldsymbol{\psi}'\mathbf{w}_{it-5}, q_i\boldsymbol{\beta}'\mathbf{x}_{it-5}; -q_i\rho_1). \tag{A.3}$$

Multivariate normal c.d.f.'s of order 3 and 4 are computed via simulation applying the GHK simulator.

The cross-equations correlation coefficients have the following meaning:

- ρ_1 = correlation between 1993 unconditional low pay probability and retention
- ρ_2 = reduced form correlation between low pay probabilities in 1993 and 1995 (1995 conditional on retention)
- ρ_3 = correlation between 1993 unconditional low pay probability and conditional 1998 low pay probability
- ρ_4 = correlation between retention and 1995 low pay probability (conditional on retention)
- ρ_5 = correlation between retention and 1998 conditional low pay probability
- ρ_6 = correlation between 1998 conditional low pay probability and 1995 low pay probability (conditional on retention).

Notes

1. The allocation of households to the panel sub-group is carried out on a random basis among households who report availability for re-interview. Roughly 90 per cent of households were available for re-interview in 1993 and 1995.
2. Some of the observed characteristics are amalgamated at a rather aggregate level, for example, in the case of education or occupation. The choice of the level of aggregation is aimed at avoiding small cells size problems, which are particularly likely to arise in a model of low pay transitions where some of the parameters of interest are estimated conditionally on being low paid.
3. Information on employer size is available only for private sector employees.
4. The earnings information available in the SHIW refers to yearly earnings, inclusive of extra-time compensations and fringe benefits, net of income taxes and social security contributions. On the working time side, the survey reports the number of months worked in the year and the number of hours worked

on average in a week, including extra-time. No information is available on the number of weeks worked on average in a month. In order to derive hourly earnings, I have assumed that each individual worked 52/12 weeks per month. Cappellari (2000) analyses low pay transitions using monthly and hourly earnings in parallel, showing that there are not dramatic differences in results between the two cases.

5. Major changes in the system of wage indexation took place at the beginning of the 1990s, whereby ex-ante wage compensations for inflation where substituted by bargained ex-post compensations. The figures reported in Table 2.2 suggest that this system was not entirely effective in protecting real wages against inflation.
6. See Heckman (1981a) for a general discussion and Stewart and Swaffield (1999) for an illustration in the context of low pay transitions.
7. As discussed in Stewart and Swaffield (1999) genuine state dependence might, for example, result from bad signalling, if employers use salary histories to assess the quality of prospective employees. Also human capital depreciation or alterations of search behaviour could cause past low pay to raise future low pay probabilities.
8. As pointed out when commenting Table 2.1, the bulk of exits from the earnings distribution occurs between 1995 and 1998, with an overall exit rate of 46 per cent.
9. The three equations structure resembles the one in Bingley *et al.* (1995). In that paper, however, the main equation is an ordered probit for the direction of movements across wage deciles, rather than a probit for low pay transition probabilities. Moreover, while Bingley *et al.* included in the attrition equation also employees who enter the earnings distribution during the transition, here I follow the approach of other attrition studies and only consider exits (e.g. Lillard and Panis, 1998). The inclusion of entries implies that personal attributes can be observed only after the 'decision' to remain in the sample has taken place, while for exits they are observed before such decision takes place.
10. Observed attributes are measured at the beginning of the transition in order to avoid simultaneity between changes in attributes and changes in wages. Note that since this equation refers to earnings conditional on lagged pay states and attrition, the error term differs from the one for unconditional earnings in (1).
11. Geweke-Hajivassiliou-Keane. See Hajivassiliou and Ruud (1994) and Gourieroux and Monfort (1996, pp. 93–107) for discussions of simulation methods and their application to maximum likelihood estimation of multivariate limited dependent variable models. The simulator is not used for bivariate c.d.f.'s which are normally available within statistical packages.
12. Alternatively, one could rely on the functional form of the model.
13. For those employees who were 'child' in the interviewed household, the information has been recovered from the household questionnaire, while for 'other relatives' or 'non relatives' information has been coded as missing.
14. In a dynamic random effect probit in which the effect of lagged states is subsumed into a dummy variable GSD is tested by testing the significance of the estimated coefficient on that dummy, see for example, Arulampalam *et al.* (2000). The test proposed in this chapter generalises that framework to the case

in which the whole parameter vector associated to personal characteristics switches according to lagged states.

15. I assume that observations from the two transitions are independent. I also experimented with a robust variance estimator which accounts for repeated observation on the same individual in the two transitions and found differences in results to be irrelevant.
16. I generalise the procedure proposed by Stewart and Swaffield (1999) for the bivariate probit case.
17. There are few cases (42 observations) of 're-joiners', that is, employees who re-enter into the earnings distribution in 1998 after having left in 1995. As explained above (see Section 3) I treat earnings attrition as an absorbing state (I borrow this definition from Zabel, 1998); consequently I ignore re-entries into the distribution and consider these cases as 'attritors' also in estimation of the 1998 distribution.
18. Estimates precision is not particularly high. Besides the aforementioned cell size problem, estimates imprecision could also be due to the use of regressors measured at the start of the transition, that is, five years before the outcome of interest.

References

Arulampalam, W., Booth, A.L. and Taylor, M.P. (2000) 'Unemployment Persistence', *Oxford Economic Papers*, 52, pp. 24–50.

Bingley, P., Bjørn, J. and Westergård-Nielsen, N. (1995) 'Determinants of Wage Mobility in Denmark 1980–1990', *CLS* Working Paper, University of Aarhus, pp. 10–95.

Cappellari, L. (2000) 'Low Wage Mobility in the Italian Labour Market', *International Journal of Manpower*, 21, pp. 264–90.

D'Alessio, G. and Faiella, I. (2000) 'I Bilanci delle Famiglie Italiane nell'Anno 1998', *Supplementi al Bollettino Statistico*, 22, Banca d'Italia.

Dickens, R. (2000) 'Caught in a Trap? Wage Mobility in Great Britain: 1975–1994', *Economica*, 67, pp. 477–97.

Freeman, R.B. (1996) 'The Minimum Wage as a Redistributive Tool', *The Economic Journal*, 106, pp. 639–49.

Gregory, M. and Elias, P. (1994) 'Earnings Transitions of the Low Paid in Britain, 1976–91: a Longitudinal Study', *International Journal of Manpower*, 15, pp. 170–88.

Gourieroux, C. and Monfort, A. (1996) *Simulation-based Econometric Methods*, Oxford: Oxford University Press.

Hajivassiliou, V. and Ruud, P. (1994) 'Classical Estimation Methods for LDV Models Using Simulation', in Engle, R. and McFadden, D. (eds), *Handbook of Econometrics, vol. IV*, Amsterdam: North Holland.

Heckman, J.J. (1981a) 'Heterogeneity and State Dependence', in Rosen S. (eds), *Studies in Labour Markets*, Chicago: Chicago University Press.

Heckman, J.J. (1981b) 'The Incidental Parameters Problem and the Problem of Initial Conditions in Estimating a Discrete Time – Discrete Data Stochastic Process', in Manski, C.F. and McFadden, D. (eds), *Structural Analysis of Discrete Data with Economic Applications*, Cambridge, MA: MIT Press.

Jenkins, S.P. (2000) 'Modelling Household Income Dynamics', *Journal of Population Economics*, 13, pp. 529–67.
Lillard, L.A. and Willis, R.J. (1978) 'Dynamic Aspects of Earnings Mobility', *Econometrica*, pp. 985–1012.
Lillard, L.A. and Panis, C.W.A (1998) 'Panel Attrition from the PSID', *Journal of Human Resources*, 33, pp. 437–57.
Lucifora, C. (1998) 'Working Poors? An Analysis of Low Wage Employment in Italy', in *Low Pay and Earnings Mobility in Europe*, Asplund, R., Sloane, P. and Thedossiou, I. (eds), Cheltenham, UK: Edward Elgar.
OECD (1993) 'Earnings Inequality: Changes in the 1980s', *Employment Outlook*, pp. 157–84.
OECD (1996) 'Earnings Inequality, Low-paid Employment and Earnings Mobility', *Employment Outlook*, pp. 59–108.
Smith, R.E. and Vavricheck, B. (1992) 'The Wage Mobility of Minimum Wage Workers', *Industrial and Labour Relations Review*, 46, pp. 82–8.
Stewart, M.B. (1999) 'Low Pay, No Pay Dynamics', in *Persistent Poverty and Lifetime Inequality: The Evidence*, Centre for Analysis of Social Exclusion, London School of Economics, Report n. 5.
Stewart, M.B and Swaffield, J.K. (1999) 'Low Pay Dynamics and Transition Probabilities. *Economica*', 66, pp. 23–42.
Zabel, J.E. (1998) 'An Analysis of Attrition in the PSID and the Survey of Income and Program Participation', *Journal of Human Resources*, 33, pp. 479–506.

3

Low-pay Mobility in the Swiss Labour Market

Augustin de Coulon and Boris A. Zürcher

1 Introduction

During the 1980s and 1990s the Swiss labour market has forfeited much of its former flexibility at the aggregate level (defined as the capacity of aggregate labour demand and supply to rapidly adapt to external shocks). Many factors account for this, but the most documented ones are a higher attachment of women to the labour market, an increased assimilation of foreign workers with low skills in the labour force and legislative changes towards eligibility criteria for unemployment benefits. These developments rather specific to the Swiss situation were accompanied by an accelerated structural change common to most industrialized economies, reflected by continuously shrinking employment opportunities in manufacturing, an increasing employment share of the service sector and an accelerated skill-biased technological change. The decline in labour market flexibility at the aggregate level, has implied greater flexibility at the individual level, either in terms of wage or labour volume adjustments. The share of part-time jobs has indeed steadily increased over the past decade, and other forms of flexible work arrangements have gained importance (Swiss Federal Statistical Office (SFSO), 1997). The discussion on job quality was further stimulated by the exceptionally long lasting period of economic stagnation during the 1990s with its consequent high level of structural unemployment among the low skilled. Some have argued that a growing proportion of the labour force is either faced with the choice of being low paid or durably excluded from employment. Generally doubts have arisen on the ability of the Swiss labour market to provide sufficient earnings opportunities for a large proportion of the labour force.

Several studies have analysed changes of the wage distribution in Switzerland. Quite surprisingly, a general decrease of job quality in terms of wages does not yet really show up. They rather show that the wage distribution has remained stable in Switzerland over the past decade.[1] For the period 1991–95 the OECD, for instance, reports an increase in the ratio of the 9th to the 5th decile by 3 per cent only and a slight decrease in the ratio of the 5th to the 1st decile by 2 per cent for male and female workers. Moreover, investigating low-pay proportions, Deutsch *et al.* (1999) find that the overall share of low-paid workers ('Bas salaires'), defined as those workers whose wage falls short of half the median wage, has remained constant at roughly 19.5 per cent between 1991 and 1997.[2] Considering only full-time workers they even find a slight decrease from 5.1 per cent in 1991 to 3.4 per cent in 1997.

In this study we address these puzzling contradicting piece of evidences by introducing a panel approach as opposed to comparisons of cross-sections. Take a simple example: a group of workers (of proportion p) is low paid at a certain point in time ($t-1$). If there is no mobility within the wage distribution (there is no change in the relative position of workers within the wage distribution), then this same group of workers is low paid throughout the entire period of observation. If there is complete mobility, then this group of workers is low paid at $t-1$ but then move to higher paid job, and another group of workers (of the same proportion p) moves down to the low-pay segment.

The figures for Switzerland mentioned by Deutsch *et al.* (1999) could, therefore, be consistent with a situation in which only few workers have dropped to the low-pay segment, but where low-pay persistence has been high. Or they could be consistent with a situation where every low paid worker in 1991 has moved to higher paid jobs and were replaced by the same number of individuals moving down to low-paid jobs. Our study investigates whether individuals are trapped in a low-pay career or whether they are just temporarily caught in a low-paying job. To address this issue we need to follow the same individuals over a certain period of time and to investigate their movements within the wage distribution. This exercise provides a complementary view to the computation of low-pay proportions. We look at the dynamics of becoming and remaining low-paid; computing simple low-pay proportions, by contrast, places emphasis on the determinants of being in a low-pay state at some point in time.

We first propose some descriptive and comparative statistics on low-pay incidence and mobility within the wage distribution. We also briefly look at movements to and out of the labour force, as it may well be that workers' mobility does not primarily manifest itself through wage adjustments, but rather through labour supply adjustments with fluctuations between different states on the labour market (employment to unemployment or withdrawal of the labour force). We observe that on an average initially low-paid workers have a much higher propensity of being low paid again in the subsequent period than initially high-paid workers.

To investigate this finding, we follow Stewart and Swaffield (1999) and model transitions into and out of the low-pay segment using a bivariate endogenous selection model. This econometric approach is based on a Markovian concept of mobility as defined by Heckman and Borjas (1980).[3] We need to take into account the potential selection bias arising when treating the initial state as exogenous (Heckman, 1981) as the available data cover a relatively short time period, so the initial state may still have a considerable impact on the subsequent state. This approach allows us to compare the difference between the probability of remaining low paid and remaining high paid.

This methodology also enables us to find out whether the higher probability of being low paid in year *t* for those initially low paid is caused by their observed characteristics (heterogeneity) or whether their experience of a low-pay spell generates lower probability to access higher paid jobs (state dependence). We may thus evaluate the factors accounting for low-pay persistence. The distinction between individual heterogeneity and state dependence is important as different policy options may apply for increasing the wages of the low-paid workers according to which of the two is the main cause for repeated low-pay spells.

The outline of the chapter is as follows: in Section 2, we present the data, define the low-pay thresholds and investigate overall mobility by means of two kinds of transition matrices. In Section 3 the econometric model is presented and discussed. The results are presented in Section 4, we first examine the determinants of the low-pay incidence. We then investigate the transition probabilities into and out of the low-wage segment. In Section 5, we evaluate whether state dependence or heterogeneity effects seem to dominate as possible explanations for low-pay persistence, and in Section 6, we give a brief summary of our results and conclude the chapter.

2 Data, descriptive and comparative statistics

The data are drawn from the Swiss Labour Force Survey (SLFS). This is a yearly survey, which is collected by the SFSO since 1991. Between 16 000 and 18 000 persons are interviewed by telephone in one of the three official languages, French, German and Italian. The survey method implies that individuals not possessing a phone and not speaking one of the official languages are not interviewed. Moreover, seasonal, and cross-border workers are not covered. The survey follows each individual over five consecutive years. This survey is used by the SFSO for displaying a wide range of official statistics on the Swiss labour market (more than 300 questions are asked).

Our approach requires some individuals being observed in year $t-1$ and then re-interviewed in year t. We chose to construct three different panels, in the first one, we select those individuals interviewed in year 1992 ($t-1$) and then re-interviewed in 1994 (t), in the second one, we select those interviewed in 1994 ($t-1$) and re-interviewed in 1996 (t), and in the third one, we select those interviewed in 1996 ($t-1$) and in 1998 (t). Then we pool theses three panels. We want to collect a data set that is representative of the entire period between 1992 and 1998. We look at individuals over a two-year period as we know that individual wage mobility tends to increase with the number of years observed (see Dickens, 2000). Extending the period to three or four years would be problematic as the number of individuals followed continuously becomes too small. So a two-year period is a compromise between data constraints (i.e. being able to track enough individuals) and underestimation of wage mobility (i.e. had we followed the individuals over a five-year period, we would have found higher mobility).

We finally obtain a raw sample of 19 636 individuals, males and females. Table 3.1 presents the averaged characteristics of those in the sample who are wage earners, of working age (15–65), whose hourly pay lies between CHF 5 and CHF 500[4] and who were interviewed in time $t-1$ and t (11 109 individuals). The means are computed for the respective pooled initial years of each panels, that is, for 1992, 1994 and 1996. We note that female workers tend to work more often in Commerce, Retail trade, Hotels and Restaurants, other Business Services and Personal and Collective Services than males. The majority of female persons work as employees; only few work as executive managers. Moreover, those women working are mainly single, have no children and tend to occupy part-time jobs more often than their male counterparts. Male workers, in turn, are more often in Manufacturing, and work more often in larger firms. Women are slightly younger in our sample than male workers; we will use this variable as a proxy for labour market experience in the analysis.

Table 3.1 Sample means (pooled data 1992, 1994, 1996)

	Male		Female	
	Mean	**Std. error**	**Mean**	**Std. error**
Education [years]	13.80	2.12	12.90	2.20
Age [years]	39.10	11.02	38.80	11.51
Agriculture, Natural Resources [share]	0.03	0.17	0.01	0.09
Manufacturing [share]	0.25	0.43	0.13	0.34
Construction [share]	0.09	0.29	0.03	0.16
Commerce [share]	0.15	0.35	0.18	0.39
Retail, Hotels, Restaurants [share]	0.01	0.12	0.03	0.18
Transport, Telecommunication [share]	0.09	0.29	0.05	0.22
Financial and Insurance Services [share]	0.07	0.25	0.07	0.25
Other Business Services [share]	0.27	0.44	0.42	0.49
Personal and Collective Services [share]	0.03	0.18	0.08	0.27
Children (yes = 1) [share]	0.46	0.50	0.37	0.48
Other Household Income [CHF]	39 177	187 526	45 892	121 361
Swiss [share]	0.85	0.36	0.85	0.35
Employee [share]	0.53	0.50	0.75	0.43
Employee with Subordinates [share]	0.32	0.47	0.18	0.38
Executive Manager [share]	0.15	0.36	0.07	0.25
Living in a city (>30 000 inhabitants) [share]	0.21	0.41	0.24	0.43
Firm size (≤20 employees) [share]	0.37	0.48	0.42	0.49
Firm size (20< employees <100) [share]	0.27	0.44	0.27	0.45
Firm size (≥100 employees) [share]	0.36	0.48	0.30	0.46
Married [share]	0.61	0.49	0.46	0.50
Full-time [share]	0.95	0.22	0.50	0.50
Size of sub-sample [share]	55.40		44.60	

Three low-pay thresholds

The choice of the low-pay cutoffs depends on the issues being addressed. If the main interest is the relationship between low pay and poverty, it may be appropriate to use an absolute measure of low pay. Relative measures seem more appropriate, in turn, when focusing on low pay that is not directly related to a subsistence wage level, but rather reflects on some kind of decency threshold (i.e. a measure of relative deprivation). In our analysis we have opted for three definitions. We adopted two widely used thresholds to perform comparisons with other studies: the first is half the median gross hourly wage, the second is two-third of the median gross hourly wage. A third threshold is defined as the level of hourly pay corresponding to a monthly nominal gross income of CHF 3000 in 1998 when working full-time. The choice of this threshold is motivated by recent discussions in Switzerland on the introduction of a legal minimum wage at this level (as there is no legal minimum wage in Switzerland).

Table 3.2 summarizes the different thresholds and also displays the corresponding full-time equivalent monthly wage when assuming an average number of 168 working hours a month. The CHF 3000 threshold has been constructed by calculating a nominal hourly wage with the Nominal Wage Index for 1992, 1994 and 1996. In 1998, this latter threshold amounts to CHF 17.86 an hour.

We can see that both relative thresholds (1/2 and 2/3 of the median) remained quite stable around CHF 14.5 and CHF 19.5 over the sample period. While the wage thresholds display only few variation, we note that the share of persons being paid less than CHF 3000 a month increased by one percentage point between 1992 and 1998 (from 8.2 to 9.2 per cent) while the share of persons earning less than 2/3 of the median wage declined by two percentage points during the same period (from 15.2 to 13.2 per cent). These results confirm previous findings that the low-pay proportions tend to move only slightly over the period in either directions depending on the thresholds considered. We observe no

Table 3.2 Low-pay thresholds, hourly wages, monthly incomes and low-pay proportions

	1992	1994	1996	1998
1/2 median	14.4	14.9	14.5	14.8
	(2 419)	(2 503)	(2 436)	(2 486)
	4.7%	4.5%	4.7%	4.4%
CHF 3 000	16.6	17.2	17.7	17.9
	(2 789)	(2 890)	(2 974)	(3 000)
	8.2%	7.8%	8.9%	9.2%
2/3 median	19.2	19.9	19.3	19.7
	(3 226)	(3 343)	(3 242)	(3 310)
	15.2%	13.5%	12.9%	13.2%

Note: First line contains hourly wages. The second line contains the monthly wage in brackets (168 hours), and the last line indicates the low-pay proportion.

significant trend towards a clear increasing proportion of the labour force experiencing low-pay spells. As these figures may be influenced by movements out of low pay to no-work, to unemployment or to apprenticeship, we devote our attention to the movements of low-paid individuals to other labour market states in the following section.

Transitions between labour market states

Four broad states are distinguished: employment, apprentice, unemployment and inactivity. The employment state is further differentiated into high paid, low paid and a situation where the wage earner refused to communicate her wage (i.e. no report). We have pooled the data such that the initial period $t-1$ and the final period t consist of all observations in the years (1992, 1994, 1996) and (1994, 1996, 1998) respectively. The transitions refer to a two-year period.

From Table 3.3 we can see that between 27 and 40 per cent of the initially low-paid workers (male and female) succeed in escaping the low-pay segment over a two-year period and that only between 18 and about 25 per cent remain low paid over two years. Compared to men, women have always a slightly lower probability of escaping lowpaid jobs. Interestingly, the probability to remain high paid is approximately 84 per cent for male workers, while it is only roughly 72 per cent for female workers. For a large share of those workers initially low paid, earnings are not reported the subsequent period (third column). We observe that low-paid persons tend to begin an apprenticeship more often than high-paid ones. Since we do not control for age and other characteristics apart from gender, this may be explained by the high-paid workers being in a different stage of their working life compared to the low-paid ones. A remarkable result, moreover, is that the probability of an initially low-paid person to drop out of the labour force is almost twice that of an initially high-paid one and that the exit rate is also about twice as high for female workers compared to male workers. The same holds for transitions into unemployment. While the higher exit rate of women may be mainly due to a voluntary retreat from the labour market, for instance to take care of children, the larger share of transitions into unemployment may be an indication of a downward rigidity of wages. Generally, these results show higher job turnover for women compared to men.

The main message of Table 3.3 is however that the probability of being low paid at time t is much higher for those low paid at time $t-1$ than for those higher paid at time $t-1$. This is precisely this aspect that we

Table 3.3 Transitions between different labour market states of low- and high-paid workers

Period $t-1$ (state in 1992, 1994, 1996)		**Period t (state in 1994, 1996, 1998)**					
		Employees			**Apprentice**	**Unemployed**	**Out of the labour force**
		High paid	**Low paid**	**No report**			
2/3 median							
Men	High paid	83.7	9.1	2.6	0.3	1.6	2.8
	Low paid	38.8	18.3	32.7	3.6	2.2	4.4
Women	High paid	71.8	13.0	6.3	0.2	1.7	7.1
	Low paid	27.0	18.0	37.7	1.1	4.4	11.7
CHF 3 000							
Men	High paid	84.2	9.2	1.8	0.3	1.6	2.8
	Low paid	37.1	22.3	29.4	4.7	1.9	4.7
Women	High paid	72.6	13.0	4.8	0.2	2.1	7.3
	Low paid	31.1	20.6	30.5	1.3	3.5	13.1
1/2 median							
Men	High paid	84.4	9.4	1.3	0.4	1.6	2.9
	Low paid	39.5	24.9	23.6	5.6	2.1	4.3
Women	High paid	73.7	13.3	3.0	0.2	2.2	7.5
	Low paid	36.4	23.6	19.5	2.1	3.5	14.9

Note: The sample consists of 11 109 individuals, aged between 15 and 65 years and whose hourly wages lies above CHF 5 and below CHF 500.

are investigating later on in Sections 3 and 4. It is also related to the issue of state dependence and heterogeneity. These higher probabilities of being low paid at time t for low paid at time $t-1$ may, on the one hand, result from worker's heterogeneity, with individual characteristics determining the low pay status over time. On the other hand, state dependence may prevail, with the experience of low pay implying a loss of human capital and/or a lower expected productivity from the point of view of the employers and therefore causing these higher probabilities of being low paid at time t, regardless of the individual characteristics. The relative importance of both these effects needs to be evaluated empirically as they imply different strategies to help individuals moving out of low-pay employment.

In the empirical part of the chapter, we will restrict our attention to those persons in employment and reporting a wage in every period considered. Therefore, only movements depicted by the first two columns of Table 3.3 will be considered. This reduces the sample size to 7617 individuals (restricted sample).[5] The other movements should nevertheless be kept in mind when discussing our empirical results. We should also mention here that our table does not tell us anything on the extent of the wage changes, so in the following section we investigate this issue.

Aggregate transition matrix

In the simple transition matrix (Table 3.4), each cell contains the conditional probability of being in state i in period t provided the state occupied in period $t-1$ was j.[6] The elements are thus given by the transition probabilities $\Pr(y_t = i \mid y_{t-1} = j) = p_{ij}$ with $t-1 \in \{1992, 1994, 1996\}$ and $t \in \{1994, 1996, 1998\}$. The income range has been partitioned into deciles.

We observe that the diagonal elements, displaying the stayer probabilities, always exceed the off-diagonal elements in magnitude. The largest stayer probabilities are observed at the tails of the wage distribution. At the lowest end of the wage distribution, approximately 56 per cent of the workers initially low paid remain low paid two years later, while at the opposite extreme of the wage distribution the share of the stayers amounts to 62 per cent. Mobility increases towards the middle range of the distribution. For example, of those initially in the 5th decile, 36 per cent move up the distribution and approximately the same amount move down. This might be due partly to the absolute wage range being higher in the upper and the lower part of the distribution (i.e. the distance measured in CHF

Table 3.4 Transition matrix, pooled data

Period $t-1$	**Period t**									
	1st decile	**2nd decile**	**3rd decile**	**4th decile**	**5th decile**	**6th decile**	**7th decile**	**8th decile**	**9th decile**	**10th decile**
1st decile	56.3	19.7	8.4	3.9	2.3	1.7	2.3	1.2	1.6	2.6
	(1.7)	(1.3)	(0.9)	(0.6)	(0.5)	(0.4)	(0.5)	(0.4)	(0.4)	(0.5)
2nd decile	19.1	40.9	18.0	8.8	4.2	2.7	1.4	1.2	1.2	2.5
	(1.3)	(1.6)	1.3)	(0.9)	(0.7)	(0.5)	(0.4)	(0.4)	(0.4)	(0.5)
3rd decile	7.5	17.1	32.7	18.3	11.8	5.6	2.8	1.1	1.3	1.8
	(0.9)	(1.3)	(1.6)	(1.3)	(1.1)	(0.8)	(0.6)	(0.4)	(0.4)	(0.4)
4th decile	4.4	8.5	19.1	27.6	20.8	10.2	4.8	2.0	0.6	1.9
	(0.7)	(0.9)	(1.3)	(1.5)	(1.4)	(1.0)	(0.7)	(0.5)	(0.3)	(0.5)
5th decile	2.7	4.6	8.9	21.6	25.8	18.8	10.3	4.5	1.9	0.9
	(0.5)	(0.7)	(1.0)	(1.4)	(1.5)	(1.3)	(1.0)	(0.7)	(0.5)	(0.3)
6th decile	2.8	2.1	4.7	9.5	19.4	29.8	18.7	8.0	2.6	2.4
	(0.6)	(0.5)	(0.7)	(1.0)	(1.3)	(1.5)	(1.3)	(0.9)	(0.5)	(0.5)
7th decile	1.5	2.1	2.7	4.4	8.4	19.7	29.6	22.5	6.8	2.3
	(0.4)	(0.5)	(0.5)	(0.7)	(0.9)	(1.3)	(1.5)	(1.4)	(0.8)	(0.5)
8th decile	1.8	1.3	1.2	2.1	3.7	7.2	21.0	35.0	20.7	5.9
	(0.4)	(0.4)	(0.4)	(0.5)	(0.6)	(0.9)	(1.4)	(1.6)	(1.4)	(0.8)
9th decile	1.7	1.3	1.1	2.1	1.3	1.5	6.4	21.2	45.5	17.8
	(0.4)	(0.4)	(0.4)	(0.5)	(0.4)	(0.4)	(0.8)	(1.4)	(1.7)	(1.3)
10th decile	2.7	1.9	3.1	1.7	2.2	2.8	2.7	3.3	17.7	61.9
	(0.5)	(0.5)	(0.6)	(0.4)	(0.5)	(0.6)	(0.5)	(0.6)	(1.3)	(1.6)

Note: Standard errors are given in parenthesis. The numbers are expressed in percentage points.

between the thresholds is not uniform across the distribution) so a given wage change implies crossing more deciles in the middle than in the tails of the distribution. The matrix also shows that there are non-zero probabilities for transitions from the lowest to the highest decile and vice versa. However, the probabilities of making larger jumps than just one decile are generally small and decrease with the number of deciles crossed. We also note that the escapees from the lowest decile mostly go to the 2nd and the 3rd decile (28.1 compared to 15.6 per cent to the 4th decile and higher). This result is interesting as the 1st decile cutpoint is situated between two thresholds that we are using for our regression analysis (i.e. between the CHF 3000 and 2/3 of the median).

International comparison

An important question within this context is whether the level and pattern of mobility in Switzerland is similar to that in other countries. Looking first at aggregate mobility, our results mirror those of Dickens (2000) who uses the British Household Panel Survey (BHPS) and the

New Earning Survey (NES) for Britain: a pronounced mobility in the middle range of the distribution, and a higher persistence in the lowest and highest deciles of the distribution.

International comparisons have been conducted by Maître and Nolan (1999), who used the European Community Household Panel and calculated the extent of mobility across quintiles for the year 1994 and 1995 in 12 European countries. Our transition matrix can be used to inquire movement between quintiles as well. We find that roughly 58 per cent of individuals stayed two consecutive years in the same quintile over the period 1992–98.[7] The share of individuals moving up or down by one quintile is 32 per cent. The share of individuals moving up or down by two and more quintiles is 10 per cent. Taking the results of Maître and Nolan as a reference point, this situates Switzerland at rank 6, 7 and 8 for the stayers, for those moving by one quintile, and for those moving more than one quintile respectively (with rank one being the most immobile country). Further comparisons can be made with Deding (2001), who compares low-pay mobility over a one-year and a three-year period (1992–93 and 1992–95) in three countries: Denmark, Germany and the United States. Movements of low pay to high pay are 41 and 48 per cent for Denmark over a one-year and three-year period respectively, similar figures are 28 and 34 per cent for Germany and 18 and 52 per cent for the United States. For Switzerland, at a similar threshold, 31 per cent of low-paid individuals left to high paid jobs over a two-year period. Stewart and Swaffield (2000) using the BHPS and computing one year transition over the period 1992–95, found higher low pay persistence. But it is difficult to assess which part of this higher persistence is due to the shorter time period used.

These comparisons allow us to classify Switzerland as displaying a slightly lower wage mobility compared to other developed countries. We should, however, stress that these results are to be interpreted with caution as the data and the definitions of low pay are not entirely comparable.

3 The econometric model

We want to investigate first the probability of being low pay. This is done without difficulty using a standard probit model. But in a second step, we want to focus on the low-pay probabilities of those who were already low paid in the previous period $t-1$ (the transition probabilities). As Stewart and Swaffield (1999) and Cappellari (1999) have shown, this problem requires additional care, we summarize here the approach proposed by these authors. The first ingredient of the model consists in defining the initial period probability of being low paid. Denote by the λ_{t-1} low pay threshold and define an indicator variable y as follows:

$$y_{t-1} = \begin{cases} 1, & \text{if } y^*_{t-1} < \lambda_{t-1} \\ 0, & \text{if } y^*_{t-1} \geq \lambda_{t-1} \end{cases},$$

y^*_{t-1} is defined as the hourly wage of part-time or full-time workers. The probability of being low paid in period $t-1$ is then given by the probit equation:

$$\Pr(y_{it-1} = 1) = \Phi(\beta' x_{it-1}), \tag{1}$$

where Φ denotes the standard normal cumulative distribution function, x_{it-1} is a vector of covariates explaining the earnings of individual i, and β' is the vector of slope coefficients. Since (1) is a simple probit equation the error term is distributed as $\varepsilon_{t-1} \sim N(0,1)$.

Now suppose that earnings of an individual in period t depend on whether he was low paid in period $t-1$. Suppose, for example, that $y_{it-1} = 1$, the probability of this individual being low paid both years is:

$$\Pr(y_{t-1} = 1, y_t = 1) = \Phi_2(\beta' x_{it-1}, \gamma_L' z_{it}; \rho) \tag{2}$$

with y_t defined similarly to y_{t-1} and where Φ_2 is the cumulative of the bivariate normal distribution. Even though this probability is only defined for those individuals with $y_{it-1} = 1$, we still maintain the assumption that the distribution of ε_t is defined over all individuals. From this it follows that the distribution of $(\varepsilon_{t-1}, \varepsilon_t)$ is bivariate standard normal with correlation ρ

$$\begin{bmatrix} \varepsilon_{t-1} \\ \varepsilon_t \end{bmatrix} \sim N\left[\begin{pmatrix} 0 \\ 0 \end{pmatrix}, \begin{pmatrix} 1 & \rho \\ \rho & 1 \end{pmatrix}\right].$$

The problem can be modelled by means of the following likelihood function:

$$L = \Pr(y_{t-1} = 1, y_t = 1)^{y_t y_{t-1}} \Pr(y_{t-1} = 0, y_t = 1)^{(1-y_t)y_{t-1}} \Pr(y_{t-1} = 0)^{(1-y_{t-1})}.$$

So the contribution of individual i to the log likelihood function is:

$$\begin{aligned} \ln L_i = {} & y_{it} y_{it-1} \ln \Phi_2(\gamma_L' z_{it}, \beta' x_{it-1}, \rho) \\ & + (1 - y_{it}) y_{it-1} \ln \Phi_2(-\gamma_L' z_{it}, \beta' x_{it-1}, -\rho) \\ & + (1 - y_{it-1}) \ln \Phi(-\beta' x_{it-1}). \end{aligned} \tag{3}$$

This model is one of partial observability, as we treat high-paid individuals in period $t-1$ as if they were not available to us in period t (see Meng and Schmidt, 1985). It is similar to the problem described by Farber (1983), in our case we can not estimate a probit on year t based on the a priori selection of those low paid in period $t-1$ as we would introduce a selectivity bias in those estimates if $\rho \neq 0$.

We note as well that the conditional distribution $\Pr(y_t = 1 \mid y_{t-1} = 1)$ is obtained by dividing the joint distribution (2) by the marginal distribution:

$$\Pr(y_t = 1 \mid y_{t-1} = 1) = \frac{\Phi_2(\beta' x_{it-1}, \gamma_L' z_{it}; \rho)}{\Phi(\beta' x_{it-1})}. \tag{4}$$

Several comments about this econometric model can be made:

(i) The model takes care of the initial conditions problem mentioned by Heckman (1981). He showed that ignoring the correlation between the initial state and the subsequent transitions and computing a simple probit model leads to a sample selection bias if the coefficient ρ is significantly different from zero. Clearly, the wage process started prior to the sampling period and its initial conditions are not observable. Hence due to serial correlation in such a process the 'arbitrarily' chosen initial period and the wage state associated with it requires that it is endogenized along the lines set out above.[8] The initial condition problem might be neglected when the panel covers a long enough time horizon because the correlation steadily declines over time and eventually fades out. A short panel over few years, however, imperatively requires controlling for the initial selection into a particular state.

(ii) For the parameter vector to be identified, some variables included in x_{it-1} must be excluded from z_{it}. Stewart and Swaffield (1999), for instance, have included family background variables in the vector x_{it-1}, which are not included in the vector z_{it}. The idea of using family background variables rests on the assumption that equation (1) reflects the selection into a particular state in the initial period – a selection that may indeed be highly dependent on inherited parental characteristics. Since the Swiss Labour Force Survey provides no such information we have used information on the nationality, the complementary income, and a dummy variable for children. Additionally, the squared age proxying for labour market experience of a worker is included in x_{it-1}, but not in z_{it}. The extra variables in

x_{it-1} can therefore be viewed as instruments for the endogenous selection into the initial state. The underlying assumption is that they do not affect the probability of being low paid, given the state in the previous period: they affect the level of the low-pay status variable, but not the change. The vector z_{it}, by contrast, should contain variables that explain wage changes. A LR-test is carried out to check for the validity of the instruments.

(iii) Notice that if the initial state is uncorrelated with subsequent transitions, then it is adequate to run for the year t a simple probit estimation *selecting only those individuals who were low paid in period* $t-1$. This is to say that if the ρ is equal to zero, the probability of being low paid in year t conditional on being low paid in year $t-1$ simplifies to

$$\Pr(y_t = 1 \mid y_{t-1} = 1) = \Phi(\gamma' z_{it}). \tag{5}$$

This, subsequently allows for a formal test of whether there is serial correlation in the wage process or whether the initial state may be treated as exogenous. In the empirical part we present estimates based on this simple model together with the estimates of the general model where $\rho \neq 0$.

We mention here that a similar model to (3) can be constructed when treating the low paid individuals at time $t-1$ as if they were not available to us at time t. The contribution of individual i in the log likelihood function of this model is

$$\begin{aligned}\ln L_i^2 &= (1 - y_{it})(1 - y_{it-1}) \ln \Phi_2(-\gamma_R' z_{it}, -\beta' x_{it-1}, \rho) \\ &\quad + (1 - y_{it-1}) y_{it} \ln \Phi_2(-\gamma_R' z_{it}, -\beta' x_{it-1}, -\rho) + y_{it-1}\Phi(\beta' x_{it-1}).\end{aligned} \tag{6}$$

Note that here a different parameter vector γ_R is estimated compared to equation (3). This equation then captures the probability of dropping into the low-wage segment given the job in the previous period was high paid.

4 Results

The results are reported in two steps. We first estimate the low-pay incidence for the period $t-1$ with a simple probit model (equation (1)). In a second step we investigate the transitions out and into low pay. We estimate equation (3) and compare the results with those obtained from estimating equation (5) where ρ is assumed to be zero. And we investigate similarly the transitions for high-paid individuals in year $t-1$, estimating equation (6) and the probit at t selecting only those high paid in $t-1$. Remember that the transitions always consist of moves over two years (between 1992 and 1994, between 1994 and 1996 and between 1996 and 1998).

Low-pay incidence

Table 3.5 shows the estimation results of the simple probit model (equation (1)) of the low-pay incidence at time $t-1$ (1992, 1994 and 1996, pooled) for the three different low-pay thresholds. The dummy variables for the firm size are defined against a medium firm size between 20 and 100 employees, the employment status is defined against middle managers, and the sectorial dummy variables are defined against manufacturing. Apart from the coefficient estimates associated with the variable we also report the marginal effects. For the variables education and experience the marginal effects are computed as the difference between the probabilities with 9 and with 12 years of schooling and between the age of 35 and 40 years respectively. For the dummy variables the marginal effects return the change of the probability associated with a switch from 0 to 1.

Looking first at the personal characteristics, we find that male workers experience a smaller incidence of low pay than female workers (between 2 and 10 per cent smaller incidence of low pay). Since we have controlled for most of the relevant characteristics usually seen as influencing individual productivity, this difference may well be taken as a sign of discrimination against female workers. The variables age and education are statistically significant and their quantitative impact varies depending on the threshold considered. A difference between 9 and 12 years of formal education reduces the low-pay incidence by at least 2.4 and by at most 7.3 per cent while a difference between 35 and 40 years of age reduces the low-pay incidence by at least 5 and by at most 14.5 per cent on average. The usual result of a concave wage profile is reflected by the positive sign associated with the age squared variable. The results further show that foreign workers seem more exposed to low-pay employment than Swiss citizens. An exception to this is the lowest threshold considered where the corresponding coefficient is statistically insignificant.[9] On average, working in an urban area or a city reduces the incidence of low pay. Working full-time also significantly reduces the low-pay incidence. Compared to Manufacturing, those economic sectors exhibiting

Table 3.5 Low-pay incidence in period $t-1$

Threshold		**2/3 median**	**CHF 3 000**	**1/2 median**
Constant		3.326 (0.218)	2.252 (0.234)	1.474 (0.260)
Personal characteristics	Male	−0.530 (0.039) *−0.107*	−0.473 (0.045) *−0.063*	−0.304 (0.052) *−0.025*
	Married	−0.002 (0.039) *0.000*	0.009 (0.043) *0.001*	0.002 (0.051) *0.000*
	Education	−0.094 (0.008) *−0.073*	−0.077 (0.009) *−0.040*	−0.071 (0.010) *−0.024*
	Age	−0.123 (0.010) *−0.145*	−0.103 (0.011) *−0.082*	−0.095 (0.013) *−0.049*
	$Age^2/100$	0.141 (0.013) *0.028*	0.121 (0.013) *0.018*	0.112 (0.015) *0.001*
	Children	0.049 (0.039) *0.010*	0.073 (0.044) *0.009*	0.101 (0.050) *0.008*
	Swiss Nationality	−0.288 (0.043) *−0.063*	−0.195 (0.049) *−0.027*	−0.076 (0.059) *−0.006*
	Other Household Income/100 000	0.003 (0.012) *0.001*	0.015 (0.012) *0.002*	0.015 (0.014) *0.002*
City	> 30 000 Inhabitants	−0.172 (0.041) *−0.031*	−0.165 (0.047) *−0.020*	−0.183 (0.056) *−0.013*
Firm size	< 20	0.304 (0.039) *0.061*	0.327 (0.044) *0.044*	0.325 (0.051) *0.028*
	> 100	−0.241 (0.046) *−0.044*	−0.283 (0.054) *−0.034*	−0.288 (0.066) *−0.021*
Employment status	Employee	0.130 (0.040) *0.025*	0.090 (0.046) *0.011*	0.095 (0.053) *0.007*
	Manager	−0.299 (0.073) *−0.050*	−0.297 (0.083) *−0.032*	−0.220 (0.097) *−0.015*
Sector	Primary Sector	1.067 (0.098) *0.327*	0.991 (0.101) *0.231*	0.966 (0.108) *0.163*

Table 3.5 Continued

Threshold		**2/3 median**	**CHF 3 000**	**1/2 median**
	Construction	−0.392	−0.348	−0.330
		(0.080)	(0.093)	(0.111)
		−0.061	*−0.035*	*−0.020*
	Wholesale/Retail Trade/Repair	0.234	0.246	0.147
		(0.051)	(0.057)	(0.067)
		0.050	*0.035*	*0.013*
	Restaurants/ Hotels	0.686	0.451	0.341
		(0.092)	(0.098)	(0.112)
		0.186	*0.078*	*0.036*
	Transport/ Communication	−0.412	−0.538	−0.407
		(0.078)	(0.101)	(0.117)
		−0.064	*−0.048*	*−0.024*
	Bank/Insurance	−0.597	−0.752	−0.621
		(0.090)	(0.123)	(0.148)
		−0.083	*−0.058*	*−0.031*
	Other Business Services	−0.384	−0.302	−0.205
		(0.049)	(0.056)	(0.066)
		−0.069	*−0.036*	*−0.015*
	Personal Services	0.060	0.180	0.232
		(0.072)	(0.077)	(0.087)
		0.012	*0.026*	*0.022*
	Full-time	−0.217	−0.251	−0.281
		(0.041)	(0.045)	(0.052)
		−0.045	*−0.035*	*−0.025*
Log likelihood		−3 941.636	−3 053.463	−2 184.007
Pseudo R^2		0.2144	0.2033	0.1776
Observed prob.		0.167	0.109	0.064
Predicted prob.		0.114	0.064	0.036

Note: Shaded cells denote statistical significance at least at the 90 per cent level. Numbers in brackets are the standard errors, numbers in italic represent the marginal effects. They are calculated as the change in the probability associated with a discrete change of the dummy variable from 0 to 1 evaluated at the mean value of the other variables. For education the marginal effect is obtained as the change in the probability associated with a change from 9 to 12 years of formal schooling. For age the marginal effect is obtained as the change in the probability associated with a change from 35 to 40 years of age.

a higher low-pay incidence are the Primary Sector, Wholesale, Retail Trade and Repair, the Personal Services as well as Restaurants and Hotels. Construction Workers and Bank and Insurance Employees and other Business Services, by contrast, seem less exposed to a low-pay occurrence. The marginal effects of the sectorial dummy variables vary considerably. Working in the Primary Sector, for instance, increases the low-pay incidence by 16 to 33 per cent compared to Manufacturing.

A similar result holds for the catering business, which exhibits a low-pay incidence that is at most 18 per cent larger than in Manufacturing. A higher low-pay incidence is also associated with working in a small firm compared to a medium sized firm. This shows that small firms tend to choose more labour-intensive technologies due to decreasing return to scale in the use of physical capital and also often make relatively intensive use of low-skilled labour. Working in a larger firm (more than 100 employees) consequently reduces low-pay incidence.

To be married and the complementary household income are found to have no systematic effect on the low-pay probability. One may thus conclude that wages are set without taking into account the broader income and family situation of a worker.

Our results are rather similar to those obtained by Cappellari (1999), and by various papers in Asplund *et al.* (1998). However the presence of children seems to affect more the low-pay incidence in Switzerland than in Italy (Cappellari, 1999). We found also insignificant effect for the married dummy whereas the opposite seems to prevail in Italy (Cappellari, 1999).

Transition probabilities

We want now to go a step further and analyse the probabilities of moves into and out of low pay. We present the estimated coefficients of the parameters $\hat{\gamma}$ of the transition equation (3) in columns 1 to 3. We compare these results with those obtained from estimating equation (5) in columns 4 to 6. So the first six columns show the results for the probability of being low paid in both years, that is, $\Pr(y_t = 1 \mid y_{t-1} = 1)$, the first three taking care of the endogenous selection into the initial low pay segment, and the next three assume that the correlation is 0. Similarly the next six columns give the estimates for the conditional probability of being low paid in period t given the person had a wage above the low-pay threshold in the preceding period $t-1$, that is, $\Pr(y_t = 1 \mid y_{t-1} = 0)$.[10]

Since the coefficients are difficult to interpret the marginal effects are reported as well. They were computed similarly as before when we looked at the low-pay incidence, and they may directly be interpreted as the percentage change in the probability of remaining low paid or dropping into the low-pay segment.

First of all we find that the probability of remaining in the low-wage segment given one was low paid in the previous period varies between 36 and 54 per cent, depending on which threshold is considered. This at the same time means that between 56 and 64 per cent of those having been low paid succeeded in escaping the low-pay segment the next period. The probability of entering the low-pay segment from a higher paid job varies between 3 and almost 5 per cent, indicating that once a worker has succeeded in establishing herself in a higher paid job the probability of dropping obviously becomes relatively small. These numbers clearly differ from those reported in Table 3.3, because the sample is restricted to workers reporting a wage and remaining in the labour force over the two-year period.

From Table 3.6 we can see that many variables that were statistically significant in the probit estimation of Table 3.5 have lost their significance now. Apparently they contain some explanatory power for the selection into a particular state, but seem not to affect transitions between wage classes.

The variables to which we attach particular importance are education and work experience. With the exception of the CHF 3000 threshold additional years of education prevent a stay in the low-wage segment. The same is observed for the probability of dropping into the low-wage segment. However, the effect is rather weak, and for the lowest threshold it is insignificant. Rather surprisingly, the acquired years of work experience measured by age are never significant in reducing the probability of remaining low paid and as well in preventing a drop into the low-wage segment (with the exception of the CHF 3000 threshold). This contrasts with the human capital approach to wage formation and only makes sense when perceiving these low-paid jobs as 'bad' jobs with no skill content. Interestingly, Cappellari (1999) found very similar results for the education and experience variables. Stewart and Swaffield (2000) found insignificant coefficients for education in their endogenous selection model, this seems not to be the case in Switzerland (except for the CHF 3000 threshold). Experience has never any effect on the low-pay transition in our estimations, whereas it has a slight effect for one of the three thresholds in Stewart and Swaffield (2000).

Figures 3.1 and 3.2 plot the effects for education and experience. While the probability plot for education conforms to our expectation this is not necessarily the case for experience. Many years of experience are not reducing the probability of remaining low paid, but as well a drop is hardly reduced with higher experience. This certainly contradicts the view that wages increase with seniority. The probability of remaining low paid and the probability of falling into the low-wage segment remain virtually the same regardless of whether a person possesses one year of work experience or whether she possesses 20 years of work experience. It is worth mentioning that the plots look similar when considering the other thresholds.

Table 3.6 Transition probabilities

Threshold		Pr(y_t = low paid | y_{t-1} = low paid)						Pr(y_t = low paid | y_{t-1} = high paid)					
		Endogenous selection model (equation 3)			Probit model (equation 5)			Endogenous selection model (equation 6)			Probit model		
		2/3 median	CHF 3 000	1/2 median	2/3 median	CHF 3 000	1/2 median	2/3 median	CHF 3 000	1/2 median	2/3 medain	CHF 3 000	1/2 median
Constant		0.700	0.196	−0.678	0.752	0.047	−0.568	−0.738	−1.041	−1.759	−0.417	−0.802	−1.642
		(0.313)	(0.386)	(0.609)	(0.319)	(0.398)	(0.568)	(0.266)	(0.266)	(0.287)	(0.249)	(0.266)	(0.292)
Personal charac-teristics	Male	−0.285	−0.149	−0.095	−0.414	−0.315	−0.057	−0.203	−0.277	−0.291	−0.263	−0.330	−0.313
		(0.116)	(0.144)	(0.202)	(0.100)	(0.129)	(0.187)	(0.073)	(0.078)	(0.085)	(0.071)	(0.078)	(0.085)
		−0.114	*−0.058*	*−0.032*	*−0.164*	*−0.124*	*−0.021*	*−0.017*	*−0.017*	*−0.013*	*−0.020*	*−0.019*	*−0.014*
	Married	−0.048	−0.111	−0.095	−0.058	−0.125	−0.083	−0.045	0.059	0.077	−0.049	0.059	0.072
		(0.081)	(0.100)	(0.154)	(0.083)	(0.105)	(0.152)	(0.060)	(0.065)	(0.071)	(0.061)	(0.066)	(0.072)
		−0.019	*−0.043*	*−0.032*	*−0.023*	*−0.050*	*−0.030*	*−0.004*	*0.003*	*0.003*	*−0.004*	*0.003*	*0.003*
	Educa-tion	−0.044	0.007	−0.073	−0.069	−0.021	−0.067	−0.051	−0.038	−0.016	−0.063	−0.048	−0.020
		(0.022)	(0.025)	(0.036)	(0.018)	(0.023)	(0.033)	(0.014)	(0.015)	(0.016)	(0.014)	(0.015)	(0.016)
		−0.053	*0.008*	*−0.008*	*−0.079*	*−0.025*	*−0.075*	*−0.016*	*−0.008*	*−0.002*	*−0.019*	*−0.010*	*−0.003*
	Age	0.002	0.005	0.005	0.000	0.003	0.005	−0.004	−0.007	0.000	−0.005	−0.007	0.000
		(0.004)	(0.004)	(0.006)	(0.003)	(0.004)	(0.006)	(0.003)	(0.003)	(0.003)	(0.003)	(0.003)	(0.003)
		0.004	*0.009*	*0.007*	*0.001*	*0.006*	*0.009*	*−0.002*	*−0.002*	*0.000*	*−0.002*	*−0.001*	*0.000*
City	>30 000 Inhabi-tants	0.077	−0.172	−0.202	0.041	−0.223	−0.183	−0.059	−0.103	−0.175	−0.076	−0.119	−0.189
		(0.104)	(0.133)	(0.213)	(0.105)	(0.137)	(0.211)	(0.071)	(0.079)	(0.090)	(0.072)	(0.080)	(0.091)
		0.031	*−0.065*	*−0.065*	*0.016*	*−0.088*	*−0.065*	*−0.005*	*−0.006*	*−0.007*	*−0.005*	*−0.006*	*−0.007*
Firm size	<20	0.285	0.220	0.774	0.332	0.287	0.760	0.246	0.329	0.377	0.270	0.357	0.395
		(0.098)	(0.123)	(0.195)	(0.097)	(0.125)	(0.195)	(0.069)	(0.076)	(0.086)	(0.070)	(0.077)	(0.087)
		0.114	*0.086*	*0.267*	*0.131*	*0.113*	*0.258*	*0.022*	*0.021*	*0.018*	*0.021*	*0.021*	*0.019*
	>100	−0.006	−0.085	0.303	−0.045	−0.143	0.325	−0.177	−0.054	−0.008	−0.195	−0.069	−0.017
		(0.116)	(0.157)	(0.271)	(0.119)	(0.164)	(0.267)	(0.080)	(0.089)	(0.101)	(0.081)	(0.091)	(0.102)
		−0.002	*−0.032*	*0.103*	*−0.018*	*−0.056*	*0.123*	*−0.014*	*−0.003*	*0.000*	*−0.014*	*−0.004*	*−0.001*

Employment status	Employee	0.220	0.190	0.547	0.249	0.216	0.544	0.183	0.165	0.049	0.194	0.172	0.054
		(0.100)	(0.125)	(0.192)	(0.102)	(0.131)	(0.194)	(0.071)	(0.078)	(0.081)	(0.072)	(0.080)	(0.082)
		0.087	*0.072*	*0.174*	*0.099*	*0.085*	*0.184*	*0.015*	*0.009*	*0.002*	*0.014*	*0.009*	*0.002*
	Manager	0.110	−0.022	0.317	0.100	−0.039	0.317	−0.261	−0.035	−0.260	−0.272	−0.043	−0.266
		(0.168)	(0.221)	(0.362)	(0.173)	(0.234)	(0.365)	(0.117)	(0.115)	(0.133)	(0.119)	(0.117)	(0.135)
		0.044	*−0.008*	*0.112*	*0.039*	*−0.016*	*0.121*	*−0.018*	*−0.002*	*−0.009*	*−0.017*	*−0.002*	*−0.009*
Sector	Primary	0.096	−0.074	0.033	0.324	0.219	−0.062	0.761	0.913	0.919	0.918	1.070	1.054
		(0.229)	(0.268)	(0.377)	(0.208)	(0.251)	(0.318)	(0.209)	(0.191)	(0.187)	(0.203)	(0.188)	(0.188)
		0.039	*−0.028*	*0.011*	*0.125*	*0.087*	*−0.022*	*0.117*	*0.121*	*0.098*	*0.143*	*0.149*	*0.123*
	Construction	−0.752	−0.937	−1.513	−0.846	−1.042	−1.493	0.277	0.138	0.046	0.248	0.118	0.035
		(0.216)	(0.306)	(0.565)	(0.215)	(0.315)	(0.567)	(0.121)	(0.137)	(0.157)	(0.123)	(0.139)	(0.159)
		−0.253	*−0.266*	*−0.282*	*−0.316*	*−0.344*	*−0.323*	*0.028*	*0.009*	*0.002*	*0.022*	*0.007*	*0.001*
	Wholesale/ Ret. Tr./Rep.	0.082	−0.103	−0.098	0.132	−0.031	−0.113	0.384	0.411	0.321	0.417	0.440	0.331
		(0.121)	(0.150)	(0.235)	(0.122)	(0.156)	(0.234)	(0.096)	(0.099)	(0.108)	(0.096)	(0.100)	(0.109)
		0.033	*−0.039*	*−0.032*	*0.052*	*−0.012*	*−0.041*	*0.040*	*0.032*	*0.018*	*0.040*	*0.032*	*0.018*
	Restaurants/ Hotels	−0.206	−0.652	−0.882	−0.101	−0.563	−0.915	0.899	0.878	0.712	1.021	0.985	0.779
		(0.190)	(0.232)	(0.393)	(0.190)	(0.242)	(0.386)	(0.177)	(0.166)	(0.171)	(0.172)	(0.164)	(0.173)
		−0.079	*−0.202*	*−0.206*	*−0.040*	*−0.210*	*−0.255*	*0.151*	*0.112*	*0.062*	*0.170*	*0.128*	*0.070*
	Trans./ Communication	−0.454	−0.406	−0.082	−0.539	−0.536	−0.052	−0.161	−0.276	−0.285	−0.197	−0.316	−0.300
		(0.208)	(0.296)	(0.406)	(0.210)	(0.307)	(0.404)	(0.142)	(0.167)	(0.191)	(0.143)	(0.169)	(0.192)
		−0.166	*−0.141*	*−0.027*	*−0.210*	*−0.200*	*−0.019*	*−0.012*	*−0.013*	*−0.010*	*−0.012*	*−0.013*	*−0.010*
	Bank/ Insurance	−0.581	−0.447	–	−0.702	−0.705	–	−0.133	−0.358	−0.272	−0.189	−0.410	−0.298
		(0.275)	(0.513)		(0.277)	(0.525)		(0.149)	(0.186)	(0.197)	(0.150)	(0.189)	(0.199)
		−0.205	*−0.153*		*−0.268*	*−0.253*		*−0.010*	*−0.015*	*−0.009*	*−0.012*	*−0.016*	*−0.009*
	Other Services	−0.309	−0.382	−0.449	−0.384	−0.460	−0.431	−0.034	−0.124	−0.098	−0.069	−0.150	−0.110
		(0.132)	(0.162)	(0.244)	(0.130)	(0.164)	(0.244)	(0.092)	(0.100)	(0.109)	(0.093)	(0.102)	(0.110)
		−0.121	*−0.142*	*−0.142*	*−0.152*	*−0.178*	*−0.148*	*−0.003*	*−0.007*	*−0.004*	*−0.005*	*−0.008*	*−0.004*
	Personal Services	−0.179	−0.233	−0.009	−0.164	−0.166	−0.009	0.061	0.056	0.117	0.079	0.087	0.143
		(0.166)	(0.196)	(0.292)	(0.170)	(0.206)	(0.291)	(0.144)	(0.149)	(0.155)	(0.146)	(0.153)	(0.158)
		−0.069	*−0.07*	*−0.003*	*−0.065*	*−0.065*	*−0.003*	*0.005*	*0.003*	*0.006*	*0.006*	*0.005*	*0.007*

Table 3.6 Continued

Threshold	$Pr(y_t = \text{low paid} \mid y_{t-1} = \text{low paid})$						$Pr(y_t = \text{low paid} \mid y_{t-1} = \text{high paid})$					
	Endogenous selection model (equation 3)			Probit model (equation 5)			Endogenous selection model (equation 6)			Probit model		
	2/3 median	CHF 3 000	1/2 median	2/3 median	CHF 3 000	1/2 median	2/3 median	CHF 3 000	1/2 median	2/3 medain	CHF 3 000	1/2 median
Full-time	0.262	0.237	0.294	0.260	0.236	0.310	−0.333	−0.317	−0.195	−0.359	−0.346	−0.221
	(0.094)	(0.111)	(0.171)	(0.097)	(0.116)	(0.168)	(0.073)	(0.079)	(0.085)	(0.074)	(0.079)	(0.086)
	0.102	*0.088*	*0.093*	*0.103*	*0.093*	*0.112*	*−0.032*	*−0.022*	*−0.009*	*−0.032*	*−0.023*	*−0.010*
ρ	−0.300	−0.381	0.131	0	0	0	0.373	0.500	0.617	0	0	0
	(0.132)	(0.153)	(0.280)				(0.149)	(0.197)	(0.309)			
Log likelihood	−3 256.5	−2 328.4	−1 456.5	−704.79	−443.8	−213.1	−3 685.4	−2 845.1	−2 030.7	−1 134.7	−961.0	−790.9
Observed. prob.	0.541	0.472	0.356	0.541	0.472	0.356	0.044	0.035	0.026	0.051	0.038	0.027
Predicted prob.	0.536	0.469	0.347	0.543	0.468	0.333	0.045	0.035	0.026	0.032	0.022	0.027
N	7 617	7 617	7 615	1 114	688	368	7 617	7 617	7 617	6 503	6 929	7 247

Note: For each variable, the first line displays the estimated coefficient, the second line the standard error in brackets, and the third line the marginal effects (in italics). The marginal effects are calculated as the change in the probability associated with a discrete change of the dummy variable from 0 to 1 evaluated at the mean of other variables. The marginal effect of education is calculated as the change in the probability associated with a change from 9 to 12 years of formal schooling. The marginal effect of experience is calculated as the change in the probability associated with a change of the age from 35 to 40 years. Cells shaded gray indicate statistical significance of the coefficients at least at the 90 per cent level. The variable bank and insurance was dropped in one equation since no individual was low paid in these sectors over two consecutive years.

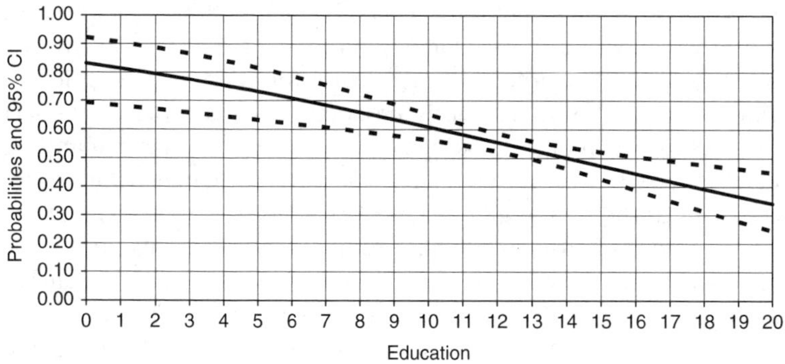

Figure 3.1 Probability plot $\Pr(y_t = 1 \mid y_{t-1} = 1)$ for the 2/3 median threshold on education[11]

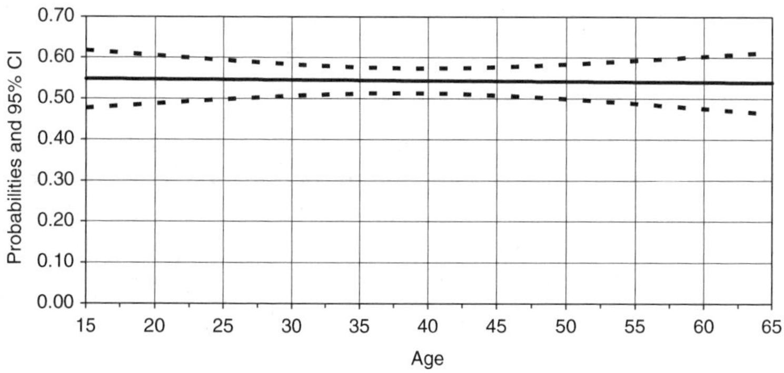

Figure 3.2 Probability plot $\Pr(y_t = 1 \mid y_{t-1} = 1)$ for the 2/3 median threshold on experience measured by the age

Working in sectors such as the Banking and the Insurance branch or Transportation and Telecommunication significantly reduces the probability of remaining or falling into a low-paid employment. Typically enough, there were not sufficient observations to assess the effect of staying below 1/2 median threshold for persons working in the Banking and Insurance business. For this reason this dummy variable had to be dropped in these equations.[12]

We find negative coefficients for most economic sectors with regard to the probability of remaining low paid over two consecutive periods on the one hand, but on the other we find some positive effects when considering the probability of dropping into the low-wage segment. This effect is particularly pronounced for the Hotel and Restaurant sector.[13] This points to a pronounced job-mobility. It seems thus very likely that only those workers remain employed in the Hotel and Restaurant business who earn sufficiently high wages. Those workers, in turn, who earn very low wages, apparently leave their job more frequently for a better paying job in another sector.[14] This subsequently produces a negative marginal effect when assessing the probability of remaining low paid. This explanation is actually endorsed by the rather high probability of dropping below any of the thresholds when coming from a higher paid job (between 6 and 15 per cent). The same as for the hotel and restaurant business seems true for the primary sector and the wholesale, retail and trade sector. Again, we can see that working in a small firm increases the probability of remaining low paid over two years, and the probability to drop below the low-pay threshold when initially high paid is positive and statistically significant.

A comparison of the probit model assuming $\rho = 0$, with the endogenous selection model shows that the initial state is often correlated with a subsequent transition (ρ is statistically different from zero in five out of six estimations), and gives signs for ρ that follow a priori expectations. The negative correlation between the initial state and a subsequent transition in the first transition equation captures the correlation between the unobservable variables in the explanation of the probability of experiencing a positive wage change and in the explanation of the probability of having a low initial wage: it is analogous to a negative coefficient in a standard regression of wage changes on their initial level. The coefficient estimates between the simple probit model and the endogenous selection model for this reason differ when ρ is significantly different from zero, which implies that we have to treat the initial state as endogenous. It is therefore not surprising to find that the instruments controlling for the initial state turn out to be jointly significant (the Likelihood Ratio (LR)-Test rejects the hypothesis of no significance at the 5 per cent level). The comparison of the two models also reveals that the coefficient estimates are sensitive to the imposition of the restriction $\rho = 0$. They are slightly inflated in the probit model compared to the endogenous selection model, that is, they tend to overestimate the effect.

5 State dependence versus heterogeneity

We may ask now, how much the explanatory variables (observed heterogeneity) account for the low-pay persistence. The state dependence effect is estimated as follows: first, the predicted conditional probability of being low paid in period t provided being low paid in period $t-1$ as given by the equation (4) is calculated for each individual, for his specific set of covariates. These (hypothetical) probabilities are subsequently averaged over first those low paid in $t-1$, and then those high paid in $t-1$. The difference between the two quantities is the contribution that is not due to state dependence. Formally this is

$$Diff = \frac{\sum_{i \mid y_{it-1=1}} \frac{\Phi_2(x'_{it-1}\hat{\beta},\, z'_{it}\hat{\gamma};\, \hat{\rho})}{\Phi(x'_{it-1}\hat{\beta})}}{\sum_{i \mid y_{it-1=0}} y_{it-1}} - \frac{\sum_{i \mid y_{it-1=0}} \frac{\Phi_2(x'_{it-1}\hat{\beta},\, z'_{it}\hat{\gamma};\, \hat{\rho})}{\Phi(x'_{it-1}\hat{\beta})}}{\sum_{it \mid y_{it-1=1}} y_{it-1}}.$$

The state dependence effect is then calculated as the residual difference between this last quantity and the raw aggregate difference of probability of being low paid in t for higher and lower paid in $t-1$. This is basically a simple difference in difference approach and seems a convenient way of computing the state dependence effect as the part not explained by observed heterogeneity. However, it should also be noted that this method equates the state dependence effect with the residuals capturing everything the model omits, including unobserved heterogeneity.[15] As a consequence, the less the model explains, the higher the state dependence effect tends to be. The decomposition results are reported in Table 3.7.

Within our specification, heterogeneity obviously plays a minor role, which is to say that the reasons for remaining low paid are mainly due to state dependence. The latter varies between 69 and 81 per cent depending on which threshold is considered (lines 8 and 13 in Table 3.7).

Comparing these results with those of Stewart and Swaffield (1999) where state dependence accounts for 56 up to 76 per cent of low-pay persistence, we have to emphasize that our results showing a higher state dependence effect may also be explained by the fact that their data set is considerably richer than ours. They were able to introduce 38 parental background variables containing attributes of the socioeconomic group of the mother and the father when the respondent was 14-years old. Moreover, they were able to control for whether the father was deceased or was not working. By this they clearly reduced the part of unobserved heterogeneity.

We can also compare our results with those of Cappellari (1999) for the Italian labour market (where the part explained by state dependence varies between 40 and 70 per cent), and observe that the part of state dependence in Switzerland is higher. However, he is also using a more comprehensive data set than the one available for our chapter.

To summarize, we find that an important share of workers low paid at a particular point in time succeeds in escaping the low-pay segment

Table 3.7 Heterogeneity and state dependence effect

Conditional probabilities	2/3 median	CHF 3 000	1/2 median
Raw transition probabilities			
(1) $\Pr(y_t = 1 \mid y_{t-1} = 1)$	54.1	47.2	35.6
(2) $\Pr(y_t = 1 \mid y_{t-1} = 0)$	5.1	3.8	2.7
(3) Difference	49.0	43.4	32.9
Probit model			
(4) $\Pr(y_t = 1 \mid y_{t-1} = 1)$ averaged over $y_{t-1} = 1$	54.1	47.2	35.6
(5) $\Pr(y_t = 1 \mid y_{t-1} = 1)$ averaged over $y_{t-1} = 0$	38.9	34.9	28.2
(6) Difference	15.2	12.3	7.4
(7) State Dependence Effect (3)−(6)	33.8	31.1	25.5
(8) (7)/(3)	69.0%	71.7%	77.5%
Endogenous selection model			
(9) $\Pr(y_t = 1 \mid y_{t-1} = 1)$ averaged over $y_{t-1} = 1$	54.1	47.2	35.6
(10) $\Pr(y_t = 1 \mid y_{t-1} = 1)$ averaged over $y_{t-1} = 0$	37.1	33.6	29.4
(11) Difference	17.0	13.6	6.2
(12) State Dependence Effect (3)−(11)	32.0	29.8	26.7
(13)=(12)/(3)	71.8%	75.5%	81.2%

two years later (between 56 and 64 per cent). According to the calculations in Table 3.7 we, in turn, also find a pronounced state dependence effect. The results in Table 3.7 also show that state dependence is larger the lower the low-pay threshold is, which indicates that those workers with personal characteristics that have a given effect on the low-pay probability are likely located higher up the wage distribution.

In order to make sense of this result it is important to recall that low-pay employment is highly concentrated in certain economically weak sectors recurring strongly either to the female or foreign workers. In the case of foreigners it seems very likely that even if they possess higher formal education or more work experience on the average they still earn lower wages. Some stigmatization effect may be responsible for this, but as well discriminatory practices.[16] A similar reasoning applies to women. Wage regressions conducted for Switzerland typically show a discriminatory component of up to 25 per cent when comparing wages of female and male workers and controlling for their different attributes (see for instance Bonjour and Gerfin, 1998). This wage differential reflects the part not explained by differences in the observed characteristics typically seen as influencing individual productivity and are thus subsumed in the state dependence effect.

6 Summary and conclusions

The chapter has investigated wage mobility in Switzerland, placing particular emphasis on those workers at the lower tail of the wage distribution. The main findings from our analysis may be summarized by the following comments:

(a) The mobility across labour states is the first issue investigated. We find that between 27 and 40 per cent of those workers initially low paid succeed in escaping the low-wage segment over a two-year period. By contrast, only roughly 9 to 13 per cent of the initially high-paid workers drop into a low-paid job. Between 20 and roughly 40 per cent of those initially low paid report no wage the next period compared to only 3 per cent of those initially high paid. The probability of being unemployed or not being in the labour force anymore in the next period is substantially higher for initially low-paid individuals than for initially high-paid individuals. This may be interpreted as a sign of higher involuntary labour supply adjustments at the lower end of the wage distribution or downward wage rigidity.

(b) The transition matrix reveals that the stayer probabilities are higher at the extremes of the wages distribution. Mobility yet increases towards the middle range of the wage distribution. This pattern conforms to what is observed in most European countries.

(c) The main determinants of low-pay incidence are years of education, work experience that both significantly reduce the probability of being low paid. We also find evidence of some wage discrimination against female and foreign workers. The low-pay probability is considerably larger for workers in the primary sector, in the catering business and to some extent in personal services than in manufacturing. The probability of being low paid is also higher in small firms. These evidences by and large agree with results obtained by standard wage equations.

(d) We investigate then the causes for low-paid workers having a higher probability of being low paid the next period than workers initially high paid. The probability of remaining low paid is positively correlated with attributes such as working in a small firm, being an employee or working full-time. A full-time employment reduces the probability of dropping into the low-wage segment. Working in a firm with less than 20 employees, in turn, significantly increases the probability of dropping into the low-wage segment. Interestingly, we find that working in the catering business and personal services reduces the probability of remaining low paid. On the other hand, working in these sectors increases the probability of dropping from an initially high-paid position into a low-paid position. This is indicative of a pronounced job mobility between economic sectors. We find also that the probability of low-pay persistence is significantly smaller for male workers than for female workers. A negative correlation of low-pay persistence is also found for Construction workers, persons working in the Banking and Insurance sector, in the Transportation and Communication sector and in the Business Service sector. A higher educational attainment reduces both the probability of remaining low paid and of dropping into the low-wage segment. However, a longer work experience has no effect on the probability of escaping the low-wage segment.

(e) Overall we find that a sizeable fraction of low pay move out of their state. However, when investigating how much the explanatory variables account for the observed low-pay persistence we find that observed heterogeneity account for only approximately 30 per cent of the probability of moving. Within our data and using our econometric approach, state dependence dominates heterogeneity.

Acknowledgements

We address our thanks to R. Dickens (Centre for Economic Performance), J. Haskel (Queen Mary, University of London) and A. Manning (London School of Economics) for their helpful comments. We would also like to thank Michel Kolly from the Swiss Federal Statistical Office for his advice on the data set. Financial support under grant no. 8210-61262 from the Swiss National Science Foundation is gratefully acknowledged by A. de Coulon. Part of the work was conducted while he was visiting the Department of Economics, Queen Mary, University of London.

Notes

1. See OECD, 1996, SFSO, 1996, Deutsch *et al.*, 1999, and Küng and Blank,2000.
2. This share is calculated on the entire active population, that is, including the self-employed and part-time workers.
3. This Markovian approach to study mobility is mainly chosen as we have no lifelong duration data at hand. This form of state dependence pertains to whether being in a certain state raises a person's probability of remaining in that state, and it should not be confused with duration dependence where the probability of remaining in a state directly depends on the *duration* spent in that state.
4. As hourly wages outside this range are highly unlikely on the Swiss labour market (only 40 individuals each year in our sample).

5. From initially 11 109 persons we subtracted 2187 individuals who were not wage earners in year *t*, and 1305 observations that were corresponding to a second initial period for the same individual. Because the panel covers some persons over a five-year period, 686 individuals were simultaneously included in the first two sub-panels and 619 in the last two sub-panels.
6. The estimation of transition probabilities may be obtained by maximizing a likelihood function (see Anderson and Goodman, 1957). The underlying assumption is that the transition matrix arises from a homogenous first-order Markov probability process. For further details about the computation of transition matrices refer to Shorrocks (1976, 1978) or Bartholomew (1967). It seems worth noting that a simple link between the probabilities and the expected duration spent in a state exists when assuming that the transition matrix represents a steady state situation (see Spillerman, 1972).
7. These 58 per cent correspond to the sum of those remaining on the diagonal of the transition matrix relative to the entire sample.
8. The true initial state of the wage process will be embedded in the wage levels in each period, causing lagged wages to be endogenous with respect to current wages.
9. This may be due to the fact that the large share of observations which have personal characteristics with a given effect on the low-pay probability is located higher up the wage distribution. Apparently at the lowest tail of the wage distribution nationality is not associated systematically with low-pay incidence.
10. Despite not showing here the estimated coefficients of the selection equation, $\hat{\beta}$, we have computed *T*-tests of the difference between their estimated values in equations (3) and (6), as these should be identical in absolute value. Of the 66 *T*-tests (23 variables for each threshold), two reject the null hypothesis of their difference being 0, six give a *p*-value between 0.15 and 0.04, one gives a *p*-value of 0.018 and the remaining 59 give *p*-values of 0 to the second decimal place or more. The econometric model is not rejected by the data.
11. The probability plots in Figures 3.1 and 3.2 were obtained with the simple probit model.
12. Some statistically insignificant results may also be due to the number of observations being quite sparse in some categories.
13. A similar effect is observed for the full-time variable.
14. An additional piece of evidence in favour of the hypothesis of a pronounced job-mobility is provided by the persistently high vacancy rate in the Restaurant and Hotel business.
15. Unobserved heterogeneity may include: ability, motivation, intelligence and so on.
16. Within this context it seems important to note that foreign workers according to the existing immigration law are attributed a working permit only if there are no Swiss workers willing to fill the vacancy.

References

Anderson, T.W. and Goodman, L.A. (1957) 'Statistical Inference about Markov Chains', *Annals of Mathematical Statistics,* 28, pp. 89–110.

Asplund, R., Sloane, P. and Theodossiou, I. (1998) *Low Pay and Earnings Mobility in Europe*, Cheltenham, UK: Edward Elgar.

Bartholomew, D.J. (1967) *Stochastic Models for Social Processes*, New York: Wiley.

Bonjour, D. and Gerfin, M. (1995) 'Einkommensungleichheit zwischen Frauen und Männern. Eine ökonometrische Analyse der Schweizerischen Arbeitskrä fteerhebung: Kommentar', *Swiss Journal of Economics and Statistics*, 4(1), pp. 701–10.

Cappellari, L. (1999) 'Low-wage Mobility in the Italian Labour Market', Warwick Economics Research Paper 531, University of Warwick.

Deding, M. (2001) 'Low Wage Mobility in Denmark, Germany and the United States', paper presented at the European Association of Labour Economists (EALE) Annual Conference, 13–16 September 2001, Finland.

Deutsch, J., Flückiger, Y. and J. Silber (1999) 'La population des "bas salaires" et des "working poor" en Suisse', in: Fluder, R., Nolde, M., Priester, T. and Wagner, A. (eds), *Armut verstehen – Armut bekämpfen*, Neuchâtel: Bundesamt für Statistik.

Dickens, R. (2000) 'Caught in a Trap? Wage Mobility in Great Britain: 1975–1994', *Economica*, 67, pp. 477–97.

Farber (1983) 'The Determination of Union Status of Workers', *Econometrica*, 51, pp. 1417–38.

Heckman, J.J. (1981) 'The Incidental Parameters Problem and the Problem of Initial Conditions in Estimating a Discrete-time Data Stochastic Process, in: Manski, C.F. and McFadden, D. (eds), *Structural Analysis of Discrete Data with Econometric Applications*, Cambridge, MA: MIT Press.

Heckman, J.J. and Borjas, G. (1980) 'Does Unemployment Cause Future Unemployment? Definitions, Questions and Answers from a Continuous Time Model for Heterogeneity and State Dependence', *Economica*, 47, pp. 247–83.

Küng Gugler, A. and Blank, S. (2000) 'Inégalité des salaires en Suisse: pas d'augmentation sensible durant les années 90', *Swiss Journal of Economics and Statistics*, 136, pp. 307–17.

Maitre, B. and Nolan, B. (1999) 'Income Mobility in the European Community Household Panel Survey', European Panel Analysis Group (EPAG) Working paper 1999–04, Institute for Social and Economic Research, University of Essex.

Meng, C.-L. and Schmidt, P. (1985) 'On the Cost of Partial Observability in the Bivariate Probit Model', *International Economic Review*, 26, pp. 71–85.

OECD (1996) *Employment Outlook*, Paris: OECD.

Shorrocks, A.F. (1976) 'Income Mobility and the Markov Assumption', *The Economic Journal*, 86, pp. 566–78.

Shorrocks, A.F. (1978) 'Income Inequality and Income Mobility', *Journal of Economic Theory*, 19, pp. 376–93.

Spillerman, S. (1972) 'Extensions of the Mover-Stayer Model', *American Journal of Sociology*, 78, pp. 599–626.

Stewart, M.B. and Swaffield, J.K. (1999) 'Low Pay Dynamics and Transition Probabilities', *Economica*, 66, pp. 23–42.

Swiss Federal Statistical Office (1996) *Niedrige Einkommen, ungeschützte Arbeitsverhältnisse und Ausschluss vom Arbeitsmarkt, Entwicklung einiger Indikatoren der SAKE 1991–1995*, SAKE News 5.

Swiss Federal Statistical Office (1997) *Le travail à temps partiel et ses répercussions sur la situation de l'emploi – Des faits et des chiffres*, SAKE News no. 97/5.

4

Low Pay, Higher Pay, Earnings Mobility and Job Satisfaction in Britain

Rannia M. Leontaridi and Peter J. Sloane

1 Introduction

Public policy concern about the position of the low paid worker has grown in the United Kingdom as earnings inequality has risen to unprecedentedly high levels and this has been reflected in the introduction of minimum wage legislation with a statutory minimum set initially at £3.60 per hour for adults in April 1999, raised to £4.10 per hour in October 2001, and further increased to £4.20 per hour in October 2002.[1] Within the European Union there has also been concern about low pay and an attempt to link this with the perceived low quality of work, with one report suggesting that 'policies towards low-wage jobs should centre on their quality at least as importantly as on the level of pay which they provide'.[2] Part-time work in particular has been the subject of attention because of its relatively low pay, poorer conditions and limited career prospects, but similar arguments apply to temporary employment and fixed term contracts.

Job quality consists of a number of elements. Thus, Beatson (2000) distinguishes between the economic contract and the psychological contract, the former focusing in the effort/reward relationship and the latter on working conditions. A further distinction is made between extrinsic and intrinsic job characteristics, the former being concerned with financial rewards, working time, work/life balance, job security and opportunities for advancement and the latter with features such as job content, work intensity, risk of ill health or injury and relationships with co-workers and managers. Because of this diversity Beaton rejects the possibility of reducing these aspects of work to a single dimension in order to rank the range of jobs according to their quality. Similarly the EU (2001) Employment in Europe report, suggests that in the absence of a single composite indicator, any analysis of job quality must be based on data with both objective and subjective evaluations of the worker–job match. We, in contrast, take the view that job satisfaction can serve as a reasonable proxy for job quality.[3] Our data set, the British Household Panel Survey (BHPS) has information not only on overall job satisfaction, measured on a seven point scale but also various facets of job satisfaction including promotion prospects, total pay, job security, relations with boss, ability to use initiative, the quality of work itself and hours worked.[4] If overall job satisfaction can be explained by these individual facets of job satisfaction, then the former should serve as a reasonable proxy for the overall quality of work as perceived by the individual worker.[5]

The European Union (2001) takes a dual labour market approach to the question of job quality, suggesting that

> there is some evidence of a two-tier labour market where the first tier is made up of jobs subject to decent pay, relative job security and career prospects, involving generally good working conditions. The second tier comprises not only unemployment and discouraged workers, but also those employed in jobs of low quality, which have low pay, precarious employment relationships or lack of further education and career prospects. (p. 79)

The Report also notes that 65 per cent of workers in jobs of good quality (and high pay) report high levels of job satisfaction, as opposed to only 30 per cent in jobs of low intrinsic quality (with low pay). EU, Employment in Europe 2002 goes further in including job satisfaction in its definition of quality of work, and claims on page 83 that in all Member States self-reported job satisfaction is strongly positively correlated with wages, job status and job related skills acquired through training. Yet econometric results contained on page 109 in Annexe 3.1 show a significant negative association between high skill and job satisfaction when controlling for the hourly wage, which calls into question the earlier claimed link between low pay and low job quality. In this chapter we test whether or not similar results apply in Britain.

In contrast to the issue of job quality, the measurement of low pay is relatively straightforward. We use a conventional two-thirds of the median for hourly earnings to identify the low paid and compare these to the remainder of the sample (higher paid), correcting earnings over the first seven waves of the BHPS for changes in the retail price index.

The determinants of job satisfaction are analysed, separately by gender, and split according to whether or not the individual is low paid. We use principal components analysis to ascertain which facets of job satisfaction are key to the explanation of overall job satisfaction. We then attempt to make use of the panel element of the BHPS to deal with the problem of unobserved heterogeneity. That is, certain reported levels of overall individual job satisfaction may be recorded because underlying unobservable characteristics, which vary across individuals, may increase the probability that a certain level of job satisfaction is reported as opposed to another. One such example may be that depending on an underlying and continuously changing emotional background, the influence of an individual's emotional state or 'mood' may influence positively or negatively his or her reported levels of job satisfaction at an interview irrespective of job, industry or other personal characteristics. The correlation over time in reported levels of job satisfaction may then simply be due to the fact that this underlying 'mood swinging' is a random variable in the sample. This type of unobserved heterogeneity or 'happiness proneness' explanation is modelled as a random effect that allows for variation in each individual's propensity for being happy in his or her job over a seven-year period. Thus, random effects ordered probit is the estimation procedure.

Finally, we consider the effect of wage mobility on job satisfaction. Does job satisfaction increase if, for example, individuals move from low paying to higher paying jobs and does it decrease if such movement is in the opposite direction? Further, is the effect similar if movements still leave the worker in the low-paid segment?

2 Some descriptives

We consider the first seven waves of the BHPS covering the years 1991 to 1997. At the start of the period the female median wage was 70.3 per cent of its male equivalent and at the end 79.2 per cent measured in hourly terms. Consequently the female share of the low paid fell over the period. While 12.82 per cent of men were low paid in 1991 by 1997 the figure had risen to 13.78 per cent; the corresponding figures for women being 33.04 per cent and 28.72 per cent respectively (Table 4.1).

Surprisingly, the overall job satisfaction of the low paid is significantly higher than that of the higher paid (Table 4.2) – 5.54 as opposed to 5.36 (t= 8.86). This is generally true for facets of job satisfaction, with the notable exception of satisfaction with pay, with a figure of 4.30 for the lower paid compared to 4.70 for the higher paid here. It is not the

Table 4.1 Median wages for men and women, 1991–97

	Median wage	Male median wage	Female median wage
Percentage of median wage			
1991	5.085	6.018	4.232
1992	5.387	6.369	4.624
1993	5.543	6.530	4.843
1994	5.633	6.711	4.938
1995	5.889	6.886	5.132
1996	6.078	7.059	5.292
1997	6.129	6.882	5.454
Percentage of low paid (2/3 of median) by year			
	All	**Men**	**Women**
1991	22.25	12.82	33.04
1992	20.75	10.79	29.61
1993	22.31	13.52	30.45
1994	21.46	12.63	29.50
1995	21.62	13.38	29.41
1996	22.72	14.05	30.95
1997	21.41	13.78	28.72

Table 4.2 Descriptive statistics for the higher pay and low-pay samples split by higher pay and lower pay

	Higher paid (HP)	Lower paid (LP)
Mean wage per hour	£8.042	£2.975
Overall job satisfaction	5.360	5.540
Job satisfaction with promotions	4.356	4.516
Job satisfaction with pay	4.695	4.303
Job satisfaction with boss	5.469	5.778
Job satisfaction with job security	5.093	5.452
Job satisfaction with initiative	5.742	5.737
Job satisfaction with work itself	5.520	5.599
Job satisfaction with hours	5.175	5.328
	% of all higher paid	**% of all lower paid**
Age 18–25	14.06	30.11
Age 26–35	33.01	23.22
Age 36–45	27.64	22.14
Age 46–55	20.60	19.20
Age 56–60	4.69	5.32

Table 4.2 Continued

	Higher paid (HP)	Lower paid (LP)
	% of all higher paid	**% of all lower paid**
Men	54.07	28.54
Women	45.93	71.46
Married	75.37	63.87
Have children	38.80	43.57
Excellent health	30.80	23.15
Good health	50.20	52.47
Fair health	14.87	19.19
Poor health	4.11	5.15
Own their home	82.33	65.53
Paid mortgage	10.31	13.22
Have a mortgage	71.99	52.29
Rent council flat	7.10	18.41
Other rented accommodation	10.47	15.79
Conservative	26.21	17.40
Labour	33.49	30.30
Libdem	8.66	5.79
Other party	2.08	2.14
No qualifications	12.62	29.18
Univ. degrees	16.28	3.31
Other higher, teach, nurse	26.78	14.49
A-levels	13.21	12.65
O-levels and equiv	22.65	26.57
Commercial and apprentice	8.47	12.98
Mean of total hrs (inc over)	37.72	33.31
Part-time work	14.44	39.77
TU coverage	56.99	27.26
TU member	43.62	16.96
Permanent contract	94.45	89.75
Promotion prospects	53.96	33.49
Managerial tasks	42.10	16.55
Bonus pay	23.57	15.47
Incremental pay	49.51	30.23
Public sector employee	31.82	13.36
Private sector employee	64.11	81.59
Size of firm 1–24	27.32	52.58
Size of firm 25–99	27.03	25.23
Size of firm 100–499	26.01	15.25
Size of firm 500 plus	19.43	6.72
Agriculture, forestry, fishing, energy, water	3.23	1.93
Manufacturing and extraction	24.12	17.68
Services	51.11	36.33
Construction, distribution and transport	21.53	44.06

Table 4.2 Continued

	Higher paid (HP)	**Lower paid (LP)**
	% of all higher paid	**% of all lower paid**
Professional occupations	6.60	0.61
Managerial and technical occupations	36.04	8.31
Skilled non-manual	21.54	44.06
Skilled manual	18.71	20.96
Unskilled and partly skilled	12.85	39.96
Have a second job	9.82	12.90
Work some parts of the day	6.08	20.67
Work shifts	12.88	14.68
Work normal day	52.35	40.97
Work at employer's premises	83.39	87.33
Live in inner and outer London	11.48	4.59
South England	32.50	31.65
North of England	25.49	28.24
Midlands	16.15	21.49
Wales	4.71	5.24
Scotland	9.26	8.38
Financial situation is comfortable	30.85	18.49
Financial situation is alright	38.58	35.30
Financial situation: getting by	24.43	33.34
Financial situation is bad	6.06	12.72
Expect finances to get better	32.78	35.11
Expect finances to get worse	12.15	8.44
Expect finances to stay the same	51.70	52.39
Finances have got better from last year	37.23	32.87
Finances have got worse from last year	23.43	25.01
Finances are same since last year	39.24	41.90

case therefore, that the lower paid are not concerned about their level of pay in determining the level of overall job satisfaction. Of course the characteristics of the lower and higher paid differ with the former containing higher proportions of young workers (aged 18–25), females, the less educated, part-time workers, non-unionists, private sector employment, employment in small firms, service sector employment and unskilled work. Since young workers, the less educated, non-unionists and those employed in smaller establishments generally exhibit high levels of job satisfaction, part of the higher level of job satisfaction among the low paid is compositional.

When the sample is split by gender (Table 4.3) overall job satisfaction is significantly higher for women than men in both low paid and higher paid segments. In fact low paid women have higher overall job satisfaction

Table 4.3 Descriptive statistics for the higher pay and low-pay samples split by gender

	HP		LP	
	Women	**Men**	**Women**	**Men**
Overall job satisfaction	5.542	5.206	5.703	5.133
Job satisfaction with promotions	4.509	4.305	4.620	4.283
Job satisfaction with pay	4.862	4.554	4.487	3.841
Job satisfaction with boss	5.603	5.355	5.911	5.446
Job satisfaction with job security	5.248	4.961	5.577	5.139
Job satisfaction with initiative	5.792	5.700	5.806	5.562
Job satisfaction with work itself	5.628	5.429	5.710	5.322
Job satisfaction with hours	5.376	5.004	5.550	4.774
Age 18–25	14.44	13.74	22.72	49.88
Age 26–35	32.42	33.51	23.52	22.49
Age 36–45	27.44	27.81	25.88	12.78
Age 46–55	21.43	19.89	22.31	11.42
Age 56–60	4.28	5.05	6.07	3.43
Mean wage (£)	7.24	8.72	2.95	3.03
Married	74.33	76.24	70.86	46.39
Have children	35.88	41.28	46.51	36.21
Excellent health	28.66	32.62	21.20	28.05
Good health	50.73	49.74	53.42	50.12
Fair health	15.51	14.33	19.83	17.57
Poor health	5.07	3.30	5.55	4.14
Own their home	83.03	81.72	67.97	59.41
Paid mortgage	10.60	10.07	13.28	13.08
Have a mortgage	72.43	71.52	54.69	46.27
Rent council flat	7.24	6.99	17.42	20.89
Other rented accommodation	9.63	11.19	14.39	19.29
Conservative	24.76	27.45	18.20	15.38
Labour	31.60	35.10	30.16	30.65
Libdem	9.42	8.02	5.65	6.15
Other party	2.27	1.92	2.10	2.25
No qualifications	11.79	12.13	32.14	24.67
Univ. degrees	15.49	16.94	2.65	4.97
Other higher, teach, nurse	26.06	27.39	13.71	16.45
A-levels	11.49	14.67	10.97	16.86
O-levels and equiv	26.26	19.58	27.09	25.27
Commercial and apprentice	8.92	8.09	13.45	11.78
Mean of total hrs (inc over)	32.19	42.42	28.01	46.56
Part-time work	29.14	1.95	52.57	7.28
TU coverage	59.73	54.66	27.51	26.63
TU member	42.12	44.89	16.07	19.17
Permanent contract	93.05	95.64	90.83	87.04
Promotion prospects	48.64	58.47	29.47	43.55
Managerial tasks	37.49	46.01	15.50	19.17

Table 4.3 Continued

	HP		LP	
	Women	Men	Women	Men
Bonus pay	18.46	27.91	12.62	22.60
Incremental pay	55.06	44.80	29.92	31.01
Public sector employee	42.55	22.69	15.74	7.40
Private sector employee	52.34	74.11	78.26	89.94
Size of firm 1–24	31.21	23.24	54.67	47.34
Size of firm 25–99	27.58	26.57	24.49	27.10
Size of firm 100–499	22.90	28.64	14.46	17.22
Size of firm 500 plus	18.09	20.56	6.17	8.11
Agriculture, forestry, fishing, energy, water	1.47	4.72	0.87	4.55
Manufacturing	13.29	33.32	13.80	27.40
Services	68.05	36.72	41.69	22.90
Construction, distribution and transport	17.18	25.24	43.63	45.15
Professional occupations	3.29	9.41	0.26	1.46
Managerial and technical occupations	38.71	33.97	8.30	8.34
Skilled non-manual	39.45	14.15	36.82	13.43
Skilled manual	6.26	28.29	13.50	39.64
Unskilled and partly skilled	12.29	13.33	41.13	37.04
Have a second job	10.79	8.99	12.93	12.84
Work some parts of the day	8.82	3.76	24.94	10.00
Work shifts	10.46	14.93	13.14	18.52
Work normal day	51.71	52.90	36.73	51.60
Work at employer's premises	90.87	77.04	91.99	75.68
Live in inner and outer London	12.83	10.38	4.42	5.03
South England	31.97	32.90	32.659	29.29
North of England	24.85	26.03	27.89	29.17
Midlands	15.09	17.05	20.99	22.73
Wales	4.43	4.95	5.06	5.68
Scotland	10.45	8.25	8.67	7.63
Financial situation is comfortable	31.27	30.50	19.52	15.92
Financial situation is alright	38.66	38.52	35.43	34.97
Financial situation: getting by	23.49	25.23	32.66	35.03
Financial situation is bad	6.52	5.67	12.31	13.73
Expect finances to get better	30.98	34.31	30.94	45.56
Expect finances to get worse	12.04	12.24	8.67	7.87
Expect finances to stay the same	53.60	50.08	56.42	42.31
Finances have got better from year	36.93	37.48	29.90	40.30
Finances have got worse from year	22.59	24.14	24.89	25.33
Finances are same since last year	40.35	38.29	45.10	33.91
Job tenure	4.39	5.27	3.89	2.95

than any of the other groups. Women have higher satisfaction than men in each of the facets of job satisfaction in both sectors.

One way of illustrating these relationships more clearly is to use cumulative density functions. From the individual responses we can calculate the response frequency for each satisfaction category $i = 1, 2, 3, 4, 5, 6$ and 7. We can then compare for each type of job satisfaction, the cumulative response frequency. Thus, let $F^j(i)$ denote the fraction of respondents in group j who report a satisfaction level less than or equal to level i. Hence if for two groups, say j and j' we find that F^j first-order dominates $F^{j'}$, that is, if $F^{j'}(i) > F^j(i)$ for all i we can say that employees in group j are *unambiguously more satisfied* than the workers in group j'.

Figures 4.1–4.16 contain the results for overall job satisfaction and seven facets of satisfaction. A group of employees is unambiguously

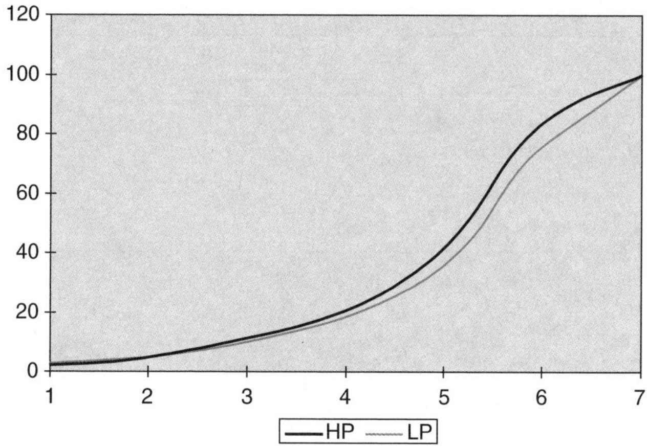

Figure 4.1 Overall job satisfaction

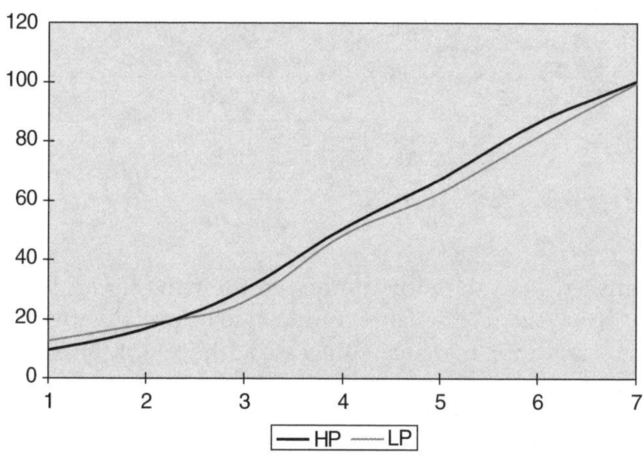

Figure 4.2 Satisfaction with promotions

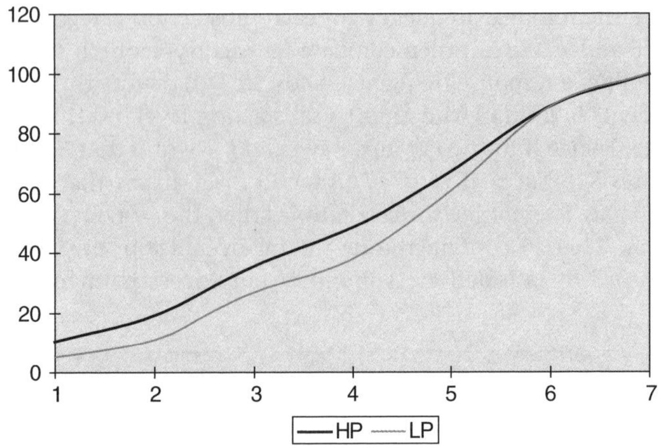

Figure 4.3 Satisfaction with pay

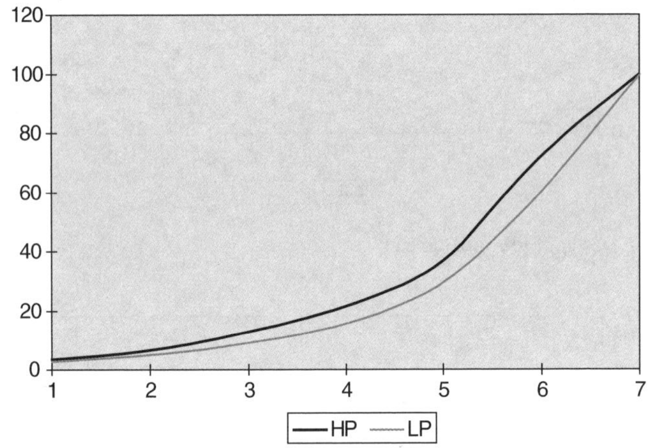

Figure 4.4 Satisfaction with boss

more satisfied than those of another group if the former's curve lies entirely below that of the latter. In the case of overall job satisfaction this is so apart from, marginally the case at the left of the distribution, implying that the low paid are more satisfied than the higher paid. The split by gender implies that women are unambiguously more satisfied at work than men.

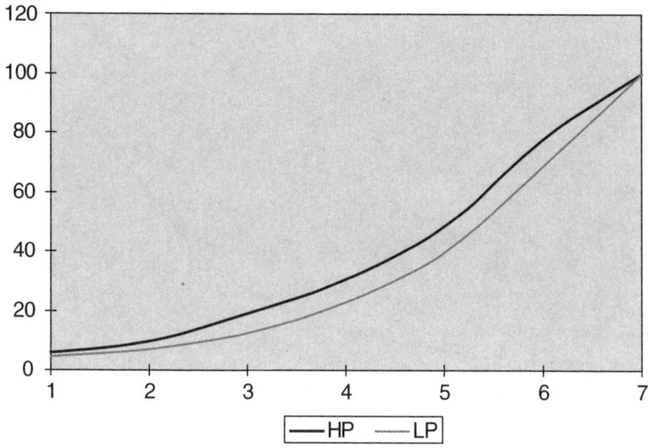

Figure 4.5 Satisfaction with job security

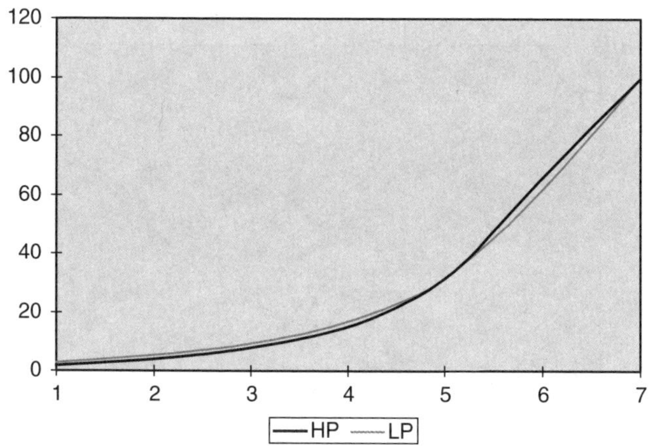

Figure 4.6 Satisfaction with job initiative

Turning to facets of job satisfaction the lower paid are unambiguously more satisfied than the higher paid with their boss and with job security. In other cases there are cross-over points, but in the case of satisfaction with promotions, work itself and hours of work more satisfied low-paid workers are more satisfied than higher paid workers with the same scores for moderate to higher satisfaction levels. The exceptional case is satisfaction with pay where the higher paid are unambiguously more

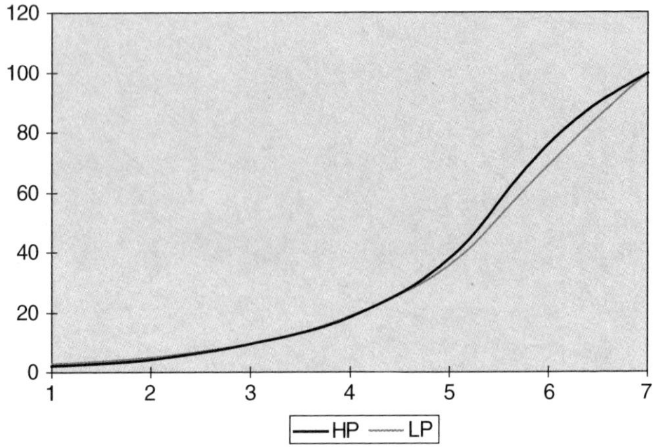

Figure 4.7 Satisfaction with work itself

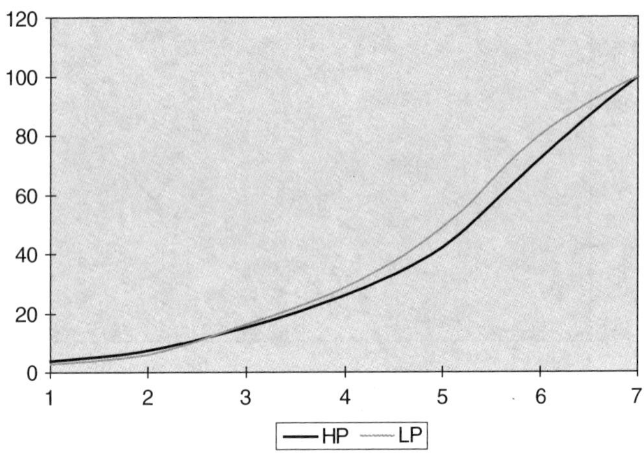

Figure 4.8 Satisfaction with hours of work

satisfied than the lower paid. Split by gender lower paid women are unambiguously more satisfied with pay than lower paid men and similarly for higher paid women relative to higher paid men.

Finally, one way to assess the relative importance of job facets in determining overall job satisfaction is to use principal components

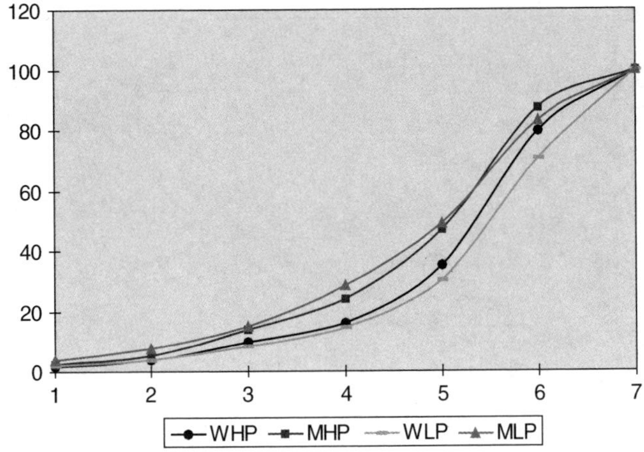

Figure 4.9 Overall job satisfaction

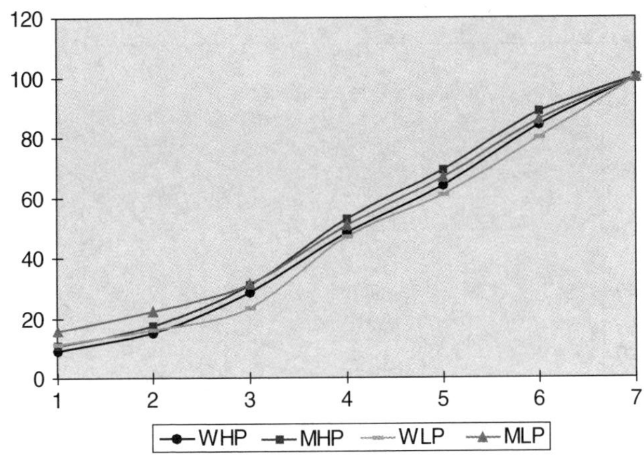

Figure 4.10 Satisfaction with promotions

analysis. The objective of this form of analysis is to find linear combinations of these variables with the greatest variance that is, identifying underlying factors which contain most of the information contained in the overall variable. Following standard practice we retained only those components which had eigenvalues greater than 1, regarding the others

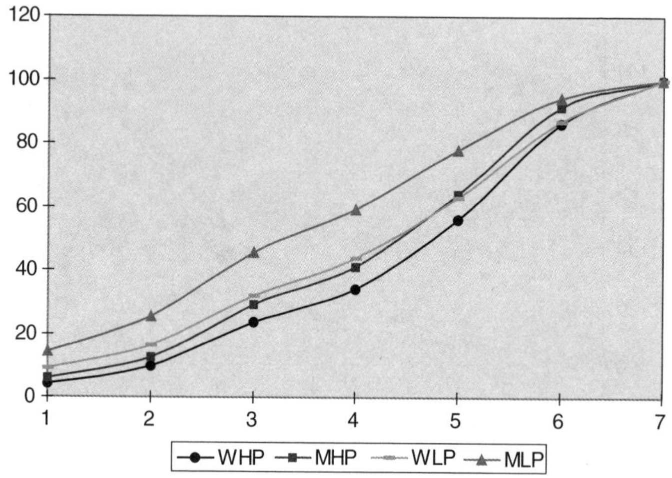

Figure 4.11 Satisfaction with pay

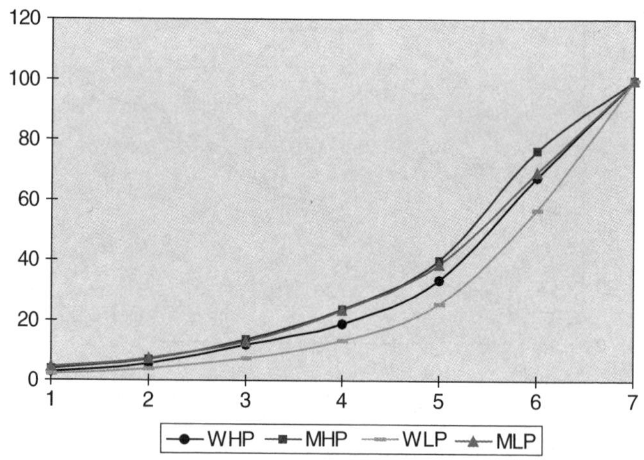

Figure 4.12 Satisfaction with boss

as sampling noise in the data. The results suggest that there are common dimensions in the subjective job characteristic measures. Three components were retained in the analysis, and the proportion of the variance in the data explained by them (the so-called communality) is consistently

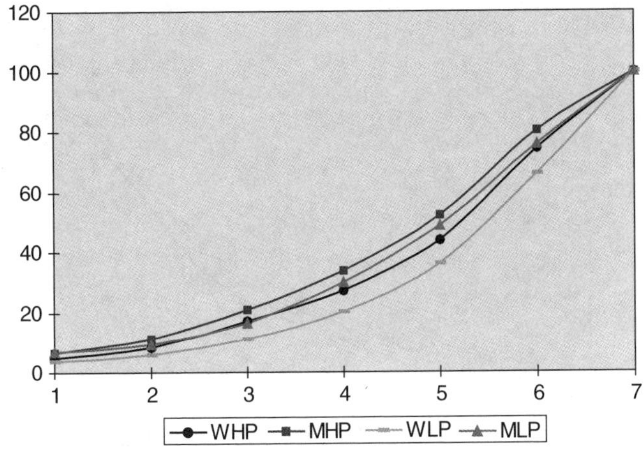

Figure 4.13 Satisfaction with job security

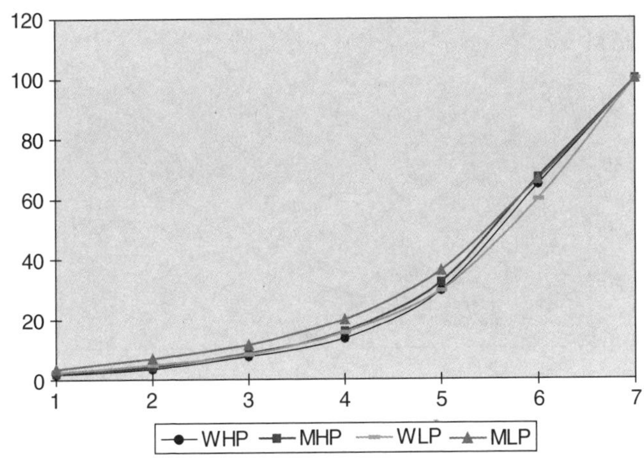

Figure 4.14 Satisfaction with initiative

above 70 per cent. As shown in Table 4.4 satisfaction with initiative, followed by satisfaction with work itself, score most highly and appear to be more important to overall job satisfaction than satisfaction with pay. This facet does, however, appear to be more important for men than for women.

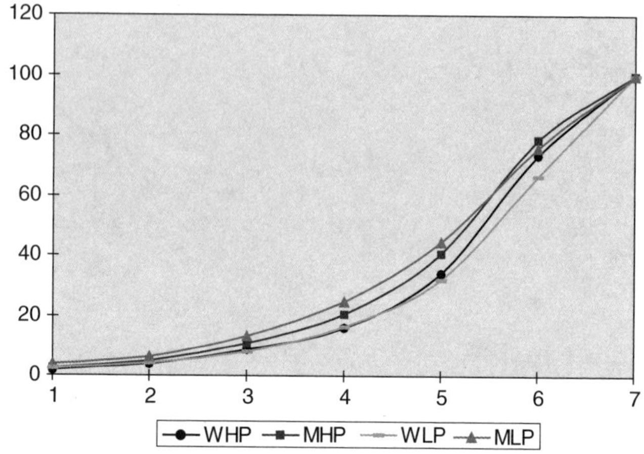

Figure 4.15 Satisfaction with work itself

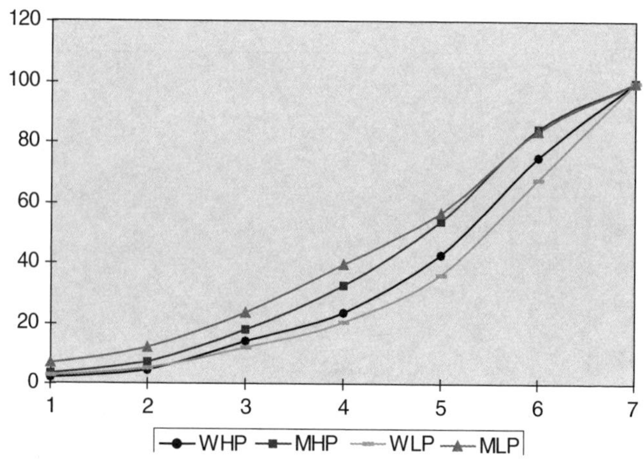

Figure 4.16 Satisfaction with hours of work

3 Model specification and estimation

It is standard in labour theory to assume that workers attempt to maximise their utility (satisfaction) in terms of wage income–leisure trade-off. Yet, even though increasing hours of work may well decrease an individual worker's utility, it is an over-simplification to assume that utility depends solely on income and hours of work, as the above analysis of

Table 4.4 Principal components analysis of job satisfaction determinants (component matrix)

	Low paid	Higher paid	Low paid		Higher paid	
			Men	Women	Men	Women
Satisfaction with promotion	0.677	0.687	0.710	0.657	0.690	0.680
Satisfaction with pay	0.640	0.597	0.655	0.619	0.620	0.556
Satisfaction with boss	0.671	0.660	0.677	0.656	0.649	0.670
Satisfaction with security	0.612	0.573	0.628	0.595	0.575	0.561
Satisfaction with initiative	0.726	0.709	0.714	0.739	0.703	0.721
Satisfaction with work itself	0.717	0.693	0.697	0.720	0.698	0.684
Satisfaction with hours	0.640	0.559	0.642	0.620	0.563	0.539

facets of job satisfaction confirms. Thus, Hamermesh (1977) and Borjas (1979) both define job satisfaction as a function of an individual's money wage and the monetary equivalent of the non-pecuniary aspects of work. Both Akerlof *et al.* (1988) and Clark (1999) find evidence that wages and hours are among the less important characteristics of a job.

Following Clark and Oswald (1996) we can represent the utility from working as a type of sub-utility function, u, contained within an overall utility function, v. Thus

$$V = v(u(y, h, i, j), \mu) \tag{1}$$

where u represents utility from work and μ is utility derived from non-work sources, being determined quite differently and dependent on factors such as family life, friendships, health and personal non-economic variables. The utility from working can then be represented as

$$U = u(y, h, i, j) \tag{2}$$

where y represents income, h is hours of work and i and j are sets of individual and job specific characteristics respectively.

It has recently become fashionable to suggest that utility is a function not only of absolute income, but also of relative income (Rees, 1993). That is, when a worker's earnings fall relative to those of others, there is a feeling of relative deprivation. Hence the utility function is expanded to incorporate an additional variable y^* which attempts to capture an individual's reference income. Hence, we have

$$U = u(y, y^*, h, i, j) \tag{3}$$

Thus utility is assumed to decline with an increase in the comparison pay level y^*. We do not know which comparisons individuals actually make, but the previous literature suggests that comparisons tend to be narrowly drawn.[6] We calculate y^* using seven years (1991–97) of the New Earnings Survey as a series of mean gross hourly wage values over population sub-groups sorted by age, gender, industrial classification and year. For example the mean gross hourly wage of male employees, working in metal manufacturing, of age 45 in 1994 is assumed to be the comparison income y_k^* against which an individual k with similar characteristics to our sample compares his income with y_k in that year. One hypothesis is that the utility of person k depends on the gap between y_k and y_k^*.[7]

To examine the impact of a job change on job satisfaction we estimate probit regressions of the increase in job satisfaction on the changes in a set of individual specific and job specific characteristics. A similar approach has been adopted by Francesconi (2001). The dependent variable is equal to one of the worker reports a higher level of job satisfaction between any year $t-1$ and t, and zero if the worker reports equal or lower satisfaction between two successive years in the panel.

4 Regression results

Random effects ordered probit

Our data are taken from the first seven waves of the BHPS, covering the period 1991–97. The sample includes 27 184 observations when individuals are aggregated across years. Of these, 21 329 are defined as higher paid and 5942 as lower paid.

We run regressions for overall job satisfaction, pay satisfaction and satisfaction with work itself. In each case we run regressions excluding and including a comparison wage variable. We estimate the log of gross hourly wages for the usual wage and usual hours of work in order to avoid the complication of overtime working, which may in some cases be required regardless of the wishes of the individual.[8]

First of all we ran the model for the whole sample and split by gender to see if our results accord with earlier work. In general this is confirmed (Table 4.5) with both absolute and relative pay being significant for the total sample, tenure and age being u-shaped, and satisfaction being negatively related to education, size of establishment and trade union membership. Particularly noticeable is the fact that overall job satisfaction is declining over time up to wave 5, recovering somewhat thereafter

Table 4.5 Overall job satisfaction

	All employees		Males only		Females only	
Log usual gross hourly wage	0.130***	0.146***	0.279***	0.294***	0.072*	0.079**
	(4.937)	(5.493)	(7.217)	(7.574)	(1.911)	(2.097)
Log comparative wage		−0.332***		−0.454***		−0.203*
		(4.802)		(3.887)		(1.897)
Log usual hours	−0.250***	−0.247***	0.073	0.080	−0.267***	−0.268***
	(6.628)	(6.559)	(0.855)	(0.931)	(6.267)	(6.299)
Job tenure	−0.028***	−0.028***	−0.038***	−0.038***	−0.019***	−0.019***
	(8.106)	(8.075)	(7.655)	(7.653)	(3.931)	(3.891)
Tenure squared	0.001***	0.001***	0.001***	0.001***	0.000**	0.000**
	(4.991)	(5.036)	(5.191)	(5.184)	(2.255)	(2.237)
Gender	−0.295***	−0.177***				
	(9.740)	(4.547)				
Age	−0.041***	−0.012	−0.052***	−0.002	0.046***	−0.032**
	(5.020)	(1.151)	(4.351)	(0.096)	(4.055)	(2.368)
Age squared	0.001***	0.000**	0.001***	0.000	0.001***	0.001***
	(6.226)	(2.408)	(4.901)	(0.853)	(5.004)	(3.186)
University degree	−0.675***	−0.664***	−0.516***	−0.503***	0.834***	−0.829***
	(12.515)	(12.278)	(6.786)	(6.613)	(10.886)	(10.819)
Vocational qualifications	−0.403***	−0.392***	−0.333***	−0.319***	−0.458***	−0.454***
	(9.473)	(9.201)	(5.432)	(5.202)	(7.731)	(7.664)
A-levels plus	−0.486***	−0.479***	−0.419***	−0.411***	−0.524***	−0.523***
	(10.124)	(9.969)	(6.188)	(6.065)	(7.633)	(7.626)
O-levels plus	−0.281***	−0.273***	−0.227***	−0.218***	−0.320***	−0.316***
	(6.685)	(6.484)	(3.598)	(3.455)	(5.670)	(5.601)
Commercial or apprentice	−0.141***	−0.133**	−0.075	−0.066	−0.190***	−0.187***
	(2.722)	(2.560)	(0.959)	(0.849)	(2.744)	(2.699)
Married	0.017	0.028	−0.029	−0.022	0.055	0.059*
	(0.662)	(1.073)	(0.710)	(0.536)	(1.578)	(1.700)

Table 4.5 Continued

	All employees		Males only		Females only	
Children	0.114***	0.113***	0.091***	0.086***	0.143***	0.141***
	(4.889)	(4.846)	(2.808)	(2.640)	(4.144)	(4.089)
Mortgage house	−0.121***	−0.123***	−0.122***	−0.118***	−0.130***	−0.131***
	(4.489)	(4.550)	(3.153)	(3.070)	(3.451)	(3.477)
Paid outright house	−0.021	−0.023	−0.036	−0.031	−0.023	−0.025
	(0.518)	(0.579)	(0.633)	(0.530)	(0.416)	(0.441)
South of England	0.162***	0.159***	0.172***	0.167***	0.148**	0.147**
	(3.759)	(3.682)	(2.697)	(2.612)	(2.548)	(2.531)
Midlands	0.182***	0.183***	0.240***	0.237***	0.130**	0.131**
	(3.756)	(3.772)	(3.366)	(3.336)	(1.983)	(1.994)
North of England	0.205***	0.204***	0.229***	0.232***	0.175***	0.175***
	(4.485)	(4.478)	(3.394)	(3.446)	(2.834)	(2.847)
Wales	0.250***	0.251***	0.399***	0.405***	0.109	0.110
	(3.644)	(3.645)	(4.055)	(4.089)	(1.144)	(1.154)
Scotland	0.036	0.038	0.174**	0.179**	−0.063	−0.060
	(0.635)	(0.685)	(2.063)	(2.122)	(0.845)	(0.815)
Fair health	−0.015	−0.018	−0.029	−0.033	−0.006	−0.008
	(0.373)	(0.447)	(0.446)	(0.495)	(0.119)	(0.151)
Good health	0.155***	0.153***	0.189***	0.187***	0.124**	0.122**
	(3.906)	(3.844)	(2.952)	(2.932)	(2.440)	(2.411)
Excellent heath	0.336***	0.335***	0.345***	0.345***	0.327***	0.327***
	(8.014)	(7.975)	(5.192)	(5.201)	(5.996)	(5.992)
Trade union member	−0.145***	−0.140***	−0.073**	−0.066*	−0.173***	−0.171***
	(5.842)	(5.630)	(2.061)	(1.854)	(4.919)	(4.864)
Permanent contract	0.156***	0.157***	0.133**	0.138**	0.142***	0.142***
	(4.478)	(4.503)	(2.433)	(2.516)	(3.123)	(3.126)

Incremental pay	0.180***	0.178***	0.219***	0.220***	0.153***	0.153***
	(9.633)	(9.567)	(8.286)	(8.340)	(5.786)	(5.768)
Managerial tasks	0.034	0.034	0.036	0.035	0.009	0.009
	(1.521)	(1.520)	(1.157)	(1.114)	(0.297)	(0.291)
Part-time	0.120***	0.117***	0.275**	0.276**	0.052	0.053
	(2.854)	(2.787)	(2.477)	(2.486)	(1.147)	(1.155)
Travel time	−0.002***	−0.002***	−0.002***	−0.002***	−0.002***	−0.002***
	(4.209)	(4.032)	(3.219)	(3.150)	(2.686)	(2.632)
Size 25–99	−0.128***	−0.125***	−0.155***	−0.151***	−0.097***	−0.095***
	(5.371)	(5.245)	(4.407)	(4.280)	(2.987)	(2.922)
Size 100–499	−0.220***	−0.215***	−0.186***	−0.180***	−0.262***	−0.260***
	(8.281)	(8.078)	(4.924)	(4.765)	(6.945)	(6.871)
Size 500 plus	−0.182***	−0.174***	−0.182***	−0.173***	−0.188***	−0.183***
	(5.954)	(5.680)	(4.174)	(3.979)	(4.305)	(4.186)
Manufacturing	−0.054	−0.083*	−0.085	−0.110*	−0.022	−0.047
	(1.113)	(1.687)	(1.376)	(1.766)	(0.273)	(0.584)
Professional services	0.056	0.122**	−0.050	0.078	0.159**	0.182**
	(1.203)	(2.509)	(0.808)	(1.115)	(2.190)	(2.483)
Other services	−0.018	−0.081*	−0.074	−0.138**	0.066	0.014
	(0.391)	(1.647)	(1.195)	(2.141)	(0.889)	(0.181)
Professionals	0.269***	0.276***	0.277***	0.286***	0.305***	0.307***
	(5.022)	(5.157)	(4.076)	(4.203)	(3.127)	(3.151)
Managerial technical	0.210***	0.210***	0.275***	0.280***	0.166***	0.165***
	(5.788)	(5.790)	(5.207)	(5.303)	(3.284)	(3.260)
Skilled non-manual	0.074**	0.077**	0.182***	0.188***	0.012	0.012
	(2.290)	(2.374)	(3.453)	(3.553)	(0.286)	(0.279)
Skilled manual	0.110***	0.111***	0.154***	0.160***	0.121**	0.120**
	(3.433)	(3.456)	(3.692)	(3.831)	(2.200)	(2.188)
Voluntarily	0.281***	0.281***	0.301***	0.300***	0.253***	0.254***
	(12.856)	(12.850)	(9.837)	(9.837)	(8.054)	(8.086)

Table 4.5 Continued

	All employees		Males only		Females only	
Wave 2	−0.054**	−0.047*	−0.034	−0.027	−0.072*	−0.068*
	(2.062)	(1.823)	(0.937)	(0.728)	(1.957)	(1.834)
Wave 3	−0.167***	−0.153***	−0.125***	−0.111***	−0.206***	−0.195***
	(6.296)	(5.748)	(3.332)	(2.939)	(5.505)	(5.150)
Wave 4	−0.216***	−0.202***	−0.188***	−0.175***	−0.244***	−0.231***
	(8.155)	(7.548)	(4.979)	(4.606)	(6.509)	(6.071)
Wave 5	−0.217***	−0.206***	−0.133***	−0.124***	−0.289***	−0.279***
	(8.077)	(7.643)	(3.500)	(3.247)	(7.602)	(7.263)
Wave 6	−0.201***	−0.184***	−0.118***	−0.105***	−0.277***	−0.262***
	(7.478)	(6.784)	(3.092)	(2.737)	(7.274)	(6.699)
Wave 7	−0.162***	−0.138***	−0.064*	−0.044	−0.241***	−0.220***
	(6.108)	(5.104)	(1.711)	(1.167)	(6.352)	(5.567)
Cut 1	−4.119***	−4.058***	−2.631***	−2.448***	−4.287***	−4.373***
	(19.686)	(19.374)	(6.834)	(6.319)	(15.774)	(15.869)
Cut 2	−3.661***	−3.600***	−2.144***	−1.961***	−3.862***	−3.948***
	(17.55)	(17.24)	(5.58)	(5.07)	(14.26)	(14.38)

Cut 3	−3.035***	−2.974***	−1.481***	−1.297***	−3.280***	−3.366***
	(14.57)	(14.26)	(3.86)	(−3.36)	(12.14)	(12.29)
Cut 4	−2.547***	−2.486***	−0.936***	−0.753*	−2.859***	−2.944***
	(12.24)	(11.93)	(2.44)	(1.95)	(10.59)	(10.76)
Cut 5	−1.718***	−1.657***	−0.074	0.108	−2.059***	−2.145***
	(8.26)	(7.96)	(0.19)	(0.28)	(7.64)	(7.85)
Cut 6	−0.092	−0.030	1.574***	1.756***	−0.445*	−0.531*
	(0.44)	(0.15)	(4.10)	(4.55)	(1.66)	(1.94)
Rho	0.442***	0.441***	0.457***	0.455	0.423***	0.423***
	(56.74)	(56.64)	(40.96)	(40.72)	(38.02)	(38.02)
No. of observations	27 184	27 184	13 186	13 186	13 998	13 998
Log likelihood	−38 794	−38 783	−19 634	−19 627	−19 046	−19 045

Notes: Absolute value of z statistics in parentheses. * Significant at 10%; ** significant at 5%; *** significant at 1%.

as indicated by the wave dummies. When the sample is split by gender we see that women report significantly higher levels of job satisfaction than men though the decline in job satisfaction over time is sharper for women, and there are also important differences in the determinants of job satisfaction. For women absolute pay is only significant at the 5 per cent level and comparative pay at the 10 per cent level. Total hours are significantly negative for women, while they are positive for men. This is consistent with pay being more important to men than to women in determining satisfaction at work. Age as well as tenure is significant for women; married women but not men have significantly higher reported levels of job satisfaction, with children having a significantly positive effect in both cases. There are significantly higher levels of satisfaction reported for both men and women in some of the regions relative to the omitted region (London), but the significant results reported for men in Wales and Scotland are not repeated for women. There are, however, some gender differences across industrial sectors and occupations which may reflect a degree of gender segregation. Finally we include a job change (voluntary quit) variable that takes the value of one if the last job move was to a better job or promotion and zero for involuntary departures on the grounds that the former is more likely to lead to a satisfactory job match. This is highly significant in all cases.

Next we split the sample according to whether individuals are low paid or higher paid (not reported here). Women are significantly happier at work than men, whether low paid or higher paid. While the log of the gross hourly wage is positive and significant for higher paid workers it is negative and significant in the satisfaction with work itself equations for the low-paid group. In order to cast more light on this perverse result the sample was split by gender (Table 4.6). For lower paid men the log hourly wage is insignificant but still negatively signed. For women the negative sign and significance remains in the satisfaction with work itself equations for the low-paid group. Though, the sign is positive for higher paid women it is not significant at conventional levels. In general these results are consistent with men's job satisfaction being driven more by pecuniary aspects of the job than that of women. The perverse sign on absolute pay for low-paid women might reflect the fact that to earn more such women have to sacrifice substantial non-pecuniary benefits within this segment of the labour market.[9]

The equations for satisfaction with pay cast further light on this. They confirm that higher pay has a significant effect in increasing satisfaction with pay for low-paid as well as higher paid workers. Splitting the sample by gender there are highly significant positive coefficients on the

Table 4.6(a) Low-paid males

	Job overall	Pay	Work itself	Job overall	Pay	Work itself
Log usual gross hourly wage	−0.080	0.324**	−0.181	−0.076	0.328**	−0.178
	(0.622)	(2.504)	(1.513)	(0.597)	(2.550)	(1.490)
Log comparative wage				−0.831***	−0.759**	−0.482
				(2.600)	(2.350)	(1.603)
Log usual hours	−0.266	−0.103	0.122	−0.269	−0.107	0.119
	(1.513)	(0.594)	(0.739)	(1.540)	(0.620)	(0.721)
Job tenure	−0.034	−0.029	0.007	−0.033	−0.029	0.007
	(1.264)	(1.068)	(0.274)	(1.234)	(1.073)	(0.287)
Tenure squared	0.002	0.002	−0.001	0.002	0.002	−0.001
	(1.212)	(1.268)	(0.570)	(1.044)	(1.168)	(0.676)
Age	−0.064**	−0.085***	−0.003	0.040	0.009	0.057
	(2.249)	(3.001)	(0.128)	(0.822)	(0.182)	(1.250)
Age squared	0.001**	0.001***	0.000	−0.000	0.000	−0.000
	(2.351)	(3.114)	(0.631)	(0.474)	(0.216)	(0.844)
University degree	−0.727***	−0.304	−0.593***	−0.693***	−0.279	−0.573***
	(3.345)	(1.393)	(3.006)	(3.220)	(1.291)	(2.910)
Vocational qualifications	−0.323**	−0.024	−0.181	−0.314**	−0.019	−0.177
	(2.186)	(0.158)	(1.368)	(2.152)	(0.131)	(1.334)
A-levels plus	−0.372**	−0.061	−0.193	−0.352**	−0.048	−0.182
	(2.472)	(0.403)	(1.417)	(2.364)	(0.320)	(1.342)
O-levels plus	−0.207	0.008	0.089	−0.181	0.028	0.103
	(1.489)	(0.056)	(0.714)	(1.313)	(0.201)	(0.830)
Commercial or apprentice	−0.099	−0.051	0.119	−0.062	−0.021	0.140
	(0.594)	(0.302)	(0.800)	(0.378)	(0.124)	(0.934)
Married	−0.021	−0.136	0.031	−0.013	−0.129	0.036
	(0.193)	(1.253)	(0.311)	(0.117)	(1.199)	(0.361)

Table 4.6(a) Continued

	Job overall	**Pay**	**Work itself**	**Job overall**	**Pay**	**Work itself**
Children	0.019	0.099	0.043	0.004	0.085	0.034
	(0.213)	(1.095)	(0.515)	(0.048)	(0.944)	(0.404)
Mortgage house	−0.249***	−0.066	−0.207**	−0.247***	−0.064	−0.206**
	(2.675)	(0.705)	(2.434)	(2.676)	(0.697)	(2.428)
Paid outright	−0.052	−0.042	−0.132	−0.037	−0.030	−0.125
house	(0.380)	(0.307)	(1.061)	(0.274)	(0.221)	(1.008)
South of	0.565***	0.616***	0.264	0.567***	0.615***	0.267
England	(2.998)	(3.187)	(1.560)	(3.034)	(3.221)	(1.581)
Midlands	0.492**	0.421**	0.300*	0.485**	0.411**	0.296*
	(2.507)	(2.097)	(1.696)	(2.497)	(2.070)	(1.680)
North of	0.579***	0.502***	0.325*	0.581***	0.500***	0.328*
England	(3.055)	(2.588)	(1.910)	(3.095)	(2.611)	(1.932)
Wales	0.976***	0.340	0.519**	0.992***	0.350	0.531**
	(3.812)	(1.312)	(2.270)	(3.914)	(1.366)	(2.329)
Scotland	0.695***	0.484**	0.393*	0.718***	0.499**	0.407*
	(2.893)	(1.978)	(1.818)	(3.015)	(2.068)	(1.887)
Fair health	−0.117	−0.168	−0.210	−0.138	−0.186	−0.221
	(0.605)	(0.885)	(1.152)	(0.719)	(0.981)	(1.214)
Good health	−0.050	−0.011	−0.147	−0.058	−0.016	−0.150
	(0.273)	(0.060)	(0.856)	(0.318)	(0.090)	(0.874)
Excellent health	0.104	0.136	0.070	0.089	0.126	0.064
	(0.546)	(0.720)	(0.391)	(0.470)	(0.674)	(0.356)
Trade union	−0.107	−0.166	−0.057	−0.099	−0.157	−0.052
member	(0.918)	(1.412)	(0.535)	(0.853)	(1.351)	(0.483)
Permanent	0.479***	0.155	0.244**	0.464***	0.141	0.237**
contract	(4.165)	(1.348)	(2.282)	(4.062)	(1.238)	(2.213)

Incremental pay	0.296***	0.148*	0.243***	0.292***	0.144*	0.240***
	(3.383)	(1.716)	(2.949)	(3.362)	(1.674)	(2.920)
Managerial tasks	0.053	0.089	−0.038	0.050	0.087	−0.040
	(0.480)	(0.802)	(0.364)	(0.458)	(0.794)	(0.388)
Part-time	0.045	0.246	0.230	0.045	0.245	0.227
	(0.223)	(1.217)	(1.196)	(0.224)	(1.219)	(1.185)
Travel time	−0.001	0.001	−0.001	−0.001	0.002	−0.001
	(0.699)	(0.741)	(0.862)	(0.433)	(0.973)	(0.693)
Size 25–99	−0.206**	−0.184*	−0.221**	−0.197**	−0.176*	−0.215**
	(2.177)	(1.950)	(2.487)	(2.098)	(1.868)	(2.418)
Size 100–499	−0.108	−0.005	−0.258**	−0.106	−0.003	−0.257**
	(0.896)	(0.043)	(2.299)	(0.888)	(0.023)	(2.291)
Size 500 plus	−0.234	−0.153	−0.420***	−0.214	−0.135	−0.408***
	(1.428)	(0.929)	(2.788)	(1.317)	(0.827)	(2.709)
Manufacturing	−0.444***	−0.257	−0.280*	−0.346**	−0.162	−0.221
	(2.583)	(1.505)	(1.762)	(1.982)	(0.931)	(1.355)
Professional services	−0.429**	−0.496***	−0.038	−0.158	−0.250	0.119
	(2.522)	(2.921)	(0.238)	(0.797)	(1.264)	(0.645)
Other services	−0.331**	−0.273*	−0.159	−0.311*	−0.249	−0.144
	(2.056)	(1.698)	(1.069)	(1.942)	(1.562)	(0.968)
Professionals	1.291***	0.936***	1.401***	1.291***	0.943***	1.403***
	(3.859)	(2.858)	(4.350)	(3.897)	(2.898)	(4.368)
Managerial technical	0.429***	0.185	0.526***	0.430***	0.190	0.530***
	(2.658)	(1.162)	(3.474)	(2.691)	(1.204)	(3.508)
Skilled non-manual	0.086	0.100	0.095	0.097	0.112	0.102
	(0.686)	(0.799)	(0.821)	(0.782)	(0.901)	(0.888)
Skilled manual	0.075	−0.094	0.271***	0.085	−0.085	0.278***
	(0.753)	(0.940)	(2.879)	(0.860)	(0.857)	(2.946)
Voluntarily	0.337***	0.291***	0.349***	0.335***	0.290***	0.349***
	(3.473)	(3.034)	(3.777)	(3.475)	(3.034)	(3.781)

Table 4.6(a) Continued

	Job overall	Pay	Work itself	Job overall	Pay	Work itself
Wave 2	−0.065	0.027	−0.233*	−0.046	0.043	−0.223*
	(0.490)	(0.205)	(1.794)	(0.347)	(0.325)	(1.722)
Wave 3	0.128	0.223*	−0.087	0.152	0.244*	−0.074
	(0.956)	(1.667)	(0.671)	(1.139)	(1.823)	(0.566)
Wave 4	−0.226*	0.154	−0.215	−0.211	0.165	−0.208
	(1.647)	(1.124)	(1.621)	(1.549)	(1.211)	(1.574)
Wave 5	0.169	0.125	−0.114	0.181	0.136	−0.109
	(1.209)	(0.898)	(0.848)	(1.302)	(0.981)	(0.811)
Wave 6	−0.099	0.150	−0.199	−0.065	0.180	−0.183
	(0.718)	(1.088)	(1.495)	(0.470)	(1.306)	(1.371)
Wave 7	−0.131	0.062	−0.153	−0.053	0.132	−0.108
	(0.952)	(0.454)	(1.160)	(0.378)	(0.944)	(0.807)
Cut 1	−4.205***	−2.384***	−1.773**	−3.642***	−1.891**	−1.457*
	(4.956)	(2.852)	(2.275)	(4.204)	(2.211)	(1.816)
Cut 2	−3.541***	−1.808***	−3.143***	−1.437*	−1.318	−1.121
	(9.45)	(2.17)	(3.64)	(1.85)	(1.55)	(1.40)

Cut 3	−2.902***	−0.984***	−2.580***	−0.905	−0.497	−0.589
	(7.76)	(1.18)	(3.00)	(1.17)	(0.58)	(0.74)
Cut 4	−2.491***	−0.510	−2.014**	−0.366	−0.025	0.049
	(6.67)	(0.61)	(2.35)	(0.47)	(0.03)	(0.06)
Cut 5	−1.643***	0.224***	−1.239	0.337	0.706	0.654
	(4.40)	(0.27)	(1.45)	(0.43)	(0.83)	(0.82)
Cut 6	0.091	1.307	0.184	1.403*	1.786**	1.718*
	(0.24)	(1.57)	(0.22)	(1.80)	(2.10)	(2.14)
Rho	0.450***	0.449***	0.423***	0.321***	0.439***	0.319***
	(33.83)	(11.35)	(9.88)	(6.93)	(10.99)	(6.89)
Log likelihood	−2 262	−2 524	−2 255	−2 258	−2 521	−2 254
No. of observations	1 411	1 408	1 408	1 411	1 408	1 408

Notes: Absolute value of z statistics in parentheses. * Significant at 10%; ** significant at 5%; *** significant at 1%.

Table 4.6(b) Low-paid women

	Job overall	Pay	Work itself	Job overall	Pay	Work itself
Log usual gross hourly wage	−0.093	0.349***	−0.184**	−0.088	0.362***	−0.184**
	(1.070)	(4.255)	(2.102)	(1.013)	(4.417)	(2.092)
Log comparative wage				−0.263	−0.616***	−0.034
				(1.446)	(3.549)	(0.185)
Log usual hours	−0.318***	−0.428***	−0.232***	−0.322***	−0.438***	−0.233***
	(4.937)	(7.052)	(3.602)	(5.004)	(7.230)	(3.607)
Job tenure	−0.009	−0.001	−0.009	−0.008	0.000	−0.009
	(1.109)	(0.067)	(1.152)	(1.070)	(0.045)	(1.146)
Tenure squared	0.000	0.000	0.000	0.000	0.000	0.000
	(0.652)	(1.022)	(0.778)	(0.638)	(0.977)	(0.776)
Age	−0.065***	−0.071***	−0.034**	−0.048**	−0.029	−0.032
	(3.838)	(4.346)	(1.973)	(2.269)	(1.470)	(1.500)
Age squared	0.001***	0.001***	0.001***	0.001***	0.001*	0.001**
	(4.334)	(4.768)	(2.713)	(2.762)	(1.945)	(2.145)
University degree	−1.249***	−0.662***	−0.959***	−1.238***	−0.636***	−0.958***
	(7.631)	(4.180)	(5.785)	(7.558)	(4.018)	(5.770)
Vocational qualifications	−0.420***	−0.184**	−0.321***	−0.414***	−0.170*	−0.320***
	(4.579)	(2.112)	(3.435)	(4.511)	(1.955)	(3.423)
A-levels plus	−0.579***	−0.397***	−0.491***	−0.581***	−0.403***	−0.491***
	(5.698)	(4.091)	(4.740)	(5.715)	(4.161)	(4.741)
O-levels plus	−0.362***	−0.274***	−0.316***	−0.357***	−0.263***	−0.316***
	(4.638)	(3.671)	(3.977)	(4.567)	(3.545)	(3.967)
Commercial or apprentice	−0.290***	−0.111	−0.282***	−0.284***	−0.097	−0.282***
	(3.100)	(1.247)	(3.000)	(3.031)	(1.096)	(2.989)

Married	−0.009	0.005	0.010	−0.003	0.018	0.011
	(0.141)	(0.079)	(0.164)	(0.055)	(0.307)	(0.175)
Children	0.174***	0.121**	0.108*	0.177***	0.128**	0.108*
	(2.896)	(2.123)	(1.778)	(2.947)	(2.248)	(1.784)
Mortgage	−0.052	−0.020	−0.042	−0.058	−0.033	−0.043
house	(0.883)	(0.351)	(0.711)	(0.978)	(0.583)	(0.722)
Paid outright	0.072	0.077	−0.015	0.069	0.069	−0.016
house	(0.830)	(0.932)	(0.172)	(0.792)	(0.840)	(0.176)
South of	0.214*	0.406***	0.085	0.215*	0.408***	0.086
England	(1.683)	(3.322)	(0.670)	(1.688)	(3.348)	(0.672)
Midlands	0.252*	0.343***	0.253*	0.255*	0.349***	0.254*
	(1.891)	(2.673)	(1.889)	(1.911)	(2.729)	(1.892)
North of	0.264**	0.307**	0.189	0.267**	0.313**	0.190
England	(2.029)	(2.458)	(1.451)	(2.052)	(2.515)	(1.454)
Wales	0.166	0.284*	0.125	0.169	0.290*	0.126
	(0.981)	(1.749)	(0.736)	(0.997)	(1.791)	(0.739)
Scotland	−0.054	0.268*	0.000	−0.049	0.283**	0.001
	(0.363)	(1.880)	(0.000)	(0.326)	(1.983)	(0.005)
Fair health	−0.130	−0.055	0.131	−0.129	−0.052	0.131
	(1.354)	(0.601)	(1.367)	(1.345)	(0.571)	(1.367)
Good health	−0.028	0.095	0.173*	−0.028	0.097	0.173*
	(0.307)	(1.076)	(1.875)	(0.299)	(1.101)	(1.875)
Excellent	0.223**	0.175*	0.434***	0.225**	0.181*	0.434***
health	(2.226)	(1.842)	(4.329)	(2.248)	(1.907)	(4.331)
Trade union	−0.178**	0.073	−0.134*	−0.175**	0.081	−0.134*
member	(2.446)	(1.030)	(1.821)	(2.405)	(1.149)	(1.815)
Permanent	0.125*	−0.071	0.250***	0.123*	−0.075	0.250***
contract	(1.680)	(0.997)	(3.363)	(1.652)	(1.047)	(3.359)
Incremental	0.184***	0.253***	0.038	0.181***	0.247***	0.038
pay	(3.703)	(5.383)	(0.767)	(3.642)	(5.258)	(0.758)

Table 4.6(b) Continued

	Job overall	Pay	Work itself	Job overall	Pay	Work itself
Managerial tasks	0.024	0.032	0.047	0.024	0.035	0.047
	(0.350)	(0.495)	(0.667)	(0.352)	(0.532)	(0.667)
Part-time	0.001	0.098	−0.148*	−0.000	0.097	−0.148*
	(0.014)	(1.371)	(1.936)	(0.003)	(1.352)	(1.939)
Travel time	−0.004**	−0.004**	−0.002	−0.004**	−0.003**	−0.002
	(2.183)	(2.075)	(1.245)	(2.170)	(2.068)	(1.243)
Size 25–99	−0.141**	−0.086	−0.127**	−0.136**	−0.076	−0.126**
	(2.515)	(1.626)	(2.251)	(2.432)	(1.439)	(2.237)
Size 100–499	−0.288***	−0.072	−0.380***	−0.286***	−0.069	−0.379***
	(3.967)	(1.027)	(5.205)	(3.945)	(0.986)	(5.201)
Size 500 plus	−0.169*	−0.278***	−0.324***	−0.163	−0.265***	−0.323***
	(1.670)	(2.857)	(3.208)	(1.613)	(2.735)	(3.198)
Manufacturing	−0.052	−0.048	−0.171	−0.075	−0.103	−0.174
	(0.372)	(0.360)	(1.206)	(0.529)	(0.763)	(1.219)
Professional services	0.240*	−0.079	0.066	0.279**	0.011	0.071
	(1.879)	(0.644)	(0.509)	(2.132)	(0.085)	(0.536)
Other services	0.115	−0.052	−0.113	0.055	−0.198	−0.121
	(0.908)	(0.432)	(0.874)	(0.407)	(1.544)	(0.888)
Professionals	1.025**	0.275	0.829*	1.037**	0.295	0.830*
	(2.283)	(0.658)	(1.849)	(2.305)	(0.708)	(1.851)
Managerial technical	0.130	−0.027	0.492***	0.128	−0.034	0.492***
	(1.385)	(0.304)	(5.055)	(1.364)	(0.383)	(5.051)
Skilled non-manual	0.029	−0.034	0.149**	0.027	−0.041	0.149**
	(0.482)	(0.607)	(2.480)	(0.452)	(0.724)	(2.475)
Skilled manual	0.031	−0.068	0.293***	0.031	−0.071	0.293***
	(0.394)	(0.910)	(3.671)	(0.394)	(0.954)	(3.670)
Voluntarily	0.233***	0.256***	0.146**	0.233***	0.257***	0.146**
	(3.627)	(4.217)	(2.267)	(3.633)	(4.229)	(2.268)

Wave 2	−0.050	0.258***	−0.117*	−0.043	0.276***	−0.116*
	(0.748)	(4.062)	(1.732)	(0.630)	(4.337)	(1.712)
Wave 3	−0.144**	0.146**	−0.164**	−0.130*	0.181***	−0.162**
	(2.102)	(2.246)	(2.370)	(1.864)	(2.748)	(2.316)
Wave 4	−0.100	0.148**	−0.172**	−0.085	0.184***	−0.170**
	(1.446)	(2.254)	(2.469)	(1.204)	(2.773)	(2.411)
Wave 5	−0.175**	0.104	−0.108	−0.161**	0.137**	−0.106
	(2.468)	(1.561)	(1.507)	(2.254)	(2.029)	(1.469)
Wave 6	−0.186***	0.138**	−0.237***	−0.162**	0.194***	−0.234***
	(2.642)	(2.080)	(3.356)	(2.242)	(2.849)	(3.224)
Wave 7	−0.099	0.170**	−0.175**	−0.068	0.242***	−0.171**
	(1.363)	(2.498)	(2.402)	(0.899)	(3.402)	(2.251)
Cut 1	−4.785***	−3.443***	−3.914***	−4.901***	−3.713***	−3.929***
	(10.986)	(8.472)	(8.966)	(11.056)	(8.993)	(8.841)
Cut 2	−4.438299***	−2.929***	−3.525***	−4.553***	−3.199***	−3.540***
	(10.24)	(7.23)	(8.11)	(10.32)	(7.77)	(8.00)
Cut 3	−3.941***	−2.238***	−3.132***	−4.056***	−2.508***	−3.147***
	(9.14)	(5.54)	(7.23)	(9.24)	(6.11)	(7.14)
Cut 4	−3.455***	−1.815***	−2.527***	−3.570***	−2.084***	−2.543***
	(8.04)	(4.50)	(5.85)	(8.16)	(5.08)	(5.78)
Cut 5	−2.707***	−1.145***	−1.807***	−2.822***	−1.415***	−1.822***
	(6.32)	(2.84)	(4.20)	(6.47)	(3.46)	(4.16)
Cut 6	−1.239***	−0.073	−0.552	−1.353***	−0.343	−0.567
	(2.91)	(0.18)	(1.28)	(3.12)	(0.84)	(1.30)
Rho	0.425***	0.407***	0.433***	0.425***	0.404***	0.433***
	(20.01)	(20.00)	(20.81)	(20.05)	(19.93)	(20.80)
Log likelihood	−6 085	−7 841	−6 288	−6 084	−7 835	−6 288
No. of observations	4 465	4 453	4 461	4 465	4 453	4 461

Notes: Absolute value of z statistics in parentheses. * Significant at 10%; ** significant at 5%; *** significant at 1%.

Table 4.6(c) High-paid males

	Job overall	**Pay**	**Work itself**	**Job overall**	**Pay**	**Work itself**
Log usual gross hourly wage	0.396***	1.356***	0.304***	0.413***	1.379***	0.321***
	(8.336)	(27.883)	(6.177)	(8.636)	(28.171)	(6.495)
Log comparative wage				−0.421***	−0.559***	−0.444***
				(3.272)	(4.419)	(3.351)
Log usual hours	0.244**	1.061***	0.341***	0.255**	1.074***	0.352***
	(2.424)	(10.766)	(3.317)	(2.536)	(10.881)	(3.424)
Job tenure	−0.042***	−0.033***	−0.025***	−0.041***	−0.033***	−0.025***
	(8.116)	(6.639)	(4.912)	(8.115)	(6.580)	(4.903)
Tenure squared	0.001***	0.001***	0.001***	0.001***	0.001***	0.001***
	(5.730)	(4.408)	(3.239)	(5.720)	(4.374)	(3.223)
Age	−0.043***	−0.100***	0.014	0.002	−0.040**	0.063***
	(3.181)	(7.542)	(1.014)	(0.124)	(2.070)	(3.117)
Age squared	0.001***	0.001***	0.000	0.000	0.001**	−0.001**
	(3.723)	(7.300)	(0.132)	(0.538)	(2.371)	(2.183)
University degree	−0.531***	−0.403***	−0.369***	−0.521***	−0.394***	−0.361***
	(6.489)	(5.013)	(4.375)	(6.364)	(4.908)	(4.286)
Vocational qualifications	−0.344***	−0.232***	−0.171**	−0.332***	−0.222***	−0.160**
	(5.153)	(3.518)	(2.515)	(4.962)	(3.371)	(2.356)
A-levels plus	−0.440***	−0.212***	−0.258***	−0.433***	−0.204***	−0.249***
	(5.887)	(2.863)	(3.355)	(5.779)	(2.761)	(3.259)
O-levels plus	−0.247***	−0.108	−0.152**	−0.238***	−0.101	−0.145**
	(3.560)	(1.606)	(2.153)	(3.420)	(1.507)	(2.044)
Commercial or apprentice	−0.054	0.029	−0.031	−0.049	0.037	−0.024
	(0.634)	(0.350)	(0.350)	(0.575)	(0.448)	(0.272)
Married	−0.027	−0.055	−0.000	−0.021	−0.047	0.008
	(0.619)	(1.290)	(0.003)	(0.494)	(1.114)	(0.174)

Children	0.063*	0.005	0.082**	0.059*	−0.001	0.079**
	(1.776)	(0.131)	(2.254)	(1.660)	(0.037)	(2.175)
Mortgage house	−0.108**	−0.070*	−0.111**	−0.103**	−0.061	−0.106**
	(2.550)	(1.684)	(2.562)	(2.447)	(1.467)	(2.439)
Paid outright house	−0.024	0.093	−0.104	−0.017	0.106*	−0.094
	(0.387)	(1.488)	(1.602)	(0.276)	(1.698)	(1.443)
South of England	0.129*	0.319***	0.154**	0.123*	0.316***	0.151**
	(1.913)	(4.838)	(2.250)	(1.828)	(4.801)	(2.205)
Midlands	0.238***	0.372***	0.359***	0.238***	0.376***	0.361***
	(3.152)	(5.042)	(4.631)	(3.153)	(5.108)	(4.662)
North of England	0.211***	0.401***	0.202***	0.215***	0.404***	0.205***
	(2.959)	(5.776)	(2.774)	(3.006)	(5.834)	(2.806)
Wales	0.302***	0.414***	0.288***	0.305***	0.423***	0.293***
	(2.856)	(3.883)	(2.656)	(2.880)	(3.969)	(2.676)
Scotland	0.128	0.336***	0.157*	0.130	0.345***	0.163*
	(1.427)	(3.838)	(1.707)	(1.453)	(3.964)	(1.767)
Fair health	0.008	0.042	0.060	0.007	0.041	0.058
	(0.109)	(0.596)	(0.825)	(0.104)	(0.584)	(0.797)
Good health	0.239***	0.204***	0.238***	0.239***	0.204***	0.237***
	(3.475)	(3.015)	(3.406)	(3.483)	(3.003)	(3.392)
Excellent health	0.401***	0.277***	0.397***	0.403***	0.279***	0.398***
	(5.624)	(3.955)	(5.478)	(5.661)	(3.974)	(5.496)
Trade union member	−0.058	−0.090**	−0.061	−0.052	−0.084**	−0.054
	(1.559)	(2.450)	(1.577)	(1.387)	(2.306)	(1.391)
Permanent contract	0.012	−0.156**	−0.032	0.018	−0.148**	−0.026
	(0.191)	(2.450)	(0.497)	(0.285)	(2.324)	(0.396)
Incremental pay	0.214***	0.165***	0.128***	0.215***	0.167***	0.129***
	(7.624)	(6.034)	(4.508)	(7.681)	(6.086)	(4.542)
Managerial tasks	0.036	−0.011	0.012	0.035	−0.013	0.010
	(1.094)	(0.332)	(0.341)	(1.043)	(0.408)	(0.286)

Table 4.6(c) Continued

	Job overall	Pay	Work itself	Job overall	Pay	Work itself
Part-time	0.440***	0.996***	0.454***	0.441***	0.998***	0.455***
	(3.155)	(7.347)	(3.226)	(3.160)	(7.356)	(3.239)
Travel time	−0.002***	−0.001*	−0.000	−0.002***	−0.001*	−0.000
	(3.529)	(1.729)	(0.474)	(3.503)	(1.686)	(0.435)
Size 25–99	−0.153***	−0.079**	−0.164***	−0.148***	−0.074**	−0.161***
	(3.941)	(2.089)	(4.143)	(3.829)	(1.972)	(4.072)
Size 100–499	−0.194***	−0.134***	−0.214***	−0.189***	−0.128***	−0.208***
	(4.770)	(3.362)	(5.152)	(4.622)	(3.197)	(5.019)
Size 500 plus	−0.186***	−0.110**	−0.237***	−0.178***	−0.101**	−0.230***
	(4.009)	(2.438)	(5.071)	(3.838)	(2.246)	(4.918)
Manufacturing	−0.017	−0.087	−0.083	−0.048	−0.129*	−0.111
	(0.249)	(1.291)	(1.180)	(0.707)	(1.905)	(1.557)
Professional services	0.021	−0.208***	−0.084	0.138*	−0.052	0.043
	(0.309)	(3.061)	(1.196)	(1.806)	(0.678)	(0.537)
Other services	−0.042	−0.218***	−0.119*	−0.110	−0.310***	−0.187**
	(0.614)	(3.198)	(1.692)	(1.545)	(4.370)	(2.522)
Professionals	0.227***	0.054	0.404***	0.236***	0.064	0.415***
	(3.128)	(0.766)	(5.446)	(3.247)	(0.903)	(5.589)
Managerial technical	0.233***	0.074	0.377***	0.239***	0.080	0.383***
	(4.007)	(1.296)	(6.390)	(4.099)	(1.404)	(6.495)
Skilled non-manual	0.170***	0.129**	0.210***	0.175***	0.136**	0.215***
	(2.864)	(2.211)	(3.511)	(2.945)	(2.345)	(3.589)
Skilled manual	0.158***	−0.023	0.245***	0.164***	−0.016	0.251***
	(3.358)	(0.494)	(5.132)	(3.480)	(0.356)	(5.257)
Voluntarily	0.295***	0.209***	0.204***	0.294***	0.210***	0.204***
	(9.039)	(6.594)	(6.194)	(9.026)	(6.623)	(6.201)

Wave 2	−0.042	0.171***	−0.053	−0.036	0.180***	−0.046
	(1.096)	(4.510)	(1.346)	(0.916)	(4.750)	(1.160)
Wave 3	−0.167***	0.079**	−0.174***	−0.153***	0.097**	−0.160***
	(4.188)	(2.028)	(4.310)	(3.830)	(2.479)	(3.938)
Wave 4	−0.191***	0.085**	−0.263***	−0.178***	0.102***	−0.249***
	(4.796)	(2.165)	(6.488)	(4.437)	(2.602)	(6.109)
Wave 5	−0.179***	0.117***	−0.298***	−0.170***	0.129***	−0.288***
	(4.451)	(2.960)	(7.278)	(4.210)	(3.271)	(7.024)
Wave 6	−0.122***	0.192***	−0.261***	−0.110***	0.208***	−0.249***
	(3.012)	(4.853)	(6.362)	(2.709)	(5.235)	(6.038)
Wave 7	−0.073*	0.164***	−0.268***	−0.055	0.188***	−0.250***
	(1.825)	(4.210)	(6.610)	(1.374)	(4.771)	(6.099)
Cut 1	−1.741***	2.561***	−0.390	−1.579***	2.770***	−0.212
	(3.861)	(5.800)	(0.843)	(3.486)	(6.238)	(0.455)
Cut 2	−1.246***	3.125***	0.0349	−1.085***	3.333***	0.213
	(2.77)	(7.07)	(0.08)	(2.40)	(7.51)	(0.46)
Cut 3	−0.557	3.993***	0.636	−0.395	4.202***	0.815*
	(1.24)	(9.03)	(1.38)	(0.87)	(9.45)	(1.75)
Cut 4	−0.007	4.472***	1.245***	0.154	4.681***	1.424***
	(0.02)	(10.10)	(2.70)	(0.34)	(10.52)	(3.06)
Cut 5	0.876*	5.343***	2.095***	1.038**	5.553***	2.274***
	(1.95)	(12.05)	(4.54)	(2.29)	(12.46)	(4.89)
Cut 6	2.573***	6.811***	3.568***	2.735***	7.021***	3.747***
	(5.71)	(15.30)	(7.71)	(6.04)	(15.69)	(8.05)
Rho	0.470***	0.453***	0.492***	0.468***	0.451***	0.491***
	(39.35)	(40.33)	(42.10)	(39.16)	(40.07)	(41.95)
Log likelihood	−17 335	−19 072	−17 040	−17 330	−19 062	−17 034
No. of observations	11 775	11 768	11 764	11 775	11 768	11 764

Notes: Absolute value of z statistics in parentheses. * Significant at 10%; ** significant at 5%; *** significant at 1%.

Table 4.6(d) High-paid females

	Job overall	Pay	Work itself	Job overall	Pay	Work itself
Log usual gross hourly wage	0.062	0.922***	0.039	0.068	0.918***	0.039
	(1.067)	(15.665)	(0.669)	(1.161)	(15.539)	(0.670)
Log comparative wage				−0.144	0.110	−0.005
				(1.056)	(0.812)	(0.036)
Log usual hours	−0.257***	−0.158***	−0.134**	−0.256***	−0.159***	−0.134**
	(4.232)	(2.632)	(2.202)	(4.211)	(2.647)	(2.202)
Job tenure	−0.036***	−0.028***	−0.031***	−0.036***	−0.028***	−0.031***
	(4.374)	(3.394)	(3.764)	(4.346)	(3.411)	(3.762)
Tenure squared	0.001***	0.001***	0.002***	0.001***	0.001***	0.002***
	(3.354)	(3.328)	(4.219)	(3.332)	(3.342)	(4.218)
Age	−0.027*	−0.043***	−0.007	−0.017	−0.051***	−0.007
	(1.766)	(2.857)	(0.467)	(0.972)	(2.872)	(0.380)
Age squared	0.001***	0.001***	0.000	0.000*	0.001***	0.000
	(2.596)	(3.336)	(1.523)	(1.676)	(3.280)	(1.280)
University degree	−0.676***	−0.714***	−0.524***	−0.672***	−0.716***	−0.524***
	(7.093)	(7.243)	(5.453)	(7.055)	(7.261)	(5.448)
Vocational qualifications	−0.362***	−0.516***	−0.132*	−0.358***	−0.519***	−0.132*
	(4.559)	(6.427)	(1.666)	(4.514)	(6.441)	(1.663)
A-levels plus	−0.375***	−0.427***	−0.240***	−0.372***	−0.429***	−0.240***
	(4.120)	(4.602)	(2.596)	(4.091)	(4.615)	(2.594)
O-levels plus	−0.201***	−0.243***	−0.206***	−0.198**	−0.246***	−0.206***
	(2.581)	(3.072)	(2.622)	(2.535)	(3.105)	(2.617)
Commercial or apprentice	−0.048	−0.218**	−0.000	−0.046	−0.220**	−0.000
	(0.498)	(2.282)	(0.002)	(0.474)	(2.303)	(0.001)
Married	0.112***	0.206***	0.078*	0.116***	0.204***	0.078*
	(2.627)	(4.757)	(1.802)	(2.696)	(4.691)	(1.800)

Children	0.115***	0.109***	0.109**	0.113***	0.111***	0.109**
	(2.687)	(2.594)	(2.526)	(2.647)	(2.626)	(2.523)
Mortgage house	−0.174***	−0.085*	−0.143***	−0.173***	−0.086*	−0.143***
	(3.541)	(1.745)	(2.893)	(3.532)	(1.753)	(2.892)
Paid outright house	−0.087	−0.021	−0.032	−0.087	−0.022	−0.032
	(1.214)	(0.301)	(0.445)	(1.216)	(0.302)	(0.445)
South of England	0.122*	0.139**	−0.001	0.121*	0.139**	−0.001
	(1.847)	(2.069)	(0.013)	(1.834)	(2.072)	(0.014)
Midlands	0.098	0.359***	0.067	0.100	0.357***	0.067
	(1.271)	(4.523)	(0.863)	(1.288)	(4.502)	(0.863)
North of England	0.146**	0.359***	0.027	0.147**	0.357***	0.027
	(2.043)	(4.922)	(0.375)	(2.054)	(4.911)	(0.374)
Wales	0.135	0.446***	0.006	0.136	0.446***	0.006
	(1.135)	(3.610)	(0.049)	(1.143)	(3.615)	(0.050)
Scotland	−0.032	0.250***	−0.124	−0.031	0.249***	−0.124
	(0.364)	(2.783)	(1.410)	(0.355)	(2.776)	(1.410)
Fair health	0.060	−0.046	0.005	0.058	−0.045	0.005
	(0.909)	(0.721)	(0.083)	(0.883)	(0.702)	(0.082)
Good health	0.202***	0.031	0.104*	0.200***	0.033	0.104*
	(3.233)	(0.513)	(1.650)	(3.209)	(0.531)	(1.649)
Excellent health	0.394***	0.112*	0.236***	0.393***	0.113*	0.236***
	(5.899)	(1.714)	(3.502)	(5.887)	(1.721)	(3.500)
Trade union member	−0.186***	−0.165***	−0.134***	−0.185***	−0.166***	−0.134***
	(4.538)	(4.016)	(3.217)	(4.513)	(4.031)	(3.215)
Permanent contract	0.173***	−0.059	0.040	0.174***	−0.059	0.040
	(2.860)	(0.993)	(0.655)	(2.861)	(0.991)	(0.655)
Incremental pay	0.136***	0.122***	0.104***	0.136***	0.121***	0.104***
	(4.213)	(3.845)	(3.225)	(4.212)	(3.838)	(3.225)
Managerial tasks	0.016	−0.017	0.141***	0.015	−0.017	0.141***
	(0.429)	(0.471)	(3.816)	(0.422)	(0.462)	(3.816)

Table 4.6(d) Continued

	Job overall	Pay	Work itself	Job overall	Pay	Work itself
Part-time	0.095	0.186***	0.081	0.096	0.185***	0.081
	(1.593)	(3.183)	(1.348)	(1.614)	(3.164)	(1.349)
Travel time	−0.002**	0.000	−0.001	−0.002**	0.000	−0.001
	(2.463)	(0.087)	(1.395)	(2.425)	(0.068)	(1.393)
Size 25–99	−0.067	−0.084**	−0.163***	−0.066	−0.085**	−0.163***
	(1.632)	(2.112)	(3.966)	(1.611)	(2.127)	(3.965)
Size 100–499	−0.239***	−0.137***	−0.262***	−0.238***	−0.138***	−0.262***
	(5.232)	(3.037)	(5.695)	(5.193)	(3.057)	(5.691)
Size 500 plus	−0.153***	−0.178***	−0.200***	−0.150***	−0.180***	−0.200***
	(3.024)	(3.586)	(3.917)	(2.965)	(3.623)	(3.912)
Manufacturing	0.005	−0.032	0.097	−0.016	−0.016	0.097
	(0.050)	(0.318)	(0.960)	(0.155)	(0.158)	(0.933)
Professional services	0.143	−0.160*	0.166*	0.158*	−0.172*	0.167*
	(1.563)	(1.770)	(1.828)	(1.709)	(1.875)	(1.812)
Other services	0.037	−0.071	0.057	−0.001	−0.041	0.056
	(0.377)	(0.732)	(0.590)	(0.012)	(0.395)	(0.537)
Professionals	0.187*	−0.203*	0.188*	0.188*	−0.204*	0.188*
	(1.696)	(1.867)	(1.694)	(1.706)	(1.876)	(1.694)
Managerial technical	0.113*	−0.157**	0.202***	0.112*	−0.156**	0.202***
	(1.668)	(2.336)	(2.954)	(1.648)	(2.324)	(2.953)
Skilled non-manual	−0.050	−0.062	−0.093	−0.051	−0.062	−0.093
	(0.810)	(1.008)	(1.488)	(0.818)	(1.002)	(1.488)
Skilled manual	0.192**	−0.107	0.167**	0.191**	−0.106	0.167**
	(2.333)	(1.326)	(2.024)	(2.320)	(1.321)	(2.024)
Voluntarily	0.243***	0.222***	0.205***	0.243***	0.222***	0.205***
	(6.453)	(6.075)	(5.420)	(6.471)	(6.058)	(5.420)

Wave 2	−0.073	0.091**	−0.163***	−0.070	0.089**	−0.162***
	(1.598)	(2.077)	(3.532)	(1.534)	(2.027)	(3.525)
Wave 3	−0.233***	−0.077*	−0.197***	−0.225***	−0.083*	−0.196***
	(5.037)	(1.724)	(4.222)	(4.813)	(1.833)	(4.164)
Wave 4	−0.316***	−0.107**	−0.354***	−0.306***	−0.114**	−0.354***
	(6.845)	(2.401)	(7.617)	(6.520)	(2.513)	(7.471)
Wave 5	−0.374***	−0.073	−0.349***	−0.366***	−0.079*	−0.349***
	(7.956)	(1.612)	(7.381)	(7.717)	(1.717)	(7.299)
Wave 6	−0.344***	−0.064	−0.329***	−0.334***	−0.072	−0.329***
	(7.275)	(1.401)	(6.906)	(6.903)	(1.542)	(6.751)
Wave 7	−0.318***	−0.083*	−0.346***	−0.304***	−0.094**	−0.345***
	(6.847)	(1.847)	(7.385)	(6.279)	(2.003)	(7.076)
Cut 1	−4.029***	−2.248***	−3.359***	−4.091***	−2.199***	−3.362***
	(10.723)	(6.011)	(8.871)	(10.760)	(5.807)	(8.758)
Cut 2	−3.7041***	−1.680***	−2.923***	−3.604***	−1.631***	−2.925***
	(4.39)	(4.50)	(7.74)	(9.50)	(4.31)	(7.64)
Cut 3	−3.1391***	−0.826**	−2.333***	−2.964***	−0.777**	−2.336***
	(3.73)	(2.21)	(6.19)	(7.83)	(2.06)	(6.11)
Cut 4	−2.5711***	−0.391	−1.855***	−2.554***	−0.342	−1.857***
	(3.06)	(1.05)	(4.92)	(6.75)	(0.91)	(4.86)
Cut 5	−1.7910**	0.432	−1.033***	−1.715***	0.482	−1.036***
	(2.14)	(1.16)	(2.74)	(4.51)	(1.27)	(2.71)
Cut 6	−0.3604887	1.820***	0.441	0.029	1.870***	0.438
	(0.43)	(4.87)	(1.17)	(0.08)	(4.94)	(1.15)
Rho	0.4340***	0.475***	0.4592652***	0.450***	0.476***	0.459***
	(10.28)	(39.06)	(35.12)	(33.80)	(39.03)	(35.10)
Log likelihood	−12 919	−15 253	−13 136	−12 919	−15 252	−13 136
No. of observations	9 533	9 525	9 529	9 533	9 525	9 529

Notes: Absolute value of z statistics in parentheses. * Significant at 10%; ** significant at 5%; *** significant at 1%.

absolute pay variable for both low-paid and higher paid men and women. For low-paid women, but not higher paid women the comparison pay variable is appropriately signed and significant.

Finally, the regressions for satisfaction with work itself are similar to those for overall satisfaction. For women neither relative nor absolute pay has a significant effect on satisfaction with work itself. Neither category of pay is significant and appropriately signed for low-paid workers or for higher paid women. Clearly pay matters much less for women than for men in determining job satisfaction.

Pay mobility – probit estimates

During the seven-year period 1991–97 there were 2328 movements either from low pay to high pay or the reverse. There were slightly more movements from low pay to high pay (1297) than from higher pay to low pay (1031). Given the nature of the sample it is possible for an individual not to move at all or to make multiple moves from one state to another. In practice, of those individuals moving from low-paid to higher paid jobs 88.13 per cent made one such move, 11.18 per cent made two such moves and 0.69 per cent three such moves. Similarly 87.49 per cent of those who moved from higher paid to low-paid jobs made a single move compared to 11.93 per cent who made two such moves and 0.58 per cent who made three moves.

Before we present the results for the impact of moving out of low pay on the probability of increasing job satisfaction, it is useful to consider the percentage of employees that make this move and the direction of change in their overall job satisfaction. Seventy-four per cent of our sample are those higher paid who remained higher paid between periods $t-1$ and t. Fourteen per cent of our sample are those low-paid workers who remained low paid. Of the low paid in the whole sample only about 7 per cent move to higher pay, which is about only 27 per cent of all low paid at $t-1$, while 5 per cent of the higher paid in the whole sample become low paid, which is about 8 per cent of all higher paid at $t-1$.

We are particularly interested in what happens to job satisfaction when such moves occur and the extent to which job satisfaction responses remain stable when no such movement occurs. In fact about one-third of those moving from low-paid to higher paid jobs report an increase in job satisfaction, but about a quarter report a reduction in job satisfaction. The latter could be explained by job changing increasing job insecurity or perhaps the more demanding nature of a higher paid job more than offsetting the increased financial compensation. For women the proportion expressing a reduction in job satisfaction when moving from a lower paid to a higher paid job is lower than that of men, but so is the proportion expressing an increase in job satisfaction.[10]

We can now present the regression results for the impact of moving out of low pay on the probability of an increase in job satisfaction (Table 4.7). Recall that the dependent variable is equal to one if the worker reports a higher level of job satisfaction between any year $t - 1$ and t, and zero if the worker reports an equal or lower level of satisfaction between any two successive years in the panel. A large number of regressions are run by gender, age and education categories as well as for part- and full-time workers. Table 4.7(a) shows the probit coefficients and standard errors, the baseline probability (i.e. the probability of experiencing an increase in job satisfaction evaluated at the sample mean of the distribution of the various groups under analysis), and marginal effects (i.e. the effect on the baseline probability of having moved out of low pay). This table does not distinguish, however, between moving out of low pay within an existing employment unit and moving out of low pay by changing employer.

Having moved out of low pay in the last year significantly increases the job satisfaction of both men and women, with the effect being slightly stronger for women. The effect is insignificant for older men, those without qualifications or with university degrees. Leaving a job voluntarily only makes a difference in the case of women. These results seem to contrast with those for the levels of job satisfaction and suggest that we should be cautious in inferring that pay does not matter.

Another series of probit results are presented in Table 4.7(b), of the impact of moving out of low pay on the probability of an increase in satisfaction with pay. Having moved out of low pay again significantly increases the satisfaction with pay of both men and women. These effects are stronger for younger men and women. These results are consistent with the earlier suggestion that the reason for the negative association between pay and satisfaction for low-paid women must be explained by a relationship between pay and unmeasured non-pecuniary benefits of work.

Movements into low pay (Table 4.8(a)) do not tend to have a significant effect on overall job satisfaction for either sex, but in the case of men this change has a significant negative effect on the level of satisfaction with pay (Table 4.8(b)).[11]

Table 4.7(a) The impact of moving out of low pay on the probability of a change in job satisfaction: probit estimates

Job satisfaction type	**Men**			**Women**		
	Baseline probability	**Probit estimate**	**Marginal effect**	**Baseline probability**	**Probit estimate**	**Marginal effect**
Overall job satisfaction:						
All	0.266	0.163*	0.056	0.246	0.182***	0.060
		(0.087)			(0.063)	
By age:						
Aged 35 or less	0.273	0.195*	0.067	0.267	0.207**	0.071
		(0.104)			(0.094)	
Aged more than 35	0.262	0.074	0.024	0.232	0.157	0.050
		(0.167)			(0.084)*	
By education:						
No qualifications	0.272	−0.095	−0.031	0.240	0.042	0.013
		(0.205)			(0.134)	
Any qualifications	0.266	0.238**	0.082	0.247	0.216***	0.073
		(0.097)			(0.071)	

A-levels, O-levels commercial etc.	0.271	0.246** (0.122)	0.086	0.255	0.260*** (0.069)	0.085
University	0.262	0.219* (0.164)	0.075	0.237	0.107 (0.131)	0.040
By working arrangements:						
Full time	0.267	0.170 (0.090)	0.056	0.253	0.212*** (0.082)	0.070
Part-time	0.273	0.378 (0.392)	0.170	0.233	0.174* (0.097)	0.055
Voluntarily left previous job	0.338	0.179 (0.161)	0.084	0.329	0.385*** (0.124)	0.146
Did not voluntarily leave previous job	0.248	0.120 (0.105)	0.038	0.227	0.095 (0.074)	0.027

Notes: The dependent variable is equal to one if the worker reports a higher job satisfaction between any two successive years $t-1$ and t, and zero if the worker reports equal or lower job satisfaction between the two years. Each regression also includes changes in: age, marital status, health, region of residence, number of children in the household, part-time employment status, union membership, hours of work, firm size, industry sector. Standard errors are in parentheses. ***, ** and * denote significance at 0.01, 0.05 and 0.10 levels respectively.

Table 4.7(b) The impact of moving out of low pay on the probability of a change in satisfaction with pay: probit estimates

Job satisfaction type	**Men**			**Women**		
	Baseline probability	**Probit estimate**	**Marginal effect**	**Baseline probability**	**Probit estimate**	**Marginal effect**
Satisfaction with pay:						
All	0.302	0.353***	0.131	0.303	0.347)***	0.129
		(0.085)			(0.060)	
By age:						
Aged 35 or less	0.319	0.399***	0.151	0.320	0.392***	0.148
		(0.101)			(0.091)	
Aged more than 35	0.289	0.152	0.054	0.292	0.314***	0.115
		(0.162)			(0.081)	
By education:						
No qualifications	0.316	0.231	0.093	0.291	0.178	0.063
		(0.188)			(0.127)	
Any qualifications	0.300	0.383***	0.143	0.306	0.402***	0.150
		(0.095)			(0.069)	

A-levels, O-levels commercial etc.	0.304	0.337*** (0.119)	0.125	0.309	0.481*** (0.068)	0.213
University	0.297	0.469*** (0.160)	0.179	0.301	0.046 (0.128)	0.013
By working arrangements:						
Full time	0.302	0.353*** (0.087)	0.128	0.312	0.397*** (0.079)	0.150
Part-time	0.353	0.612 (0.393)	0.249	0.287	0.294*** (0.093)	0.105
Voluntarily left previous job	0.382	0.394** (0.160)	0.157	0.368	0.555*** (0.123)	0.217
Did not voluntarily leave previous job	0.281	0.303*** (0.101)	0.108	0.289	0.273*** (0.070)	0.097

Notes: The dependent variable is equal to one if the worker reports a higher job satisfaction between any two successive years $t-1$ and t, and zero if the worker reports equal or lower job satisfaction between the two years. Each regression also includes changes in: age, marital status, health, region of residence, number of children in the household, part-time employment status, union membership, hours of work, firm size, industry sector. Standard errors are in parentheses. ***, ** and * denote significance at 0.01, 0.05 and 0.10 levels respectively.

Table 4.8(a) The impact of moving into low pay on the probability of a change in overall job satisfaction: probit estimates

Job satisfaction type	**Men**			**Women**		
	Baseline probability	**Probit estimate**	**Marginal effect**	**Baseline probability**	**Probit estimate**	**Marginal effect**
Overall job satisfaction:						
All	0.266	0.015	0.005	0.246	0.087	0.028
		(0.109)			(0.073)	
By age:						
Aged 35 or less	0.273	0.209	0.073	0.267	−0.065	−0.021
		(0.147)			(0.121)	
Aged more than 35	0.262	−0.218	−0.066	0.232	0.177*	0.057
		(0.166)			(0.092)	
By education:						
No qualifications	0.272	−0.034	−0.011	0.240	0.146	0.047
		(0.200)			(0.141)	
Any qualifications	0.266	0.038	0.011	0.247	0.068	0.022
		(0.131)			(0.086)	

A-levels, O-levels commercial etc.	0.271	0.028 (0.162)	0.008	0.255	−0.077 (0.085)	0.020
University	0.262	0.060 (0.229)	0.018	0.237	0.122 (0.150)	0.039
By working arrangements:						
Full time	0.267	0.044 (0.113)	0.014	0.253	0.150 (0.099)	0.048
Part-time	0.273	−0.226 (0.452)	−0.084	0.233	0.050 (0.109)	0.015
Voluntarily left previous job	0.338	0.244 (0.241)	0.106	0.329	−0.109 (0.203)	−0.038
Did not voluntarily leave previous job	0.248	−0.024 (0.123)	−0.013	0.227	0.151* (0.078)	0.043

Notes: The dependent variable is equal to one if the worker reports a higher job satisfaction between any two successive years $t-1$ and t, and zero if the worker reports equal or lower job satisfaction between the two years. Each regression also includes changes in: age, marital status, health, region of residence, number of children in the household, part-time employment status, union membership, hours of work, firm size, industry sector. Standard errors are in parentheses. ***, ** and * denote significance at 0.01, 0.05 and 0.10 levels respectively.

Table 4.8(b) The impact of moving into low pay on the probability of a change in satisfaction with pay: probit estimates

Job satisfaction type	Men			Women		
	Baseline probability	Probit estimate	Marginal effect	Baseline probability	Probit estimate	Marginal effect
Satisfaction with pay:						
All	0.302	−0.109*	−0.037	0.303	0.022	0.008
		(0.066)			(0.058)	
By age:						
Aged 35 or less	0.319	−0.093	−0.032	0.320	−0.127	−0.044
		(0.098)			(0.095)	
Aged more than 35	0.289	−0.117	−0.039	0.292	0.121	0.043
		(0.088)			(0.075)	
By education:						
No qualifications	0.316	0.060	0.020	0.291	0.071	0.024
		(0.208)	(0.270)		(0.158)	
Any qualifications	0.300	−0.125*	−0.042	0.306	0.013	0.005
		(0.069)			(0.063)	

A-levels, O-levels commercial etc.	0.304	−0.259**	−0.085	0.309	0.073	0.032
		(0.110)			(0.069)	
University	0.297	−0.035	−0.012	0.301	−0.077	−0.027
		(0.090)			(0.094)	
By working arrangements:						
Full time	0.302	−0.138**	−0.045	0.312	−0.009	−0.003
		(0.067)			(0.073)	
Part-time	0.353	0.510	0.192	0.287	0.088	0.029
		(0.339)			(0.097)	
Voluntarily left previous job	0.382	−0.289**	−0.106	0.368	0.028	0.010
		(0.132)			(0.119)	
Did not voluntarily leave previous job	0.281	−0.048	−0.018	0.289	0.016	0.003
		(0.075)			(0.067)	

Notes: The dependent variable is equal to one if the worker reports a higher job satisfaction between any two successive years $t-1$ and t, and zero if the worker reports equal or lower job satisfaction between the two years. Each regression also includes changes in: age, marital status, health, region of residence, number of children in the household, part-time employment status, union membership, hours of work, firm size, industry sector. Standard errors are in parentheses. ***, ** and * denote significance at 0.01, 0.05 and 0.10 levels respectively.

5 Conclusions

The finding that low-paid workers have higher job satisfaction than higher paid workers casts doubt on the notion that there are 'good jobs' and 'bad jobs'. Rather it appears that low-paid workers obtain compensating differences in the form of non-pecuniary benefits. There is, therefore, no justification for the European Commission's assertion that low-paid jobs are inherently jobs of low quality, at least as far as the British evidence is concerned.

It also appears that pay is not the dominating factor in terms of job satisfaction, particularly in the case of women. Facets of job satisfaction such as satisfaction with initiative and satisfaction with the nature of work itself rank more highly. Nevertheless, even for the low paid there are benefits for the average worker in escaping from the low-pay segment in the form of significantly higher overall and job satisfaction. Having moved out of low pay in the last year significantly increases the job satisfaction of both men and women, particularly those aged 35 or less. There is an even stronger effect for men with no qualifications and women with intermediate qualifications. Finally, while for women there are significant effects for both full-time and part-time women the effect is stronger for the former. However, it is not invariably the case that apparently favourable job changes lead to increased job satisfaction. There are examples of job satisfaction declining with movements out of low-paid work and there is no significant relationship between voluntary quits and increased overall job satisfaction for men. It may be that job changes lead to increased job insecurity at least in the short term.

The somewhat contrasting results for the random effects ordered probit and the standard probit equations suggest a degree of caution in interpreting the importance of pay. It may be that workers sort themselves into jobs where pay is satisfactory, given that it is more difficult to judge the non-pecuniary aspects of work without sampling them. Thus, Clark (2001), using the same seven waves of the BHPS found that satisfaction with pay (together with satisfaction with job security) was the most important determinant of quits.[12]

The appropriate conclusion may be, therefore, that where pay is satisfactory other features of work become more important in determining overall job satisfaction.

Acknowledgements

We are grateful to Richard Jones for excellent research assistance and Frances Jackson for very efficient secretarial assistance.

Notes

1. The government has accepted the recommendation of the Low Pay Commission that the adult rate should be raised to £4.50 in October 2003 and, subject to confirmation in early 2004, to £4.85 from October 2004, with corresponding increases in the young persons' rate.
2. Salverda *et al.*, p. xi.
3. Likewise, Hamermesh (2001) suggests that 'a potentially useful view is that job satisfaction is the resultant of the worker's weighing in his/her mind of all the job's aspects. It can be viewed as a single metric that allows the worker to compare the current job to other labour market opportunities' (p. 2).
4. In 1998 there was a change in the job satisfaction question and the questions on promotion prospects, job security, relations with boss and ability to use initiative were dropped.
5. For a similar approach see Clark (1998). The fact that job satisfaction measures can explain various forms of worker behaviour is also reassuring. Thus, Akerlof *et al.* (1988), Freeman (1978), Hamermesh (1977) and Clark (2001) find that job satisfaction is an important predictor of quit behaviour, while Clegg (1983) and Mangione and Quinn (1975) find a negative correlation between job satisfaction, and both absenteeism and worker productivity.
6. Thus, Major and Forcey (1985) found that individuals prefer to make comparisons within the same sex and job rather than across these dimensions. Brown (2001) found in contrast, that external market comparisons dominated over internal organisational comparisons.
7. We make no attempt to estimate whether wages are endogenous. Thus, wages and job satisfaction could be simultaneously determined if wages reflect a compensating differential for say degree of risk in a job which in turn lowers job satisfaction. Likewise if more satisfied workers increase their degree of effort, this in turn may raise their wages. However, finding appropriate exclusion restrictions in such a simultaneous system can be problematical. Lydon and Chevalier (2002) used characteristics of a respondent's partner or spouse as instruments in their sample of graduates, which produced significantly higher own wage effects in their job satisfaction equation in line with a compensating differentials story. However, their approach forces them to limit the analysis to married individuals or those with partners.
8. Fixed effects regressions were also run with the sample split into high satisfaction (5, 6, 7) and low satisfaction (1, 2, 3, 4). These produced results which were consistent with those obtained from the random effects ordered probits.
9. When regressions were run including overtime earnings the negative coefficient on absolute pay became significant in the overall job satisfaction equations for low-paid women. Thus, it appears that overtime working reduces the overall job satisfaction of women more than overtime premium payments increase it.
10. Of those moving from higher pay to low-paid jobs 40 per cent claim a reduction in job satisfaction and 38 per cent an increase. For women more claim an increase than a reduction in job satisfaction. This is consistent with pay being more critical to men than to women.
11. We also ran regressions for movements up or down the overall pay distribution with individuals in each wave assigned to 20 equal groups in the pay distribution. Then the individual's position in the distribution was compared

in consecutive waves according to whether it remained the same, moved up or moved down. This produced similar results and is not reported here.

12. Clark concludes (p. 239) 'it is not that economists have been barking up the wrong tree with the emphasis of wages and hours, but rather they have not been barking up enough of them'.

References

Akerlof, G.A., Rose, A.K. and Yellen, J.L. (1988) 'Job Switching and Job Satisfaction in the U.S. Labour Market', *Brookings Papers on Economic Activity*, 2, pp. 495–582.

Borjas, G.J. (1979) 'Job Satisfaction, Wages and Unions', *Journal of Human Resources*, 14, pp. 21–40.

Brown, M. (2001) 'Unequal Pay, Unequal Responses? Pay Referants and their Implications for Pay Level Satisfaction', *Journal Management Studies*, 38(6), September, pp. 879–96.

Clark, A.E. (1998) 'What Makes a Good Job? Evidence from OECD Countries', Universite d'Orleans, mimeo.

Clark, A.E. (2001) 'What Really Matters in a Job? Hedonic Measurement Using Quit Data', *Labour Economics*, 8(2) May, pp. 223–42.

Clark, A.E. and Oswald, A.J. (1996) 'Satisfaction and Comparison Income', *Journal of Public Economics*, 69, pp. 57–81.

Clegg, C.W. (1983) 'Psychology of Employee Lateness, Absence and Turnover: Methodology, a Critique and an Empirical Study', *Journal of Applied Psychology*, 68, pp. 88–101.

European Union (2001) *Employment in Europe 2001; Recent Trends and Prospects*, Employment and Social Affairs, Luxembourg.

European Union (2002) *Employment in Europe 2002; Recent Trends and Prospects*, Employment and Social Affairs, Luxembourg.

Francesconi, M. (2001) 'Determinants and Consequences of Promotions in Britain', *Oxford Bulletin of Economics and Statistics*, 63, pp. 279–310.

Freeman, R.B. (1978) 'Job Satisfaction as an Economic Variable', *American Economic Review*, 68, pp. 135–41.

Hamermesh, D.S. (1977) 'Economic Aspects of Job Satisfaction', in Ashenfelter, O.E. and Oates, W.E. (eds), *Essays in Labour Market Analysis*, New York: John Wiley, pp. 53–72.

Hamermesh, D.S. (2001) 'The Changing Distribution of Job Satisfaction', *Journal of Human Resources*, 36(1), Winter, pp. 1–30.

Lydon, R. and Chevalier, A. (2002) 'Estimates of the Effect of Wages on Job Satisfaction', *Centre for Economic Performance*, LSE, mimeo, May.

Mangione, J.W. and Quinn, R.P. (1975) 'Job Satisfaction, Counter-Productive Behaviour and Drug Use at Work', *Journal of Applied Psychology*, 60, pp. 114–16.

Major, B. and Forcey, B. (1985) 'Social Comparisons and Pay Evaluations; Preferences for Same Sex and Same Job Wage Comparison', *Journal of Experimental Social Psychology*, 21, pp. 393–405.

Rees, A. (1993) 'The Role of Fairness in Wage Determination', *Journal of Labor Economics*, 11, pp. 243–52.

Salverda, W. *et al.* (2001) *The European-American Employment Gap, Wage, Inequality, Earnings Mobility and Skill; A Study for France, Germany, the Netherlands, the UK and the U.S.*, Final Report, Employment and Social Affairs, European Commission, June.

Part II

Low Pay and Unemployment

5

An Econometric Analysis of Unemployment Traps for Belgium

Anna Cristina D'Addio, Isabelle De Greef and Michael Rosholm

1 Introduction

The combination of unemployment benefits, high taxes on labour income, social contributions and conditional transfers such as additional child benefits, may reduce the willingness of unemployed workers – especially the low skilled – to find and/or to accept a job (OECD, 1996, 1999). Low returns associated with being employed rather than unemployed may thus affect the decision of moving into employment.

The situation in which households or individuals have no – financial and/or non-financial – incentives to leave unemployment for employment is termed an 'unemployment trap'. The computation of the replacement rates, that is, the ratios between the household/individual disposable income when employed and the household/individual disposable income when unemployed, is crucial to assess whether unemployment traps exist and affect the transition into employment. This task is particularly important for policy concerns, raising the participation rate in the labour market being one of the priorities of most European countries.

Two main approaches have been adopted in the study of financial unemployment traps.[1] The first is based on representative households/individuals and computes replacement rates using specific assumptions (see e.g. OECD, 1996, 1997). The second approach exploits real data and econometric techniques in doing so (see e.g. Gregg *et al.*, 1999; Holm *et al.*, 1999; Kyyrä, 1999; Gurgand and Margolis, 2001; Pedersen and Smith, 2001; OECD, 2002). For Belgium, in which we are interested, most of the evidence on unemployment traps has been provided within the former approach (Defeyt, 1998; De Greef, 2000; De Lathouwer, 2000; De Lathouwer and Bogaerts, 2001; Valenduc, 2001). Despite the usefulness of this literature, which provides a sort of benchmark identifying those households/individuals that are more likely to be trapped, it is based on some ad hoc assumptions not necessarily met in the real world. Mainly for this reason, we have adopted in our study the approach based on real data.

In this article we investigate whether unemployment traps exist in the transition into employment in Belgium. In doing this, we use the data extracted from the waves 3 to 7 (covering the years 1993–97) of the Panel Study of Belgian Households (PSBH) about individuals who have experienced at least one spell of unemployment during the survey period.

The available data are therefore longitudinal. Most of the empirical analyses on unemployment traps based on this kind of data, assume that the sample selection process is constant over time, and the argument crucial to this assumption is that fixed effect type estimators eliminate sample selection bias since they difference out both the unobserved individual-specific effect and the sample selection effect (see e.g. Jensen *et al.*, 2002). There is no reason to believe that the sample selection process is time-invariant: Unobservable time-varying variables may occur in both the selection equation and the equation of interest, and they may exhibit a complex correlation structure. We have therefore used panel data estimation techniques and explicitly accounted for the sample selection problem in that framework.

In doing so, we first specify and estimate by maximum likelihood techniques a parametric panel data random effects model composed by a wage equation and a selection equation. If the decision to work is affected by expected earnings, it is likely that individuals who are currently working have higher wages than those that would be earned by unemployed individuals. In that sense, the correction for potential selection bias (Heckman, 1979) accounts for the non-randomness of the selection process into employment: Wages are observed only for those who are employed, that is, those who have received job offers and for whom the offered wage exceeds the reservation wage. In other words, the sample selection correction is meant to avoid a potential bias caused by unobserved heterogeneity that affects both the probability of being employed and the wage level.

Based on the estimations of the wage equations corrected for sample selectivity, we compute expected wages and use them to calculate replacement rates for all individuals in the sample (including those that have not moved out of unemployment during the survey period). In this way we obtain an observed and an estimated income ratio as in Kyyrä (1999). While the observed income ratio is based on the observed wage earned by workers who move into work, the estimated one is based on the expected wage for workers who have not moved into employment. The introduction of time-varying regressors in the selection equation as well as in the wage equation allows us to compute expected wages yearly and to consider their trend during the observation period. In a previous version of the paper, the lack of those data prevented us of doing so (see D'Addio *et al.*, 2002). Finally, in order to assess the effect of the replacement rates on the probability of moving into employment we estimate a logit model with fixed effects separately for men and women.

The chapter is organized as follows. Section 2 briefly describes the Belgian tax system as well as its unemployment insurance scheme. In Section 3 we survey some of the previous evidence on unemployment traps. In Section 4 we present the econometric model applied. Section 5 describes the dataset. In Section 6 we report and discuss the estimation results. Some conclusions are drawn in Section 7.

2 Unemployment insurance and tax schemes in Belgium during the 1990s

Different studies have shown how important and persistent the problem of unemployment is in Belgium. Besides arguments about the structural nature of the problem, the features of the existing tax scheme are likely to make people less willing to accept jobs. In addition to this, the sudden removal of conditional transfers (such as additional child benefits) occurring when moving into employment reduces work incentives, especially so for temporary jobs. Since January 2000 some measures have been taken up in order to make work more attractive. According to some authors (see De Lathouwer, 2002) many of them have had a positive impact on the willing of individuals to enter the labour market.

The data used in this study cover the years 1993–97, therefore we describe the unemployment insurance scheme as well as the tax system prevailing over that period. All the amounts reported in this section are about the year 1997.

Unemployment insurance scheme

The Belgian unemployment insurance scheme is characterized by a generous level of benefits (see De Lathouwer, 2000; De Lathouwer and Bogaerts, 2001) especially for persons with low incomes, and by an indefinite entitlement period. The payment of unemployment benefits may however be suspended for unemployed people who are 'cohabitants', that is, live with a working partner or their parents, depending on various conditions (see De Greef, 2000). In addition, unemployed people may be sanctioned for a wide range of reasons for example, administrative reasons, unavailability to take on jobs and the like (see OECD, 1997; Grubb and Martin, 2001).

In order to be eligible for unemployment benefits, a worker must have been employed for a relatively long period. The length of the required employment period depends on the age of the worker. For instance, individuals aged less than 36 must have been employed for 312 days during the latest 18 months on the first day of unemployment. To receive unemployment benefits, unemployment should be involuntary, the worker should be available for and actively seeking employment. The entitlement to unemployment benefits depends on schooling curricula and on the receipt of unemployment benefits in the past. The level of unemployment benefits depends on four characteristics: the composition of the household, the length of unemployment, the age, and the previous wage of the individuals.[2]

Concerning household composition, three categories are identified; heads of household, singles, and cohabitants. Heads of household are entitled to a high level of benefits, singles are qualified to a medium level of benefits, and cohabitants receive the lowest level of unemployment benefits. In addition, the amount of the unemployment benefits is constant over time for the heads of the household (60 per cent of the previous wage) while it decreases for singles (from 60 per cent the first year to 42 per cent the second year) and for cohabitants (from 55 per cent the first year to 35 per cent the first quarter of the second year and to a lump sum the second quarter of the second year). However, if a cohabitant has been employed for more than 20 years, he/she benefits indefinitely of the second period compensation (35 per cent of the previous wage). Unemployment benefits depend on previous earnings however they are upwards and downwards bounded; for example for heads of household they are set between a maximum of 864.9 euros and a minimum of 759.3 euros. Finally, the level of benefits depends on the age. Unemployed individuals aged more than 50 receive an additional amount. This supplement, conditional on having worked more than 20 years, varies with the household type and the age of the individual.

The tax system

The tax system consists of social security contributions and a progressive income tax. Social security contributions paid by the employees

Table 5.1 Belgian tax schedule: year 1997

Annual earnings in euros	**Marginal income tax rate in per cent**
0–6 271.7	25.0
6 271.7–8 304.4	30.0
8 304.4–11 849.3	40.0
11 849.3–27 268.3	45.0
27 268.3–40 902.4	50.0
40 902.4–59 990.2	52.5
⩾59 990.2	55.0

correspond to 13.07 per cent of gross earnings. Spouses are taxed separately. However, if they have no labour income or if the labour income of one of the spouses is less than 30 per cent of the household's labour earnings, 30 per cent of the net household labour income (minus the labour income of the spouse) is attributed to the partner. The amount that may be fictionally transferred to the spouse with low or no labour income is limited to a maximum of 7362.4 euros.

Several tax allowances exist in the Belgian tax scheme. Each individual is granted a personal income exemption that depends on household's composition. The other main tax allowances are related to the number of children, childcare costs, work related expenses. The amount of the tax exemption is higher for replacement incomes (e.g. pensions, unemployment benefits) than for labour earnings. Table 5.1 details the tax schedule prevailing in Belgium in 1997. An additional local income tax is levied on taxable income at an average rate of 7 per cent.

3 Survey of the literature

Most of the evidence on unemployment traps has been provided within the approach using representative households/individuals (see e.g. OECD, 1997). Making assumptions on the level of (potential) wages, this approach computes the change in the household/individual's disposable income associated with the transition from unemployment into employment, with the aim of identifying family/individual types with high probabilities of being financially trapped. This way of proceeding is relevant and rich on details. However it is based on specific, and somewhat arbitrary, assumptions concerning for example, the hourly wage rate and the previous length of unemployment. In addition, the unemployed are assumed to have a fully rational behaviour, although this does not always correspond to the reality (e.g. owing to a lack of knowledge of the rules of the tax and benefits systems) and their unobserved heterogeneity is not accounted for. Furthermore, commuting costs, additional intervention in health care and social housing that are likely to increase the occurrence of financial traps are frequently ignored in this literature. For Belgium, the main results can be summarized as follows: Single-parent families and some households with only one source of income are more exposed to unemployment traps than other types of households (Defeyt, 1998; De Greef, 2000; De Lathouwer, 2000; De Lathouwer and Bogaerts, 2001; Valenduc, 2001).

Fewer studies have adopted the approach based on real data and econometric techniques, mainly owing to the lack of appropriate data on earnings as well as to some methodological problems. Most of those studies have focused on the earning losses associated with the experience of unemployment (e.g. Arulampalam, 2000).[3] Some of them have analysed the impact of unemployment schemes on the decision of moving into work (e.g. Gurgand and Margolis, 2001). Only very few authors have explicitly investigated how the transition into employment is affected by potential unemployment traps (e.g. Kyyrä, 1999; Pedersen and Smith, 2001).

A large part of the literature has conventionally assumed that the wages of workers who have experienced an unemployment spell are equal to those earned by employed individuals with the same observable characteristics (see Layard *et al.*, 1991). In this strand of the literature, however, expected wages of individuals who are currently out of work are either estimated or derived from the surveys' questionnaire and are not 'arbitrarily' assumed. Some studies have used the wage earned in the last job prior to unemployment. Others have exploited the unemployed workers' own expectations about the wages they would get in a future job (Pedersen and Smith, 2001), or the average wage obtained by people who are employed. Some are based on the expected wage adjusted for selectivity, on the wage obtained by workers after an unemployment experience (post-unemployment wages), and finally, some are based on post-unemployment wages corrected for sample selection bias in a cross sectional framework (Holm *et al.*, 1999; Kyyrä, 1999).

Three important results should be emphasized on the grounds of the studies mentioned above. First, some transitions from unemployment to employment are associated with a decrease or only a modest increase of the disposable income. Second, unemployed workers get re-employed at lower wages than the ones they enjoyed in their previous job.

Third, the wage losses suffered by workers who have experienced a period of unemployment are persistent; the average wage rate tends to remain below the expected average wage rate without job loss for several years after the unemployment spell.

There are several ways to explain why it may be meaningful in some cases to accept a job associated with negative short-term financial returns. Unemployed people may give a lot of importance to the inter-temporal perspectives; they are likely to expect higher wages in the future (promising career prospects) or to anticipate falling unemployment benefits simultaneously with a depressing effect of long unemployment periods on the post-unemployment wage. Some individuals may even be willing to accept a job that is associated with long-term income losses if they enjoy working or if they simply feel 'ashamed' about being unemployed.

Theory also suggests several reasons for why a period of unemployment may be followed by wage losses. The first one concerns job tenure; jobs associated with post-unemployment wages are by definition short-tenure at the time at which one observes them (no tenure effect). Lower post-unemployment wages may also result from a deterioration of skills or a loss of firm-specific (or sector-specific) human capital that is not transferable to a new job. A reduction in the post-unemployment wages may also be caused by a lower quality of the job match between the worker and the firm. Further, a decrease in the reservation wage over time can lead to acceptance of a job with a lower wage. The decline of the reservation wage can be justified for instance by a (expected) decrease in the level of unemployment benefits (e.g. see Van den Berg, 1990). Finally employers may rank workers on the grounds or their employment/unemployment experience.

4 Methodology

Sample selection correction for panel data

The selection process into employment may be non-random. Sample selectivity may bias the parameters of interest if not adequately controlled for. From a methodological point of view, the longitudinal structure of data makes it more difficult to control it.

Two main approaches have been followed in the development of panel data sample selection model estimators: Two-step estimators based mainly on Heckman (1979) and maximum likelihood estimators.[4] We have chosen the latter. Further, although one can choose between random and a fixed approach in the modelling, we have preferred a random effects specification. With fixed effects, only time-varying variables are useful in the estimation process. Time-invariant covariates cannot therefore be used to gather insights into the factors determining the dependent variable of interest.

The model we consider can be formulated as follows:

$$y_{it}^* = x_{it}'\beta + \alpha_i + \varepsilon_{it}, \tag{1}$$

$$d_{it}^* = z_{it}'\gamma + \eta_i + \upsilon_{it}, \tag{2}$$

$$d_{it} = \begin{cases} 1 & \text{if } d_{it}^* > 0, \\ 0 & \text{otherwise,} \end{cases} \tag{3}$$

$$y_{it} = y_{it}^* \cdot d_{it}, \tag{4}$$

where i ($i = 1, \ldots, N$) denotes the individual and t ($t = 1, \ldots, T$) denotes the time period; d_{it} is an indicator for having an observed wage, y_{it} denotes the log of the observed wage, x_{it}' and z_{it}' are vectors of explanatory variables, possibly with common elements, and definitely with an exclusion restriction. The equation of interest is (1) and the selection process is described by (2). β and γ are the unknown parameter vectors to estimate. The α_i and η_i are unobservable time-invariant individual-specific components which are possibly correlated with each other. Finally, ε_{it} and υ_{it} are unobserved disturbances, possibly correlated with each other. The variable y_{it}^* is observed only if the indicator variable $d_{it} = 1$, that is, if the person i is employed in period t.

To estimate (1) and (2) simultaneously by maximum likelihood, one has to specify the joint distribution of the error components ε_{it} and υ_{it}. We assume that the idiosyncratic error terms follow a bivariate normal distribution

$$(\varepsilon_{it}, \nu_{it}) \sim N(0, 0, \Sigma), \quad \text{where } \sum = \begin{bmatrix} \sigma_\varepsilon^2 & \rho\sigma_\varepsilon \\ \rho\sigma_\varepsilon & 1 \end{bmatrix}. \tag{5}$$

Let $\theta = [\beta, \gamma, \sigma_\varepsilon, \rho, p, \alpha, \eta]$ denote the parameter vector. The likelihood of a single observation, conditional on the random effects is then

$$\begin{aligned} L_{it}(\theta) &= f(\varepsilon_{it}, \upsilon_{it} \,|\, \alpha_i, \eta_i, x_{it}, z_{it}) \\ &= [(1-\phi_{\nu|\varepsilon}(-z_{it}'\gamma - \eta_i \,|\, y_{it} - x_{it}'\beta - \alpha_i)) \cdot \phi_\varepsilon(y_{it} - x_{it}'\beta - \alpha_i)]^{c_{it} \cdot d_{it}} \\ &= [\Phi_\upsilon(z_{it}'\gamma + \eta_i)]^{(1-c_{it}) \cdot d_{it}} \cdot [\Phi_\upsilon(-z_{it}'\gamma - \eta_i)]^{(1-d_{it})} \end{aligned} \tag{6}$$

where the conditional distribution $\nu|\varepsilon \sim N\left[(\rho_\varepsilon/\sigma_\varepsilon), (1-\rho^2)\right]$; Φ and ϕ are the standard normal distribution and probability density function respectively for the variables referred by subscripts. The random effects are assumed to follow a bivariate discrete distribution with 2×2 points of support, and we assume independence between idiosyncratic errors and random effects. c_{it} is an indicator taking the value 1 if the wage is observed for an individual who finds employment (in some cases, it is not, see Section 5).

Let $\alpha = \{\alpha_1, \alpha_2\}$, $\eta = \{\eta_1, \eta_2\}$, $p = \{p_{11}, p_{12}, p_{21}, p_{22}\}$, where $p_{kj} = \Pr[\eta_k, \alpha_j]$. For a single individual, the likelihood contribution is then

$$
\begin{aligned}
L_i(\theta) &= \int_{-\infty}^{\infty}\int_{-\infty}^{\infty}\left[\prod_{t=1}^{T_i} f(\varepsilon_{it}, \upsilon_{it} \mid x_{it}, z_{it}, \alpha_i, \eta_i)\right] dG(\eta_i, \alpha_i) \qquad (7)\\
&= \sum_{j=1}^{2}\sum_{j=1}^{2} p_{kj}\prod_{t=1}^{T_i} f(\varepsilon_{it}, \upsilon_{it} \mid x_{it}, z_{it}, \alpha_i, \eta_i)
\end{aligned}
$$

where $G(\cdot)$ is the joint c.d.f. of the random effects.

Estimated income ratios

To compute the income ratios for each individual in the sample (i.e. also for the individuals who never find employment) we derived the expected (log) wages as in Husted *et al.* (2001a,b). Conditional on the entire path of participation indicators, the expected log wage for an individual is

$$
\begin{aligned}
&E[y_{it} \mid d_{i1}, \ldots, d_{iT_i}, x_{it}, z_{i1}, \ldots, z_{iT_i}] \qquad (8)\\
&\quad = x_{it}\beta + E[\alpha_i \mid d_{i1}, \ldots, d_{iT_i}, z_{i1}, \ldots, z_{iT_i}] + E[\varepsilon_{it} \mid d_{it} \cdot z_{it}],
\end{aligned}
$$

where T_i is the maximum number of time periods over which an individual is observed.

The expected values of the error components of the wage equation are

$$E[\alpha_i \mid d_{i1}, \ldots, d_{iT_i}, z_{i1}, \ldots, z_{iT_i}] = \sum_{j=1}^{2} \alpha_j q_{ji}^{\alpha}, \qquad (9)$$

$$E[\varepsilon_{it} \mid d_{it} = 1, z_{it}] = \rho\sigma_\varepsilon \sum_{k=1}^{2} q_{kit}^{\eta} \frac{\phi(z_{it}\gamma + \eta_k)}{\Phi(z_{it}\gamma + \eta_k)}, \qquad (10)$$

$$E[\varepsilon_{it} \mid d_{it} = 0, z_{it}] = -\rho\sigma_\varepsilon \sum_{k=1}^{2} q_{kit}^{\eta} \frac{\phi(z_{it}\gamma + \eta_k)}{1 - \Phi(z_{it}\gamma + \eta_k)}, \qquad (11)$$

The term q^{α}_{ji} denotes the parameters of the individual specific probabilities of α_i. It is expressed as

$$q^{\alpha}_{ji} = \frac{\sum_{k=1}^{2} p_{kj} \prod_{t=1}^{T_i} [\Phi_v(z'_{it}\gamma + \eta_i)]^{(1-c_{it})\cdot d_{it}} \cdot [\Phi_v(-z'_{it}\gamma - \eta_i)]^{(1-d_{it})}}{\sum_{l=1}^{2} \left[(p_{l1} + p_{l2}) \prod_{t=1}^{T_i} [\Phi_v(z'_{it}\gamma + \eta_i)]^{(1-c_{it})\cdot d_{it}} \cdot [\Phi_v(-z'_{it}\gamma - \eta_i)]^{(1-d_{it})} \right]}. \tag{12}$$

The term q^{η}_{kit} denotes the parameters of the individual and time specific probability of η_i and it writes as

$$q^{\eta}_{kit} = \frac{\sum_{j=1}^{2} p_{kj}\Phi_v(z_{it}\gamma + \eta_k)}{\sum_{j=1}^{2} [(p_{1j}\Phi_v(z_{it}\gamma + \eta_1)) + p_{2j}\Phi_v(z_{it}\gamma + \eta_2)]}. \tag{13}$$

A fixed effects logit model

In order to assess the effect of replacement rates on the probability of moving into employment we have estimated, for men and women separately, a logit model with fixed effects (FE). Under certain assumptions on the distribution of the transitory errors, one can sometimes avoid making stochastic restrictions on the individual effects by treating them as fixed effects and conditioning them out. In such cases, the individual effects are allowed to have an arbitrary correlation with the observed covariates, k'_{it}. This doesn't happen in random effects models, where one has to specify the distribution of the unobserved individual effects, conditional on the observed covariates. Our latent model is written as

$$d^*_{it} = k'_{it}\,\omega + \tau_i + \zeta_{it},$$
$$d_{it} = \begin{cases} 1 & \text{if } d^*_{it} > 0, \\ 0 & \text{otherwise,} \end{cases}$$

where τ_i is the time-invariant individual specific effect, k'_{it} is a vector of explanatory variables, ω is the vector of parameters to be estimated and ζ_{it} is the unobserved disturbance. Rather than observing d^*_{it}, we observe d_{it} that is equal to one whether the individual is observed at time t to move into employment, and to 0 otherwise.

For ζ_{it} independently and logistic distributed we have

$$\Pr(d_{it} = 1 \mid k_{it}, \tau_i) = \frac{\exp(\tau_i + k'_{it}\omega)}{1 + \exp(\tau_i + k'_{it}\omega)}. \tag{14}$$

Chamberlain (1980, 1984) shows that such a model can be estimated by conditional maximum likelihood. In particular, the probability of a particular sequence $(d_{i1}, \ldots, d_{iT})$ conditional on $s_i = \sum_{t=1}^{T} d_{it}$,

$$\Pr(d_{i1}, \ldots, d_{iT} \mid k_{i1}, \ldots, k_{iT}, \tau_i, s_i) = \frac{\prod_{t=1}^{T} \exp(k_{it}' \omega d_{it})}{\sum_{d \in D_i} \prod_{t=1}^{T} \exp(k_{it}' \omega d_t)} \tag{15}$$

where D_i, the set of all possible combinations of s_i ones and $T - s_i$ zeros, is independent of τ_i.

5 Data

The sample

The empirical analysis is based on PSBH. This survey was carried out for the first time in the spring of 1992 (wave 1). Since the questions about incomes and individuals' employment status have been modified from 1994 onwards, we considered the waves 3 to 7 (spring 1994 to spring 1998) that contain information about 9398 individuals aged at least 16.

The information we use is retrospective, therefore the analysis covers the years 1993 to 1997. At each survey date, individuals report their labour market status at that time and for each of the preceding 12 months. They also declare (if they work) their annual income for the previous year net of taxes and social contributions.

The sample used in this study consists of individuals who have experienced at least one unemployment spell. They are followed from that moment until the end of the observation period. The sample thus consists of both unemployed individuals having moved towards employment and unemployed persons who remain unemployed throughout the observed period. Individuals who moved from unemployment into self-employment have been excluded from the analysis. The reason for discarding those individuals resides mainly in the fact that for them it is difficult to distinguish the wage from other income sources.

1338 persons have been unemployed at least once during the observation period experiencing 1948 unemployment spells. We focus only on those spells involving unemployment benefits payment (1661). Half of the unemployment spells end with a transition into employment (paid work and self-employment); 35 per cent of the unemployment spells are right-censored. The 12 per cent of the unemployment spells that end with a transition into non-participation (retirement, housekeepers and students) and the 3 per cent ending in a so-called 'other activity' have been discarded. After that, our sample consists of 1341 spells of unemployment, experienced by 959 individuals. We will use separate samples for men (601 spells) and women (740 spells). The sample is unbalanced and individuals are observed from one to five times.

The dependent variables

... in the selection and wage equation

The dependent variables are an employment indicator and the individuals' monthly net (log)-wage.

The employment indicator takes a value of 1 if the individual moves from compensated unemployment into paid work in a given year, and it is 0 if the individual remains unemployed in that year. To be considered as employed in the PSBH, people have to work at least 15 hours per week. To determine this status, we have used the hours actually worked since labour income covers also extra-hours worked.

The dependent variable of the wage equation is the (log) monthly net wage including tips, commissions, bonus and holiday earnings that we deflated by the consumer price index (base 1997). Its introduction is justified here in the context of labour supply theory (see D'Addio and De Greef, 2001).

At each survey date the interviewed individuals report wages net of taxes and social contributions. However, for 25 per cent of the unemployment spells that ended with a transition into employment, the information concerning the wages is missing. This problem is accounted for in the estimation procedure (see Section 4). For each of the five waves, we use the number of months in which the individual is unemployed or employed to compute the monthly in-work and out-of-work income. Monthly wages are then computed by dividing annual salaries by the real number of months worked.[5] This way of proceeding does not allow us to separate the wages associated with different jobs when the worker has been employed in more than one job during a year.

... in the FE logit model

In the fixed effect logit model the dependent variable is equal to 1 if the individual moves from compensated unemployment into paid work in a given year, and it is 0 if the individual remains unemployed in that year.

The explanatory variables

Before going further, we should say a word about exclusion restrictions (see Rendtel and Pötter, 2001). For the order condition to hold we know that we should have at least one variable excluded from the wage equation. However, this is not sufficient for identification. To this purpose, we also need the rank condition to hold. This means that one of the excluded variables should be significant in the selection equation. Testing the rank condition is a test of the coefficients of the excluded variables in the reduced form regressions. In our case, they are health status for men and the degree of social activity for women.

... in the wage and selection equation

Broadly speaking, only human capital and work-related variables (i.e. experience and its square, educational attainments, a part-time indicator, a supervision-tasks indicator, an indicator of previous professional experience) have been used in the wage equation. In order to capture the effects of financial (and to some extent non-financial) incentives, many other variables appear in the selection equation. The unemployment rate over the relevant period has been added in both equation to broadly account for business cycle conditions Tables 5.2 and 5.3 present descriptive statistics for available samples of men and women.

We start with the description of the variables used in the wage equation.

Experience refers to 'potential' work experience and it is computed as the difference between the age at the survey date and the age when the individual left school. We also introduced its quadratic form to capture concavity in the experience–wage profiles as postulated by human capital theory. Another variable indicates whether the individual had any actual work experience in the past. Further, to capture the level of responsibility associated with previous job-experience we have introduced an indicator taking on the value 1 if the individual has never supervised other workers in the past. To verify whether the experience of previous long unemployment spells has a 'scarring' effect on subsequent earnings, we have included an indicator taking the value of 1 if the individual has been unemployed for more than 12 months at the start of the year t.

We have used an indicator for part-time employment only for women, since this is a striking feature in female labour market participation.

Education is introduced in our specification through a set of indicators for the highest level of formal education attained. Five educational levels are considered; primary school or without education

Table 5.2 Descriptive statistics: men

Variable	Obs.	Mean	Std. dev.	Min.	Max.
Age	601	34.6	11.17	18	64
Social activity	601	46.92	49.95	0	1
House allowances	601	13.81	34.53	0	1
Long-term unemployment	601	48.92	50.03	0	1
Having loans	601	35.27	47.82	0	1
Financial difficulties	601	37.44	48.44	0	1
Mental distress	601	12.15	32.69	0	1
Kids less than 3 years	601	9.98	30	0	1
Bad health	601	16.31	36.97	0	1
Financial satisfaction	601	34.28	47.5	0	1
Not head of the household	601	59.4	49.15	0	1
Householder	601	59.23	49.18	0	1
Number of children	601	0.58	1	0	6
Belgian nationality	601	87.02	33.63	0	1
Primary school or no education	601	15.81	36.51	0	1
Lower secondary school	601	29.62	45.69	0	1
Upper secondary school	601	32.11	46.73	0	1
High school	601	13.81	34.53	0	1
University	601	8.65	28.14	0	1
Married	601	43.43	49.61	0	1
Lone parenthood	601	28.12	45	0	1
Additional child benefits	601	3.66	18.79	0	1
Living in Flanders	601	33.11	47.1	0	1
Unemployment rate	601	9.3	3.99	8.6	9.8
Potential experience	601	16.03	12.48	0	50
No responsibility	601	87.85	32.69	0	1
Part-time	601	3.33	17.95	0	1
Previous professional experience	601	92.35	26.61	0	1

(the reference), lower secondary school (3 years after primary school), upper secondary school (6 years after primary school), high school (2–4 years after the secondary school) and university. An indicator for marriage has also been used.

Other variables commonly thought to have an effect on wages such as type of job, sector of the firm, firm size and union coverage have not been introduced mainly owing to the lack of information about them in the available dataset.

Besides the individual's age, its square, educational attainments and the long-term unemployment indicator, the variables listed here below are used in the selection equation.

Table 5.3 Descriptive statistics: women

Variable	Obs.	Mean	Std. dev.	Min.	Max.
Age	740	33.06	9.73	18	59
Social activity	740	47.43	49.97	0	1
House allowances	740	14.19	34.92	0	1
Long-term unemployment	740	57.3	49.5	0	1
Having loans	740	31.89	46.64	0	1
Financial difficulties	740	32.16	46.74	0	1
Mental distress	740	22.57	41.83	0	1
Kids less than 3 years	740	17.84	38.31	0	1
Bad health	740	10.41	30.55	0	1
Financial satisfaction	740	28.11	44.98	0	1
Not head of the household	740	88.38	32.07	0	1
Householder	740	52.43	49.97	0	1
Number of children	740	0.81	0.98	0	5
Belgian nationality	740	92.84	25.8	0	1
Primary school or no education	740	10.9	31.24	0	1
Lower secondary school	740	24.46	43.01	0	1
Upper secondary school	740	38.11	48.6	0	1
High school	740	21.35	41.01	0	1
University	740	5.14	22.09	0	1
Married	740	47.3	49.96	0	1
Lone parenthood	740	18.92	39.19	0	1
Additional child benefits	740	10.54	30.73	0	1
Living in Flanders	740	40.81	49.18	0	1
Unemployment rate	740	9.3	3.76	8.6	9.8
Potential experience	740	14.43	11.01	0	47
No responsibility	740	94.73	22.36	0	1
Part-time	740	12.3	32.86	0	1
Previous professional experience	740	88.78	31.58	0	1

Two variables account for the health of the individuals. While the first states their degree of physical health, the second refers to individuals' mental distress (see De Greef, 2000).

A measure of social involvement (see Sweeney, 1998) is used to differentiate people socially active from the others. Individuals are ranked as socially active if they are member of an association (e.g. a sport club, a cultural or a humanitarian association) or if they have a very active network of friends.

To measure the effect of additional public financial support received when unemployed, a dummy variable has been introduced. It takes the value of one if the unemployed or his household is granted for example, social housing with low rent or food stamps.

Three variables related to pecuniary difficulties have been used. First, a dummy indicates if the individual, or another member of his/her household, is in debt (excluding mortgage loans). A second dummy takes the value 1 if the person has any financial difficulties in paying bills related to for example, rent, heating and so on. The third dummy is equal to 1 if the person is unsatisfied about his financial situation.

A home ownership dummy indicates whether the individual owns the accommodation he/she is living in.

Some variables are included to account for household composition. These are the number of children, the presence of children aged less than three, being married, being a single parent, not being head of the household and being entitled to additional child benefits. The variable for nationality indicates Belgian nationality.

Finally, we have introduced a dummy stating whether the individual lives in Flanders.

... in the FE logit model

The explanatory variables introduced in this model are time varying and they are the unemployment rate and the income ratio. However, for the latter we have introduced separately the numerator and denominator (expressed in logs) and not the ratio per se. This choice has been motivated by the potential non-linearity implicit in the ratio and by the willing of assessing separately the impact of in-work and out-of work incomes.

6 Estimation results

Wage and selection equation

The estimation of (1) and (2) simultaneously by maximum likelihood on the samples of men and women gives the results reported in Tables 5.4–5.6. In order to test their robustness, we also estimated an ordinary random effects probit model of the selection equation and a random effects generalized least squares (GLS) wage equation. These results show that most of the parameter estimates are very robust across the two different specifications. The main gain from the panel data sample selection model thus consists in the modelling of the correlation structures of the error components, which are used in the calculation of expected wages. Only the results from the estimation of the panel data model are reported in the following tables, the others are available upon request.

Table 5.4 Results of the estimation of (1) and (2) by ML: selection equation

Selection equation	**Men**		**Women**	
η_1	−5.4717*	(2.4543)	−9.115**	(2.6699)
η_1	−3.2338	(2.78)	−7.6093**	(2.6063)
Age	0.1377*	(0.0677)	0.1064	(0.0967)
Age^2	−0.024*	(0.0094)	−0.02311	(0.0145)
Social activity	−0.0561	(0.1859)	−0.4716**	(0.1887)
House allowances	0.2037	(0.2778)	−0.3561	(0.2687)
Long-term unemployment	−1.1541**	(0.1805)	−1.6859**	(0.2262)
Having loans	0.1181	(0.178)	−0.0589	(0.179)
Financial difficulties	0.0865	(0.1768)	−0.1163	(0.2106)
Mental distress	−0.0718	(0.2423)	0.1317	(0.1832)
Kids less than 3 years	−0.1125	(0.3354)	−0.1702	(0.2307)
Bad health	−0.6468**	(0.2445)	−0.1148	(0.3187)
Financial satisfaction	−0.3289	(0.1824)	−0.3202	(0.204)
Not head of the household	−1.1616**	(0.2171)	−0.9234**	(0.2948)
Householder	0.4969**	(0.1941)	0.1016	(0.1919)
Number of children	−0.3302**	(0.1266)	−0.0068	(0.1032)
Belgian nationality	−0.1271	(0.2635)	0.2514	(0.3276)
Lower secondary school	0.3353	(0.2889)	0.3403	(0.3226)
Upper secondary school	0.8211**	(0.3154)	0.5064	(0.3127)
High school	0.6183	(0.36)	0.6679	(0.363)
University	0.839*	(0.3828)	1.0928*	(0.4806)
Married	−0.2414	(0.2147)	0.4592*	(0.2151)
Lone parenthood	−0.0364	(0.2231)	0.2332	(0.2825)
Additional child benefits	0.3505	(0.4102)	−0.8155*	(0.3861)
Living in Flanders	0.3012	(0.1994)	−0.0295	(0.1838)
Unemployment rate	−0.5278*	(0.2111)	−0.9504**	(0.2293)

Notes: * Significant at 5%; ** significant at 1%.

We first notice some significant differences in the behaviour of males and females. Moreover sample selectivity seems to affect women more than men. These issues are discussed further below.

Considering the parameters of the selection equation, we notice that previous long-term unemployment status reduces dramatically the transition probability into employment for both men and women. Not being the household head is also associated with a much lower transition probability into employment for both samples, while being married leads to an higher transition probability for women. For them, eligibility to additional child benefits strongly reduces the transition probability. Male homeowners have higher transition probabilities, but their transition probability is reduced the more children they have. Bad health

Table 5.5 Estimation results of (1) and (2) by ML: wage equation

Wage equation	Men		Women	
α_1	9.8113**	(0.4362)	9.3132**	(0.4451)
α_2	10.426**	(0.4339)	9.8029**	(0.4333)
Experience (# years)	0.2615**	(0.065)	0.3582**	(0.0949)
Squared experience	−0.5385**	(0.2116)	−0.9584**	(0.3661)
Long-term unemployed	−0.1683**	(0.0507)	−0.1823**	(0.0577)
Part-time worker			−0.1525**	(0.0407)
Responsibility	0.023	(0.0551)	−0.0445	(0.0739)
Married	−0.1823	(0.2047)	−0.1684	(0.2015)
Previous professional experience	−0.0018	(0.0741)	−0.0168	(0.0747)
Lower secondary school	−0.1835*	(0.0844)	0.1215	(0.138)
Upper secondary school	−0.0687	(0.0897)	0.0935	(0.1359)
High school	0.1311	(0.0927)	0.3636**	(0.1404)
University	0.1192	(0.1002)	0.4651**	(0.1476)
Unemployment rate	0.0196	(0.041)	0.0451	(0.0435)

Note: * Significant at 5%; ** significant at 1%.

Table 5.6 Estimation results of (1) and (2) by ML: other parameters

	Men		Women	
ρ	0.0049	(0.3565)	0.0594**	(0.0083)
σ_ε^2	0.0608**	(0.0047)	0.615**	(0.1582)
P11	0.1646**	(0.0509)	0.1193	(0.102)
P12	0.7457**	(0.0886)	0.3161**	(0.1313)
P21	0.0174	(0.0267)	0.2243**	(0.075)
P22	0.0722	(0.079)	0.3403**	(0.1177)
Log likelihood	−328.057		−384.118	
Number of cases	601		740	

Note: ** Significant at 1%.

is also an important hindrance to finding employment for men, but apparently not for women. University education is associated with better employment prospects for both samples.

To summarize, many variables associated with financial incentives are highly important in the transition from unemployment to employment, particularly for women. However, some non-financial variables are also significant. It is the case for the degree of social activities for women. For men, it is the feeling about their own health status that matters heavily. Finally, we notice that the higher the unemployment rates, the lower is the probability of finding a job.

Let us turn now to the wage equation results. For both sub-samples, the experience of long-term unemployment in the past has a significant negative effect on earnings prospects, through lowering the post-unemployment (log)-wage. Similar results have been found by Gregory and Jukes (1997) and Nickell *et al.* (1999) who point at the fact that in the United Kingdom, long unemployment spells are associated with larger wage losses (see also for converse evidence Arulampalam, 2000).

For women, the best earnings prospects are associated with the highest educational attainments. The wages of men having lower secondary school degrees are negatively affected. Women working part-time are also likely to have lower wages.

Potential work experience improves considerably the earnings prospects of unemployed individuals. As suggested by human capital theory, the significance of the quadratic term of work experience confirms concave experience–wage profiles for both samples.

Let us consider now to the issue of sample selection. We notice from Table 5.6 that the correlation coefficient of the idiosyncratic error terms is positive although significantly different from 0 only for women. For them, the probabilities associated with the support points of the random effects are significant, while for men only one of them is. This suggests that the sample selection issue is particularly important for women. The significant correlation coefficient and its positive sign is consistent with good economic sense; those who find wage offers relatively high with respect to their characteristics are also more likely to be hired.

To summarize the overall results, we notice that previous long-term unemployment experience has a negative and significant impact for the two samples considered; it reduces individuals' probability of moving into employment and it lowers the earnings prospects. The hypothesis concerning the depreciation of human capital during unemployment is thus confirmed in our study; long-term unemployment is likely to have a scarring effect on subsequent earnings.

The results also suggest that more experienced workers earn higher wages and that workers holding higher qualification levels perform better in terms of earnings compared to those holding only a basic educational level. Marriage has the expected sign but it is not significant.

Let us turn now to the discussion of unemployment traps.

Estimated and observed income ratios

We have computed three different income ratios, in the spirit of Kyyrä (1999). The key tool in computing them is the wage. However, it is

Table 5.7 Mean observed and expected wages

Variable	Obs.	Mean	Std. dev.	Min.	Max.
Men					
Employed					
OW	288	1074.518	372.7809	314.0316	2202.965
EW_1	363	1020.369	163.7628	676.1897	1429.57
EW_2	363	1060.963	342.5847	314.0316	2202.965
Fictionally employed					
OW	0				
EW_1	238	946.9023	148.6394	659.8068	1432.033
Women					
Employed					
OW	278	842.0187	319.1293	307.3102	2195.356
EW_1	398	778.8627	139.0472	502.8323	1248.542
EW_2	398	818.687	280.1794	307.3102	2195.356
Fictionally employed					
OW	0				
EW_1	342	757.7837	126.8071	466.7278	1360.449

observed only for those who move into work. To be able to compute the income ratios also for the individuals who either have been unemployed over the entire survey period (i.e. those we term 'fictionally' employed) or have not reported the wage at the date of the interview, we have used the expected wage calculated on the basis of (8) in Section 4. For individuals moving into work we used both the observed (OW) and the expected (EW) wage.

In Table 5.7, we present the mean wages used in the computation of the income ratios. Three mean wages have been calculated for those who find jobs. These are (a) the mean observed wages; (b) the mean expected wage; and (c) the mean expected wage for those with a missing wage observation. For those who do not move into work, we could only compute the mean expected wage.

The mean predicted wage is close to the mean observed one. However, those who do not work have a considerably lower mean expected wage than the overall mean. This holds for both men and women, but the difference is larger for women. Furthermore, those who do not find jobs have expected wages that are on average (around) 9 per cent below the expected wages of those that do find employment. In addition, there are remarkable differences between men and women. In fact, the wages earned by women who manage to obtain employment are 22 per cent lower than those of men.

In computing the three different income ratios the numerator is the individuals' disposable income when employed (obtained by summing up the wages and other non-related work incomes, NWI) and the denominator is the individuals' disposable income when unemployed (derived by summing up the unemployment benefits, UB, and other NWI). For those observations having missing unemployment benefits we estimated their amount (251 spells). Since we don't know the wage earned in the last job prior to employment, this estimation is based only on three components out of four, that is, age, unemployment duration and household composition. In the ratios below we imputed the maximum and minimum unemployment benefit on the basis of the previous estimation. Ratios relating to the maximum amounts of benefits are indexed by letter (a), those computed by imputing the minimum amount of benefits are indexed by letter (b).

The ratios computed are:

(a) an observed income ratio (OIR) that can only be computed for the individuals that move into jobs during the observation period and who have an observed wage,

$$\text{OIR} = \frac{\text{NWI} + \text{OW}}{\text{NWI} + \text{UB}} \tag{16}$$

(b) an estimated income ratio (EIR_1) calculated imputing the expected wage to the entire sample

$$\text{EIR\_1} = \frac{\text{NWI} + \text{EW\_1}}{\text{NWI} + \text{UB}} \tag{17}$$

(c) a combination of both of them (EIR_ 2): for those who find employment and have an observed wage we used the observed wage and for the remainder of the sample we use the expected wage as follows

$$\begin{aligned}\text{EW\_2} = {} & \text{OW} \cdot 1_{\{\text{job found and wage observed}\}} \\ & + \text{EW\_1} \cdot 1_{\{\text{job not found or wage not observed}\}}.\end{aligned}$$

We write then EIR_2 as

$$\text{EIR\_2} = \frac{\text{NWI} + \text{EW\_2}}{\text{NWI} + \text{UB}}. \tag{18}$$

To account for family composition, we have distinguished five classes of households. They are: (1) singles; (2) couples, that is, those living with a partner and without children aged less than six; (3) couples with young children, that is, those living with a partner and having at least one child aged less than six; (4) single parents with old children, that is, individuals living alone with children aged more than six; (5) single parents with young children, that is, individuals living without a partner and having at least one child aged less than six.

The presence of unemployment traps is likely to be revealed by an income ratio smaller than 1. When the ratio equals 1, individuals could choose between working and not working on the basis of their preferences for leisure, the social network associated with employment and so on. When the ratio is above 1, individuals could have a financial incentive to move into work. Obviously according to the value that a person gives to the fact of having a job, different scenarios may appear.

The introduction of the variable 'unemployment rate' in both the wage and selection equations allows us to account for broad labour market conditions over the years covered by the observation period. Therefore, we have computed the c.d.f. of EIR and OIR for the different samples of men and women yearly (see Tables 5.8 and 5.9). For men, the issue of unemployment traps doesn't seem very important. It should however be noticed that over the observation period the share of men getting a gain when moving into work is relatively small.

For women, things are considerably different. For instance, over the years covered by the observation period, around 20 per cent of the employed women accept either a reduction or less than a 25 per cent increase in their disposable income.

We have summarized the results obtained when each of the previous ratios is smaller or equal to 1 in Tables 5.10–5.17. Tables 5.10–5.12 present results for OIR_a, EIR_1a, EIR_2a. Tables 5.13–5.15 present results for OIR_b, EIR_1b, EIR_2b. Finally Table 5.16 summarizes the results for the 'fictionally employed'. In the discussion, we only focus on the results obtained by imputing the maximum amounts of unemployment benefits, when those are missing. That is, we discuss Tables 5.10–5.12 and 5.16. As a note remark that, as we expected, a lower amount of benefits affects the statistics about the ratios since the number of those having an income ratio smaller than 1 decreases.

From Table 5.10 reporting the ratio lower or equal to 1 for those that move into employment (i.e. the OIR), we learn that 4.17 per cent of men and 12.95 per cent of the women who have accepted employment, experienced a reduction in their disposable income. There is not much variation in the ratio across household types, but we remark that 19 per cent of women having experienced long-term unemployment in the past accept a reduction in their disposable income when moving to employment compared to only 4 per cent of the men.

Table 5.8 C.d.f. of observed and estimated income ratios by year: men

EIR_1a			EIR_2a			OIR_a		
0.5	Frequency	Cumulative %	0.5	Frequency	Cumulative %	0.5	Frequency	Cumulative %
1993								
0.75	0	0.00	0.75	0	0.00	0.75	0	0.00
1	2	1.96	1	3	2.94	1	2	1.96
1.25	12	13.73	1.25	15	17.65	1.25	7	8.82
More	88	100.00	More	84	100.00	More	93	100.00
1994								
0.75	0	0.00	0.75	2	2.00	0.75	0	0.00
1	1	1.00	1	2	4.00	1	1	1.00
1.25	10	11.00	1.25	9	13.00	1.25	4	5.00
More	89	100.00	More	87	100.00	More	95	100.00
1995								
0.75	0	0.00	0.75	0	0.00	0.75	0	0.00
1	1	1.09	1	5	5.43	1	1	1.09
1.25	10	11.96	1.25	13	19.57	1.25	7	8.70
More	81	100.00	More	74	100.00	More	84	100.00
1996								
0.75	0	0.00	0.75	1	1.00	0.75	0	0.00
1	1	1.00	1	3	4.00	1	1	1.00
1.25	15	16.00	1.25	16	20.00	1.25	7	8.00
More	84	100.00	More	80	100.00	More	92	100.00
1997								
0.75	0	0.00	0.75	0	0.00	0.75	0	0.00
1	14	6.76	1	15	7.25	1	12	5.80
1.25	58	34.78	1.25	54	33.33	1.25	49	29.47
More	135	100.00	More	138	100.00	More	146	100.00

When considering Table 5.11 reporting EIR_1, we observe that for around 4 per cent of the men, and 13 per cent of the women, finding employment is (or will be) associated with a financial loss. This situation is even worse for single women with or without children aged less than six (around 23 per cent) and for those having experienced a long unemployment spell in the past (16 per cent). The numbers for the combined income ratio EIR_2 in Table 5.12 are very close to those in Table 5.11.

In Table 5.16 we summarize the results for those who have been unemployed throughout the survey period. We remark that 6.72 per cent of the men and 12.9 per cent of the women would have no immediate financial incentive to move into work since this transition would be associated with a considerable reduction in the disposable income. Men living in couples (8.33 per cent), single women with and without children aged less than six (23 and 24 per cent respectively) are those more

Table 5.9 C.d.f. of observed and estimated income ratios by year: women

EIR_1a			EIR_2a			OIR_a		
0.5	Frequency	Cumulative %	0.5	Frequency	Cumulative %	0.5	Frequency	Cumulative %
1993								
0.75	3	2.63	0.75	6	5.26	0.75	3	2.63
1	10	11.40	1	10	14.04	1	5	7.02
1.25	27	35.09	1.25	23	34.21	1.25	11	16.67
More	74	100.00	More	75	100.00	More	95	100.00
1994								
0.75	0	0.00	0.75	1	1.00	0.75	0	0.00
1	11	11.00	1	11	12.00	1	3	3.00
1.25	16	27.00	1.25	17	29.00	1.25	11	14.00
More	73	100.00	More	71	100.00	More	86	100.00
1995								
0.75	1	0.96	0.75	4	3.85	0.75	0	0.00
1	13	13.46	1	11	14.42	1	8	7.69
1.25	21	33.65	1.25	14	27.88	1.25	20	26.92
More	69	100.00	More	75	100.00	More	76	100.00
1996								
0.75	1	1.04	0.75	4	4.17	0.75	0	0.00
1	17	18.75	1	12	16.67	1	8	8.33
1.25	19	38.54	1.25	15	32.29	1.25	13	21.88
More	59	100.00	More	65	100.00	More	75	100.00
1997								
0.75	4	1.23	0.75	6	1.84	0.75	2	0.61
1	35	11.96	1	37	13.19	1	23	7.67
1.25	79	36.20	1.25	67	33.74	1.25	64	27.30
More	208	100.00	More	216	100.00	More	237	100.00

Table 5.10 Observed income ratios: OIR_a (workers with observed wage)

	Men (No. of cases)		Women (No. of cases)		Men (%)	Women (%)
	Total	OIR < 1	Total	OIR < 1		
Everybody	288	12	278	36	4.17	12.95
Singles	27	1	33	3	3.7	9.09
Couples	70	4	50	7	5.71	14
Couples with children	164	5	163	22	3.05	13.5
Single parents	3	0	2	0		
Single parents with children	24	2	38	4	8.33	10.53
Long-term unemployment	81	4	90	17	4.94	18.89

Table 5.11 Estimated income ratios: EIR_1a (whole sample)

	Men (No. of cases)		Women (No. of cases)		Men (%)	Women (%)
	Total	**EIR < 1**	**Total**	**EIR < 1**		
Everybody	601	19	740	95	3.16	12.84
Singles	69	3	59	14	4.35	23.73
Couples	164	11	151	17	6.71	11.26
Couples with children	329	4	390	33	1.22	8.46
Single parents	5	0	4	0	0	0
Single parents with children	34	1	136	31	2.94	22.79
Long-term unemployment	294	17	424	68	5.78	16.04

Table 5.12 Estimated income ratios: EIR_2a (whole sample)

	Men (No. of cases)		Women (No. of cases)		Men (%)	Women (%)
	Total	**EIR < 1**	**Total**	**EIR < 1**		
Everybody	601	31	740	102	5.16	13.78
Singles	69	4	59	11	5.8	18.64
Couples	164	15	151	20	9.15	13.25
Couples with children	329	10	390	40	3.04	10.26
Single parents	5	0	4	0	0	0
Single parents with children	34	2	136	31	5.88	22.79
Long-term unemployment	294	22	424	69	7.48	16.27

Table 5.13 Observed income ratios: OIR_b (workers with observed wage)

	Men (No. of cases)		Women (No. of cases)		Men (%)	Women (%)
	Total	**OIR < 1**	**Total**	**OIR < 1**		
Everybody	288	11	278	22	3.82	7.91
Singles	27	1	33	3	3.7	9.09
Couples	70	3	50	3	4.29	6
Couples with children	164	4	163	12	2.44	7.36
Single parents	3	0	2	0	0	0
Single parents with children	24	2	38	4	8.33	10.53
Long-term unemployment	81	3	90	13	3.7	14.44

Table 5.14 Estimated income ratios: EIR_1b (whole sample)

	Men (No. of cases)		Women (No. of cases)		Men (%)	Women (%)
	Total	EIR < 1	Total	EIR < 1		
Everybody	601	17	740	52	2.83	7.03
Singles	69	1	59	10	1.45	16.95
Couples	164	11	151	10	6.71	6.62
Couples with children	329	4	390	13	1.22	3.33
Single parents	5	0	4	0	0	0
Single parents with children	34	1	136	19	2.94	13.97
Long-term unemployment	294	16	424	42	5.44	9.91

Table 5.15 Estimated income ratios: EIR_2b (whole sample)

	Men (No. of cases)		Women (No. of cases)		Men (%)	Women (%)
	Total	EIR < 1	Total	EIR < 1		
Everybody	601	27	740	58	4.49	7.84
Singles	69	2	59	8	2.9	13.56
Couples	164	14	151	9	8.54	5.96
Couples with children	329	9	390	21	2.74	5.38
Single parents	5	0	4	0	0	0
Single parents with children	34	2	136	20	5.88	14.71
Long-term unemployment	294	19	424	44	6.46	10.38

Table 5.16 Estimated income ratios for the 'fictionally' employed (EIR for those who don't find jobs)

	Men (No. of cases)		Women (No. of cases)		Men (%)	Women (%)
	Total	EIR < 1	Total	EIR < 1		
Everybody	238	16	342	44	6.72	12.87
Singles	36	3	26	6	8.33	23.08
Couples	82	9	77	10	10.98	12.99
Couples with children	113	4	163	10	3.54	6.13
Single parents	2	0	2	0	0	0
Single parents with children	5	0	74	18	0	24.32
Long-term unemployment	186	15	294	41	8.06	13.95

exposed to the risk of these traps. Women having experienced long-term unemployment are very likely to have no incentives to accepts jobs since the wages they would earn will be lowered by the negative influence of their previous career. This confirms once again how important is the previous labour market history for this population.

The impact of in-work and out-of-work incomes on the probability of moving into employment

In order to assess whether unemployment traps affect the transition into employment, we have estimated for each of the sub-samples of men and women a fixed effects logit model. The results are reported in Tables 5.17 and 5.18.

It can be seen that while for women, the denominator of the ratio, that is, the amount of income while unemployed, has a strong impact on the probability of moving into employment, for men it is not the case. More particularly, the higher this income, the lower the probability of moving into employment. In other words, it seems that women are more likely than men to stay unemployed when the amount of the unemployment benefits increases.

Table 5.17 FE logit model: men

EIR_1a		**EIR_2a**	
Ln(Numerator of EIR_1a)	1.8375*	Ln(Numerator of EIR_2a)	0.8634
	[0.96]		[1.05]
Ln(Denominator of EIR_1a)	−0.5320	Ln(Denominator of EIR_2a)	−0.2577
	[0.70]		[0.43]
Unemployment rate	−0.4397	Unemployment rate	−0.4795
	[0.86]		[0.95]
EIR_1b		**EIR_2b**	
Ln(Numerator of EIR_1b)	2.9683*	Ln(Numerator of EIR_2b)	1.0656
	[1.49]		[1.25]
Ln(Denominator of EIR_1b)	−1.2445	Ln(Denominator of EIR_2b)	−0.6992
	[1.49]		[1.11]
Unemployment rate	−0.4025	Unemployment rate	−0.4516
	[0.79]		[0.90]

Notes: Absolute value of z statistics in brackets.
* Significant at 5%; ** significant at 1%.

Table 5.18 FE logit model: women

EIR_1a		**EIR_2a**	
Unemployment rate	−0.7334	Unemployment rate	−0.7334
	[1.36]		[1.40]
Ln(Numerator of EIR_1a)	0.0702	Ln(Numerator of EIR_2a)	0.3720
	[0.03]		[0.31]
Ln(Denominator of EIR_1a)	−2.0537*	Ln(Denominator of EIR_2a)	−1.9867*
	[2.41]		[2.41]
EIR_1b		**EIR_2b**	
Ln(Numerator of EIR_1b)	0.2563	Ln(Numerator of EIR_2b)	0.2430
	[0.12]		[0.21]
Ln(Denominator of EIR_1b)	−2.2064*	Ln(Denominator of EIR_2b)	−2.0888*
	[2.22]		[2.22]
Unemployment rate	−0.4661	Unemployment rate	−0.4587
	[0.89]		[0.88]

Notes: Absolute value of z statistics in brackets.
* Significant at 5%; ** significant at 1%.

The amount of 'in-work' income does not affect significantly the transition into job of both men and women. This suggests, in the light of the results discussed in the previous sections, that the individuals present in the available sample are likely to move into jobs not only for financial reasons.

7 Conclusion

In this chapter we investigated whether unemployment traps affect the transition into employment of Belgian individuals interviewed in the waves 3 to 7 of PSBH. To compute replacement rates, we have specified and estimated their post-unemployment wage and a selection equation (for finding employment) using a panel data sample selection model. For this task, we have adopted a parametric random effects specification that has been estimated simultaneously by maximum likelihood techniques on (unbalanced) samples of men and women. The estimates have been subsequently used to predict wages, for all individuals in our sample, and to compute income ratios that is the ratios between income as employed and as unemployed. Further, to assess whether the amount of incomes in and out-of work affects individuals' transition into employment, we have estimated a fixed effects logit model.

Compared to a previous version of the study (see D'Addio *et al.*, 2002), the introduction of a time-varying regressor, that is, the unemployment rate, allowed us to account for broad labour market conditions. In addition, we could describe the income ratio (observed and estimated) over the survey period, year by year. Moreover, we could gather further insights into the incentives of individuals to move into jobs mainly through the FE logit model. Significant differences exist in the participation behaviour of men and women. However, a common striking factor is the experience of long periods of unemployment in the past: long-term unemployed people have higher difficulties in (re)-integrating into the labour market and they obtain lower wages when they succeed in finding jobs. Still, more experienced workers have the best earning prospects on the labour market. It should be noticed that despite this, better-educated women who participate more and earn more compared to those holding a basic educational level, always receive lower wage than men, *ceteris paribus*.

The issue of sample selectivity seems also more important for women. This suggests that their transition back into work is highly selective. Moreover, a high proportion of their transitions into work are associated with important financial losses. This problem also affects men, but to a lower extent. Looking more particularly at the results reported in Table 5.16 for the fictionally unemployed, we notice that quite a high share of unemployed men and women are 'potentially trapped' financially in the unemployment state since their transition into work would be accompanied by a substantial reduction in their disposable income. This is particularly true for single women with and without young children.

Finally the results of the FE logit model suggest that women are particularly sensitive to the amount of the income they are granted when out of work. 'In-work incomes' do not seem to have a significant impact on the potential transition into jobs.

Our analysis opens the way to various comments. First, since long-term unemployment significantly (and negatively) affects both the earnings and the participation decisions, policies oriented in preventing people from becoming long-term unemployed could improve the incentives of these people to enter the labour market and eventually to lower unemployment itself.

Second, since experience matters significantly, it would probably be possible to increase the propensity of people to integrate into the labour market by making them more experienced, even through temporary jobs which interrupt unemployment and allows them to accumulate general human capital.

Third, since the transition into work is very frequently associated with a loss or a very small increase in the disposable income, it seems to us that the value given to the fact of having a job matters strongly. In other words, individuals don't look likes 'myopic', on the contrary they are likely to give a lot of importance to inter-temporal perspectives. 'Having a job today' is probably felt as more useful compared to the choice of being unemployed. This at least if unemployment benefits are not too high.... Indeed, especially for women the significant impact of unemployment benefits on their transition decisions suggests the importance of this component in their participation behaviour. In this sense, general abandonment of the right to eternal unemployment benefits, or a more dramatic time-variation in unemployment benefits could help in providing the right incentives to take employment, as could the abandonment of the right to 'unemployment-state-specific' additional support.

Finally, the fact that women are granted lower wages on the labour market and are those more at risk to be 'trapped' in the unemployment state, is very important for policy concerns. Increasing the employment of women through the design of incentives schemes like those linked to childcare, and family support in general, could contribute to alleviating their labour market problems and to lowering the overall unemployment rate.

Acknowledgements

The authors acknowledge financial support from the Marie Curie Fellowship Scheme of the European Commission and from the Danish Research Agency. We are grateful to Bruno van der Linden and to the participants at the AFSE 2002, the AEA Conference 2002, the Panel Data Conference 2002, the ESEM 2002 and the EALE 2002. The usual disclaimer applies.

Notes

1. Many studies have also focused on whether past unemployment experience has a scarring effect on subsequent earnings, a phenomenon which would contribute to the explanation of the existence of unemployment traps for individuals, some of whom have previously been successful in the labour market (see e.g. Ruhm, 1991; Jacobson *et al.*, 1993; Stevens, 1997; Nickell *et al.*, 1999; Arulampalam, 2000; OECD, 2002).
2. Since 1987, unemployed have had the opportunity to increase the amount of benefits by working for an *Agence locale pour l'emploi* (ALE or Local Agency for Employment) with a maximum of 45 hours per month and they receive

3.72 euros for each hour worked. With some exceptions, people working for these agencies are registered as unemployed.

3. See also Pedersen and Westergard-Nielsen, 1993; Laurent, 2001. For the literature on displaced workers, see for example, Fallick, 1996; Kletzer, 1998.
4. See for example, Wooldridge, 1995; Verbeek and Nijman, 1996; Kyriazidou, 1997; Vella and Verbeek, 1999; Jensen *et al.*, 2002.
5. The same methodology is applied for unemployment benefits.

References

Arulampalam, W. (2000) 'Is Unemployment Really Scarring? Effects of Unemployment Experience on Wages', *IZA Discussion Paper* n. 189.

Chamberlain, G. (1980) 'Analysis of Covariance with Qualitative Data', *Review of Economic Studies*, 47, pp. 225–38.

Chamberlain, G. (1984) 'Panel Data', in Griliches, Z. and Intriligator, M.D. (eds), *Handbook of Econometrics*, 2, Amsterdam: Elsevier Science.

D'Addio, A.C. and De Greef, I. (2001) 'Un modèle d'offre de travail pour l'étude des incitants financiers liés à la transition chômage-emploi pour la Belgique', Université catholique de Louvain, Belgique, miméo.

D'Addio, A.C., De Greef, I. and Rosholm, M. (2002) 'Assessing Unemployment Traps in Belgium with Panel Data Sample Selection Models', *Working Paper* n. 669, IZA, Bonn.

De Greef, I. (2000) 'Les pièges financiers en Belgique. Aperçu de la legislation du chômage, des spécificités institutionnelles et études de cas types', *Revue Belge de Sécurité Sociale*, June.

De Lathouwer, L. (2000) 'Les pièges à l'emploi en Belgique', Antwerpen: CSB-Berichten.

De Lathouwer, L. (2002) 'Le piège au chômage: quelles rèformes sociales pour augmenter l'offre de travail?', *Reflets et Perspectives*, 3, pp. 61–75.

De Lathouwer, L. and Bogaerts, K. (2001) 'Financiële incentieven en laagbetaald werk. De impact van hervormingen in de sociale zekerheid en de fiscaliteit op de werkloosheidsval in België', Antwerpen: CSB-Berichten.

Defeyt, P. (1998) 'Lutter contre les pièges financiers: Analyse et propositions', *Institut pour un Développement durable*, Belgique.

Fallick, B. (1996) 'A Review of the Recent Empirical Literature on Displaced Workers', *Industrial and Labour Relations Review*, October, pp. 142–55.

Gregg, P., Johnson, P. and Reed, H. (1999) 'Entering Work and the British Tax and Benefit System', *Institute for Fiscal Studies*, London.

Gregory, M. and Jukes, R. (1997) 'The Effects of Unemployment on Subsequent Earnings: A Study of British Men 1984–1994', *CEPR, Discussion Paper* n. 21.

Grubb, D. and Martin, J.P. (2001) 'What Works and for Whom: A Review of OECD Countries Experiences with Active Labour Market Policies', *Working Paper* n. 2001–14, IFAU, Paris: OECD.

Gurgand, M. and Margolis, D. (2001) 'RMI et revenus du travail: une évaluation des gains financiers à l'emploi', *Economie et Statistique*, 6/7, pp. 346–7.

Heckman, J. (1979) 'Sample Selection Bias as a Specification Error', *Econometrica*, 47, pp. 153–61.

Holm, P., Kyyrä, T. and Rantala, J. (1999) 'Household Economic Incentives, the Unemployment Trap and the Probability of Finding a Job', *International Tax and Public Finance*, 6(3), pp. 361–78.

Husted, L., Nielsen, H., Rosholm, M. and Smith, N. (2001a) 'Qualifications, Discrimination, or Assimilation? An Extended Framework for Analyzing Immigrant Wage Gaps', *IZA Discussion Paper* n. 365, Bonn.

Husted, L., Nielsen, H.S., Rosholm, M. and Smith, N. (2001b) 'Employment and Wage Assimilation of Male First-Generation Immigrants in Denmark', *International Journal of Manpower*, 22(1/2), pp. 39–68.

Jacobson, L.S., Lalonde, R.J. and Sullivan, D.G. (1993) 'Earnings Losses of Displaced Workers', *American Economic Review*, 83, pp. 685–709.

Jensen, P., Rosholm, M. and Verner, M. (2002) 'A Comparison of Different Estimators for Panel Data Sample Selection Models', *Working Paper* 2002–1, Denmark: University of Aarhus.

Kletzer, L. (1998) 'Job Displacement', *The Journal of Economic Perspectives*, 12, pp. 115–36.

Kyriazidou, E. (1997) 'Estimation of a Panel Data Sample Selection Model', *Econometrica*, 65, pp. 1335–64.

Kyyrä, T. (1999) 'Post-Unemployment Wages and Economic Incentives to Exit from Unemployment', *Valtion Taloudellinen Tuktimuskeskus Research Report* n. 56, Helsinki.

Laurent, S. (2001) 'Capital Humain, emploi et salaire en Belgique et ses régions', *Quatorzième Congrès des Economistes Belges de Langue Française*, Liège.

Layard, R., Nickell, S. and Jackman, R. (1991) *Unemployment, Macroeconomic Performance and the Labour Market*, Oxford University Press.

Nickell, S., Jones, T. and Quintini, G. (1999) 'A Picture of the Job Insecurity Facing British Men', in The Labour Market Consequence of Technical and Structural Change, *CEPR Discussion Paper* n. 42.

OECD (1996) *Employment Outlook*, Paris: OECD.

OECD (1997) *Employment Outlook*, Paris: OECD.

OECD (1999) *Benefit Systems and Work Incentives*, Paris: OECD.

OECD (2002) *Income Changes When Moving in and out of Work*, OECD, Social Policy Division.

Pedersen, P. and Smith, N. (2001) 'Unemployment Traps: Do Financial Dis-Incentives Matter?', *IZA Discussion Paper* n. 274, Bonn.

Pedersen, P. and Westergard-Nielsen, N. (1993) 'Unemployment: A Review of the Evidence from Panel data', *OECD Economic Studies*, 20, pp. 65–95.

Rendtel, U. and Pötter, U. (2001) 'The Behaviour of OLS, the Heckman 2-Step Procedure and ML Estimates When the Sample Selection Model is Misspecified', Manuscript, University of Frankfurt.

Ruhm, C. (1991) 'Are Workers Permanently Scarred by Job Displacements?', *American Economic Review*, 81, pp. 319–24.

Stevens, A. (1997) 'Persistent Effects of Job Displacement: The Importance of Multiple Job Losses', 15, pp. 165–88.

Sweeney, J. (1998) 'Why Hold a Job? The Labour Market Choice of the Low Skilled', Leuven: Katholique Universiteit Leuven, p. 263.

Valenduc, C. (2001) 'La réforme de l'impôt des personnes physiques: ses effets sur l'imposition des salaires, l'incitation à l'emploi et sur la distribution des revenus', Belgique, p. 36.

Van den Berg, G.J. (1990) 'Search Behaviour, Transitions to Non-Participation and the Duration of Unemployment', *Economic Journal*, 100(402), pp. 842–65.

Vella, F. and Verbeek, M. (1999) 'Two-Step Estimation of Panel Data Models with Censored Endogenous Variables and Selection Bias', *Journal of Econometrics*, 90, pp. 239–63.

Verbeek, M. and Nijman, T. (1996) 'Incomplete Panels and Selection Bias', in Mátyás, L. and Sevestre, P. (eds) *The Econometrics of Panel Data*, 1st edition, New York: Kluwer Academic Publishers.

Wooldridge, J. (1995) 'Selection Corrections for Panel Data Models under Conditional Mean Independence Assumptions', *Journal of Econometrics*, 68, pp. 115–32.

6
Outsourcing and the Demand for Low-skilled Labour: Exemplary Evidence from German Manufacturing Industries

Ingo Geishecker

1 Introduction

During the past decades, the fortunes of less skilled workers have deteriorated substantially in most OECD countries. In the United States, the United Kingdom and various other countries, low-skilled workers have experienced large decreases in their relative earnings when compared with those of high-skilled workers (see OECD, 1994). For Germany however empirical evidence on the development of the relative earnings position of low-skilled workers is not conclusive. Blau *et al.* (1997), Christensen and Schimmelpfennig (1998) and Fitzenberger (1999) find mixed evidence. Estimation of the change in the relative earnings position of low-skilled workers seems to be sensitive to the definition of educational categories, the differentiation between production and non-production workers, and to the data set. However German unemployment and employment trends for low-skilled workers are far clearer and mirror somewhat the development of relative earnings in the United States and the United Kingdom. Reinberg (2001) reports that, while the overall German unemployment rate increased between 1976 and 1998 from around 4 per cent to almost 9 per cent, the increase for less skilled workers without any vocational training was from around 6 per cent to over 23 per cent. These figures are confirmed by Christensen and Schimmelpfennig (1998) who report that, while the average unemployment rate for low-skilled workers increased from 9.8 per cent (1983–89) to 13 per cent (1992–95), the average unemployment rate for high-skilled workers only increased from 2.3 per cent to 3.4 per cent and for medium-skilled workers from 4.5 per cent to 5.6 per cent respectively. Thus for Germany, there is only weak support for a deteriorating earnings position of low-skilled workers, but strong evidence for a substantial worsening of their employment opportunities.

While country-specific supply shocks may partially explain these developments, the parallel deterioration of either the earnings or the employment position of less skilled workers in most OECD countries has led some authors to conclude that both relative wage and employment aspects can be attributed to a common demand shock. As Freeman (1995, p. 19) states:

> The rise in joblessness in Europe is thus the flip side of the rise in earnings inequality in the U.S. The two outcomes reflect the same phenomenon – a relative decline in the demand against the less skilled …

As persuasive this idea indeed is, what then is the driving force behind this demand shift? Against a backdrop of increasing international trade, we must ask whether trade is at the least to some extent responsible for the decline in the relative demand for low-skilled workers. As is discussed in Section 2, empirical applications of standard trade theory generally fail to provide a strong link between the relative factor demand and international trade. In particular, the occurrence of skill upgrading within industries seems to contradict the hypothesis that international trade is a main culprit for the observed decline in the relative demand for low-skilled labour. However the analysis of trade with intermediate goods and outsourcing may provide new insights. Various production stages that were initially carried out domestically can be outsourced to newly industrialised and developing countries or to Central and Eastern European transition economies. In Section 3 international outsourcing is defined and its magnitude is measured. Using input–output tables, international outsourcing by German manufacturing industries is measured by imported intermediate inputs from the respective industries abroad. In what follows the relevance of international outsourcing for the domestic demand for low-skilled labour will be accessed empirically for the years 1978 to 1993.[1] An econometric model based on a translog cost function with quasi fixed input factors is derived. The empirical findings are discussed in Section 6. International outsourcing is found to be of high relevance for the relative demand for low-skilled labour in various industries, explaining between 14 per cent and 47 per cent of the observed demand shift in the respective industry. Section 7 draws some conclusions from the results.

2 Links between trade and the demand for labour

According to the Stolper–Samuelson theorem, negative demand shifts for low-skilled labour can be caused by trade-induced declines in relative prices for products intensive in the use of low-skilled labour. However Slaughter (1998) surveys empirical work on product price changes for the United States. Generally he finds that the results of different price studies are not conclusive and furthermore it is an open issue whether '[...] these product-price changes have anything to do with international trade' (Slaughter, 1998, p. 34). Empirical evidence for Germany is provided by Lawrence (1994) and Neven and Wyplosz (1996) who find that prices for low-skill-intensive products have indeed not decreased and therefore have not mandated negative demand shifts for low-skilled labour. In addition, the process of skill upgrading can be observed in many OECD countries in nearly all industries (see Berman *et al.*, 1998). Standard trade theory however predicts that, with flexible wages, as low-skilled labour becomes relatively cheaper, the relative input of low-skilled labour should increase within all industries. However, even in the United States, an economy with very high wage flexibility, this was not the case. Berman *et al.* (1994) report on shift-share analysis[2] for the United States. Their findings suggest that between 1979 and 1987 the share of high-skilled labour increased throughout the economy on average by 0.552 percentage points each year. From this, 70 per cent can be attributed to skill upgrading within industries, a result that clearly contradicts the implications of standard trade theory. Similar results can be obtained for Germany. Schimmelpfennig (1998) reports that while the share of high-skilled labour in total employment increased by 6.53 percentage points between 1984/86 and 1994/96, around 85 per cent of this change can be attributed to skill upgrading within industries.[3] The authors own calculations on the basis of more disaggregated industry data with manual and non-manual workers taken as proxies for low- and high-skilled labour largely confirm these findings. While the overall share of high-skilled labour of total employment increased by 5.6 percentage points, around 88 per cent of this change can be attributed to skill-upgrading within industries.

Many authors (see for instance Berman *et al.*, 1994, 1998) therefore conclude that skill-biased technological change rather than international trade, is the driving force behind the negative demand shift for low-skilled labour. It may, however, be misleading to focus solely on skill-biased technological change. First, skill-upgrading within industry does not necessarily violate the predictions of standard trade theory if rigid wages are assumed. A lack of wage flexibility prevents the substitution of low-skilled workers, who are then driven out of the market. Second, while standard trade theory mainly focuses on trade with final goods, trade with intermediate goods may yield quite different results, as this chapter shows.

3 Trade with intermediate goods

Trade with intermediate goods has become increasingly important over the past decades. This reflects an *'[...] increasing interconnectedness of production processes in a vertical* trading chain that stretches across many countries, with each country specialising in particular stages of a good's production sequence' (Hummels *et al.*, 2001, p. 76).

The rapid evolution of assembly plants ('maquiladoras') in the Mexican border region provides an example of interconnectedness of production. US firms economise on low-skilled labour by outsourcing production stages with low-skill intensity to foreign plants that are either owned by the US firm itself or by a subcontractor. Subsequently the produced goods are imported and are then further processed domestically.

Outsourcing is distinguished from classical trade by the intermediate character of the imported goods requiring further domestic processing, research and development and marketing activities. Campa and Goldberg (1997) quantify the scale of outsourcing by the ratio of imported intermediate inputs to the total value of domestic production. They report that between 1974 and 1993 this ratio increased from 13.4 per cent to 21.6 per cent in the United Kingdom, from 15.9 per cent to 20.2 per cent in Canada and from a comparably low 4.06 per cent to 8.2 per cent in the United States. Feenstra and Hanson (1999) apply a similar procedure. They calculate the share of imported intermediate inputs in total intermediate inputs for several US manufacturing industries. Between 1979 and 1990 the average share increased from 7.3 per cent to 11.6 per cent. A narrower definition of international outsourcing, which restricts the imported intermediate inputs to imported inputs from the same industry abroad, yields somewhat weaker results. Between 1979 and 1990 the average share increased from 3.1 per cent to 5.6 per cent. The discrepancy between the figures for the wide and narrow definitions of outsourcing raises the issue of how to precisely measure outsourcing. Input–output tables provide a valuable data basis, with which to solve this problem. They contain the value of imported intermediate goods for each industry from each industry abroad. Campa and

Goldberg (1997) and others assume that the total sum of imported intermediate goods in each industry represents a reasonable indicator for outsourcing. But following Feenstra and Hanson (1999) this 'definition' seems too broad. Outsourcing should be understood as the result of a make or buy decision. The decision of a domestic car producer, for instance, to buy steel or car tyres from a foreign supplier is therefore clearly not related to outsourcing, since the car producer just does not have the opportunity to make steel or tyres himself. Of course employment in the domestic steel or rubber industry may be affected adversely by this decision but this is due to import competition with final goods and not due to international outsourcing. If one instead focuses on the imported intermediate goods for each industry from the same industry abroad, represented by the main diagonal in the input–output-matrix, the effects of trade in final goods and outsourcing can be more accurately separated. Accordingly, in this chapter international outsourcing is narrowly defined as the shift of an industry's *core activities* abroad. A theoretical model showing how international outsourcing can affect the relative demand for low-skilled labour within industries has been developed in Feenstra and Hanson (1996). Their model rests on the assumption of different relative factor prices for low- and high-skilled labour in two regions (North and South). The North is assumed to have a lower relative wage for high-skilled labour and thus an absolute cost advantage in the production of skill intensive intermediate goods. According to the model, capital growth or Hicks-neutral technological progress in the South relative to the North results in a cost advantage of the South in the production stages with a higher skill intensity in which the North initially had a cost advantage. Hence the North specialises in increasingly skill intensive production stages, which leads to an increased (decreased) relative demand for high (low) skilled labour.

It should be stressed however that the above model only assumes one final goods sector. Applying the model to a whole economy with many sectors abstracts from the possibility of factor movements between sectors which is only plausible in the short run. The model forms the theoretical basis for this chapter's empirical assessment of the short run impact of international outsourcing on the relative demand for low-skilled labour in German manufacturing industries.

4 Previous empirical research

Feenstra and Hanson (1996) provide one of the first empirical assessments of the impact of international outsourcing on the relative demand for low-skilled workers. In their study on the United States they approximate international outsourcing by the share of imports from a particular industry abroad in total domestic demand for that industry's products. Thus, outsourcing is actually measured as import penetration. Their empirical model is based on a translog cost function with capital as an quasi fixed input along the lines of Brown and Christensen (1981). From this cost function, a cost share equation for non-production workers is derived. In order to assess the impact of outsourcing, Feenstra and Hanson extend the cost share equation to include the calculated industry's import penetration ratio in an ad hoc fashion. Following this procedure, the authors report that approximately 15 per cent to 33 per cent of the increase of the cost share of non-production labour over the period 1979–87 can be explained by international outsourcing. In a follow-up study Feenstra and Hanson (1999) apply a more accurate definition of international outsourcing by focusing on imported intermediate inputs of an industry from the same industry abroad. According to this study international outsourcing can explain between 11 per cent and 15 per cent of the observed decline in the cost share of production labour in US manufacturing between 1979 and 1990.

A similar study was undertaken by Anderton and Brenton (1999) for the United Kingdom. They estimate the impact of outsourcing for a panel of 11 disaggregated textile and mechanical engineering industries. In contrast to Feenstra and Hanson (1996), they do however distinguish between imports from low- and high-wage countries. As might be expected, only the coefficient of import penetration from low-wage countries is statistically significant.[4] Furthermore, the impact differs between the high-skill intensive mechanical engineering and the low-skill intensive textiles industry. While the coefficient of the import penetration variable is, in general, not statistically significant for the mechanical engineering industries, in the textiles industry up to 40 per cent of the observed rise in the cost share and up to 33 per cent of the rise in the employment share of skilled workers between 1970 and 1983 can be explained by import penetration from low-wage countries.

Diehl (1999) provides some empirical evidence for the impact of international outsourcing on German manufacturing industries. He uses an ad hoc model for relative labour demand, as well as a well-specified empirical model that is also based on a translog cost function. In contrast to Feenstra and Hanson (1996) and Anderton and Brenton (1999), Diehl uses relative import prices instead of import quantities. While his model contains capital as a quasi fixed input reflecting adjustment costs, to allow that capital can differ from its long run equilibrium, imported and domestic imports are implicitly assumed always to be at their long run equilibrium. To calculate the prices for domestic and imported inputs for each industry, Diehl uses sectoral data for domestic producer and import prices, weighted with the respective foreign and domestic industries share in total inputs. These weights can be obtained from the biannual input–output tables, which distinguish between imported and domestic inputs. Diehl (1999) uses constant weights from the input–output table for 1978. This results, in all probability, in an overestimation of imported input prices. Consider the case of a decline in the price of imported relative to domestic inputs.[5]

A further problem with the above approach is the rather broad definition of international outsourcing. As highlighted in Section 3, when dealing with the relative demand for low-skilled workers, one should focus on the imported intermediate inputs from the same industry abroad, thus applying a narrower definition of international outsourcing. Diehl finds that international outsourcing has only a weak impact on the skill structure of employment in German manufacturing. In 16 out of 28 industries the coefficient of the price variable for imported intermediate inputs is statistically insignificant, implying a substitution elasticity of just one between imported inputs and production workers. Furthermore, the elasticity of substitution between non-production workers and imported intermediate inputs is not significantly lower than that of production workers. In addition, the coefficient of the imported input price is statistically significant and negative in 12 out of 28 industries, implying an even lower elasticity of substitution between production labour and imported intermediate inputs. Thus no empirical evidence exists for a shift in the relative demand for production (low-skilled) workers due to international outsourcing. Diehl (1999) compares his findings with those of Anderton and Brenton (1999) by using import penetration ratios as a proxy for international outsourcing. In general, this variable performs somewhat better than the price variable. Empirical evidence for the impact of international outsourcing on the relative demand for low-skilled labour remains ambiguous: 9 out of 28 estimated coefficients are statistically significant, of which only five have the expected sign.

Falk and Koebel (2000) use a similar approach. Using a Box Cox cost function, which nests the normalised quadratic as well as the translog functional form, they estimate elasticities of substitution between the variable input factors: high-, medium- and low-skilled labour as well as imported intermediate materials, domestic non-energy intermediate materials, energy and intermediate services. However their findings suggest that neither imported material inputs nor intermediate services substitute for unskilled labour. In a second step Falk and Koebel (2000) compare their results with those of Feenstra and Hanson (1999), applying a similar translog cost function. Again outsourcing is found to be statistically insignificant for the cost share of unskilled labour.

In the following section a somewhat different empirical model is developed. The model captures the impact of narrowly defined international outsourcing by including imported intermediate inputs as a quasi fix production factor.

5 The empirical model

The starting point for the econometric model is an arbitrary aggregated production function for each industry *i*:

$$Y_i = Y(L_i^{HS}, L_i^{LS}, K_i, I_i, T_i), \tag{1}$$

with L_i^{HS} and L_i^{LS} denoting the variable high and low-skilled labour input,
K_i the quasi fixed capital input,
I_i the quasi fixed inputs of imported intermediates from industry *i* (abroad) and
T_i a technology parameter in industry *i*.

Assuming that capital and imported intermediate inputs are quasi fixed takes account of the fact that, due to adjustment costs, both input factors may differ from their long run equilibrium. If firms are profit maximising and if isoquants of the production function are convex, there exists a dual variable cost function for each industry:

$$CV_i = CV(W_i^{HS}, W_i^{LS}, K_i, I_i, T_i), \tag{2}$$

with W_i^{HS} and W_i^{LS} representing the respective wage rates for high- and low-skilled labour in industry *i*. The cost function can be approximated by a general translog function with variable and quasi fixed input factors that was introduced by Brown and Christensen (1981). In order to reduce complexity, the industry subscripts are temporarily dropped.

$$\begin{aligned}\ln CV = {} & \alpha_0 + \beta_{HS} \ln W^{HS} + \beta_{LS} \ln W^{LS} \\ & + 1/2\gamma_{HSLS} \ln W^{HS} \ln W^{LS} + 1/2\gamma_{LSHS} \ln W^{LS} \ln W^{HS} \\ & + 1/2\gamma_{HSHS} \ln W^{HS} \ln W^{HS} + 1/2\gamma_{LSLS} \ln W^{LS} \ln W^{LS} \\ & + \delta_Y \ln Y + 1/2\delta_{yy} \ln Y \ln Y \\ & + \delta_K \ln K + 1/2\delta_{KK} \ln K \ln K + \delta_I \ln I + 1/2\delta_{II} \ln I \ln I\end{aligned}$$

$$+ \chi_{\mathrm{YLS}} \ln Y \ln W^{\mathrm{LS}} + \chi_{\mathrm{YHS}} \ln Y \ln W^{\mathrm{HS}} + \chi_{\mathrm{KLS}} \ln K \ln W^{\mathrm{LS}}$$
$$+ \chi_{\mathrm{KHS}} \ln K \ln W^{\mathrm{HS}} + \chi_{\mathrm{ILS}} \ln I \ln W^{\mathrm{LS}} + \chi_{\mathrm{IHS}} \ln I \ln W^{\mathrm{HS}}$$
$$+ \mu_{\mathrm{YK}} \ln Y \ln K + \mu_{\mathrm{YI}} \ln Y \ln I + \mu_{\mathrm{KI}} \ln K \ln I$$
$$+ \eta_{\mathrm{T}} T + 1/2 \eta_{\mathrm{TT}} TT + \eta_{\mathrm{YT}} T \ln Y + \mu_{\mathrm{KT}} T \ln K$$
$$+ \eta_{\mathrm{IT}} T \ln I + \eta_{\mathrm{LST}} T \ln W^{\mathrm{LS}} + \eta_{\mathrm{HST}} T \ln W^{\mathrm{HS}}. \quad (3)$$

Differentiation of the variable cost function with respect to prices of the variable factors gives the respective factor demand equation. Since the cost function is in logarithmic form, differentiation yields the factor's share in total variable costs:

$$\frac{\partial \ln CV}{\partial \ln W^{\mathrm{HS}}} = \frac{W^{\mathrm{HS}}}{CV} \times \frac{\partial CV}{\partial W^{\mathrm{HS}}} = \frac{W^{\mathrm{HS}} L^{\mathrm{HS}}}{CV} = S^{\mathrm{HS}} \quad (4)$$

$$\frac{\partial \ln CV}{\partial \ln W^{\mathrm{LS}}} = \frac{W^{\mathrm{LS}}}{CV} \times \frac{\partial CV}{\partial W^{\mathrm{LS}}} = \frac{W^{\mathrm{LS}} L^{\mathrm{LS}}}{CV} = S^{\mathrm{LS}}, \quad (5)$$

where S^{HS} and S^{LS} denote the cost share of high- and low-skilled labour in variable costs. Since high- and low-skilled labour are the only variable inputs, both factor share equations have to add up to one and only one of them is linearly independent. Equation (5) can be written out more explicitly with industry again being indexed with i:

$$S_i^{\mathrm{LS}} = \beta^{\mathrm{LS}} + 1/2 \gamma_{\mathrm{LSHS}} \ln W_i^{\mathrm{HS}} + 1/2 \gamma_{\mathrm{HSLS}} \ln W_i^{\mathrm{HS}}$$
$$+ \gamma_{\mathrm{LSLS}} \ln W_i^{\mathrm{LS}} + \chi_{\mathrm{YLS}} \ln Y_i + \chi_{\mathrm{KLS}} \ln K_i + \chi_{\mathrm{ILS}} \ln I_i + \eta_{\mathrm{TLS}} T_i. \quad (6)$$

The result is a linear equation expressed in the logarithmic of the wage for high- and low-skilled labour, output, the quasi fixed input factors capital and imported intermediates, as well as a non-logarithmic technology parameter for each industry.

Adding a time dimension and a stochastic error term u_{it} with $E(u_{it}) = 0$ yields a fully specified econometric model:

$$S_{it}^{\mathrm{LS}} = \beta^{\mathrm{LS}} + 1/2 \gamma_{\mathrm{LSHS}} \ln W_{it}^{\mathrm{HS}} + 1/2 \gamma_{\mathrm{HSLS}} \ln W_{it}^{\mathrm{HS}}$$
$$+ \gamma_{\mathrm{LSLS}} \ln W_{it}^{\mathrm{LS}} + \chi_{\mathrm{YLS}} \ln Y_{it} + \chi_{\mathrm{KLS}} \ln K_{it} + \chi_{\mathrm{ILS}} \ln I_{it} + \eta_{\mathrm{TLS}} T_{it} + u_{it}. \quad (7)$$

The error term can be further decomposed into:

$$u_{it} = \nu_i + \lambda_t + \omega_{it} \quad (8)$$

where ν_i denotes a constant unobservable industry specific effect, λ_t the unobservable effect of a single time period, which is common across industries, such as the macro economic shock of German unification and ω_{it} the remaining stochastic error term with

$$\text{Var}(\omega_{it}) = \sigma^2.$$

In imposing the restriction that the coefficients of the independent variables are equal across industries, the estimation can be pooled, hence utilising time and cross section variation. It should be noted, however, that it seems questionable as to whether the wage variables W_i^{HS}, W_i^{LS} are indeed exogenous. If industry wages and the relative demand for low-skilled labour are simultaneously determined, which cannot be ruled out even with high wage coordination across German manufacturing industries, estimation of the model would deliver biased coefficients. The wage variables are therefore excluded from the regression.

It could be furthermore argued that due to the different sizes of the industries, the stochastic error term is likely to be heteroscedastic. A further concern is whether the stationarity of the variables is given. Applying the Im-Pesaran-Shin panel unit root test, the H_0 of non-stationarity cannot be rejected at least for the output variable. Both of the above problems can be tackled by transforming the model into the first differences form:

$$\begin{aligned} dS_{it}^{LS} &= S_{it}^{LS} - S_{it}^{LS}L \\ &= \chi_{YLS}d\ln Y_{it} + \chi_{KLS}d\ln K_{it} + \chi_{ILS}d\ln I_{it} + \eta_{TLS}t_{it} + \lambda_t + \omega_{it}. \end{aligned} \tag{9}$$

The independent variables are thus: the log growth rates of output, net capital stock and imported intermediate inputs. The technology parameter, t, captures technological change and is approximated by a common linear time trend for all industries. The parameters λ_t are a set of time dummies and capture common macro-economic effects.

The coefficient of the growth rate of output should take on a positive sign, because increases in production are associated with an increased input of production labour among whom low-skilled workers are more predominant. The coefficient of the growth rate of capital is expected to have a negative sign, as it is well established that, while labour and capital are in general substitutes, capital is more readily substituted for low-skilled than for high-skilled labour (see for instance Griliches, 1969). As a result, the cost share of low-skilled labour should decrease as capital increases. Technological change is likely to have a negative impact on the relative demand for low-skilled labour, the coefficient of the trend variable is therefore expected to have a negative sign. Following the model of Feenstra and Hanson (1996) international outsourcing is expected to have a negative impact on the relative demand for low-skilled labour. Hence, the coefficient of imported intermediate inputs is expected to take on a negative sign.

6 Empirical results

The results of the FGLS regression are shown in Table 6.1. For the years 1991 and 1993, which are the years after German unification, time dummies are included, due to a structural change in the data (see Appendix A). In general the coefficients have the expected signs. Increases in output result in a higher cost share of low-skilled labour in total variable costs, as suggested by the positive, statistically significant coefficient of the output variable. Furthermore, the hypothesis that capital and low-skilled labour are negatively correlated is confirmed by the significant and negative coefficient of the capital variable (see Table 6.1 columns a–c).

The coefficient of the trend variable has the expected sign, but although it is statistically significant, it is noteworthy that the estimated impact of technological change on the cost share of low-skilled labour is very small (Table 6.1 column a). In addition the time trend is likely to capture also other variations than pure technological progress. The author therefore has also experimented with industrial research and development expenditures as a proxy for technological change. However this proxy was found to be statistically insignificant an the results are not reported. One likely explanation is that, as technological progress and the capital stock are highly positively correlated, the capital variable captures most technological progress, leaving little explanatory power for the technology variable. In the following specifications the technology variable is therefore excluded from the regression.

However the coefficient of imported intermediate inputs is statistically not significantly different from zero, in both specifications with and without the technology variable (see Table 6.1 columns a and b). Regarding the coefficient of the growth rate of imported intermediate inputs, a few more comments are necessary. Input–output tables do not allow to distinguish between imported intermediates by their country of origin or by their skill intensity. Imported intermediated goods, as measured here, therefore include low-skill intensive intermediates from developing and newly industrialising countries, as well as intermediates with the same skill intensity from other developed countries. It is clear that both types of imported intermediates have significantly different effects on the relative demand for low-skilled workers. According to the model by Feenstra and Hanson (1996) only in industries where low-skill intensive intermediates are the dominant imported intermediate inputs,

Table 6.1 FGLS regression results

	a		b		c	
dln*Y*	0.064	(10.91)***	0.042	(6.37)***	0.044	(10.23)***
dln*K*	−0.043	(4.38)***	−0.063	(5.53)***	0.053	(3.62)***
dln*l*	0.001	(−0.65)	−0.002	(−0.88)		
Trend	0	(12.06)***				
dln*l*: Petroleum					−0.011	(−0.77)
dln*l*: Stone and earth products					0.032	(−1.42)
dln*l*: Iron					−0.001	(−0.05)
dln*l*: Non-ferrous metals					−0.008	(−0.86)
dln*l*: Foundries					0.001	(−0.20)
dln*l*: Cold rolling mills					−0.004	(−0.20)
dln*l*: Structural metal products, railroad					−0.001	(−0.51)
dln*l*: Mechanical engineering					0.019	(−0.59)
dln*l*: Road vehicles					0	(−0.02)
dln*l*: Air- and spacecraft					−0.014	(−1.35)
dln*l*: Electrical engineering					−0.042	(1.81)*
dln*l*: Instruments					−0.004	(−0.27)
dln*l*: Finished metal products					0.002	(−0.17)
dln*l*: Toys, musical instruments etc.					0.002	(−0.21)
dln*l*: Chemicals					−0.119	(3.56)***
dln*l*: Office machinery, computers					−0.047	(2.15)**
dln*l*: Ceramic goods					0.017	(−1.27)
dln*l*: Glass					−0.003	(−0.12)
dln*l*: Wood working					0.017	(−1.40)
dln*l*: Wood products					0	(−0.07)
dln*l*: Pulp, paper					−0.045	(5.77)***
dln*l*: Paper products					−0.004	(−0.48)

Table 6.1 Continued

	a		b		c	
dln*l*: Printing					−0.005	(−0.58)
dln*l*: Plastic products					0.003	(−0.41)
dln*l*: Rubber products					0.003	(−0.34)
dln*l*: Leather, Shoes					0.02	(−0.39)
dln*l*: Textiles					0.035	(2.27)**
dln*l*: Clothing					−0.004	(−0.72)
dln*l*: Food, Beverages					−0.007	(−0.34)
dln*l*: Tobacco					0.005	(−0.43)
year 91	0.007	(4.20)***	0.001	(−0.54)	−0.003	(2.16)**
year 93	−0.004	(1.82)*	−0.011	(−7.31)***	−0.018	(9.31)***

Note: t-statistics in parentheses, * significant at 10%, ** at 5%, *** at 1%.

Table 6.2 Decrease in cost share of low-skilled workers explained by outsourcing

	Industry decrease in cost share (in percentage points)	**Total growth of outsourcing (%)**	**Explained proportion (%)**
Electrical engineering	−9.3	92.8	41.9
Chemicals	−8.5	33.7	47.2
Office machinery	−14.2	43.6	14.4
Paper and pulp	−4.8	27.9	26.2
Textiles	−8.4	−48.1	

one would expect a negative impact on the cost share of low-skilled workers. The pooling of imported intermediate inputs over all industries might therefore be not appropriate. A third model specification therefore takes account of industry specific impacts of international outsourcing allowing the coefficient χ_{ILS} to take on a separate value for each and every industry (see Table 6.1 column c).

Although one should be cautious in interpreting the results because of only eight observations over time for each industry it is clear that outsourcing plays a very different role in determining the relative demand for low-skilled labour across industries. For most industries, outsourcing does not play a significant role in determining the cost share of low-skilled labour. However, there are five industries where international outsourcing is important: electrical engineering, chemicals, office machinery/computers, paper and pulp and textiles.

In all of the above industries, except textiles, international outsourcing is not only statistical significant at least 10 per cent, but the coefficient also has a negative sign. This provides some evidence that the relative demand for low-skilled labour in these industries is indeed negatively affected by international outsourcing. However the coefficient of the outsourcing variable is also statistically significant at 5 per cent for the textiles industry but has a positive sign. This suggests that as imported intermediate goods rise, the cost share of low-skilled labour also increases in this industry. This result is somewhat puzzling and contradicts the implications of the model by Feenstra and Hanson (1996). In order to understand the processes that are going on in this industry further research at a more disaggregated industry level is required.

While a statistically significant coefficient actually only indicates which part of the overall variation of the dependent variable can be explained by variations in the respective independent variable, it is now possible on the basis of the point estimates to assess the economic importance of international outsourcing in greater detail. Table 6.2 shows the overall growth of imported intermediate goods between 1978 and 1993, the overall decrease in the cost share of low-skilled labour and the proportion of this decrease in the cost share that can be explained by international outsourcing for total manufacturing and each of the above industries.[6] As column 2 of Table 6.2 indicates, international outsourcing gained substantial importance for most industries between 1978 and 1993. In particular in Electrical engineering a massive growth of imported intermediate inputs of 93 per cent can be observed.

While international outsourcing appears to be of very little importance for determining the relative demand for low-skilled workers in manufacturing as a whole, Table 6.2 indicates that this quite low overall effect masks the fact that for certain industries international outsourcing is of much higher importance. For specific industries international outsourcing indeed can explain between 14 per cent and 47 per cent of the observed decrease in the industry cost share of low-skilled labour between 1978 and 1993.

It is worth noting, however, that many industries in which international outsourcing is important have in fact been high-skill intensive industries from at least 1978 onwards. Table 6.3 shows the share of high-skilled labour in total employment for the years 1978 and 1993. The office machinery and computer industry is in particular very skill intensive. The empirical results suggest that international outsourcing contributed to an even further demand shift away from low-skilled workers in these industries. In the office machinery and computer industry for instance, mainly less skill intensive production stages, such as the production of power supply units or enclosures have been shifted abroad recently, reducing the demand for low-skilled employees even further.

Conclusion

There is indeed some empirical evidence for the hypothesis that between 1978 and 1993 international outsourcing was an important factor in determining the relative demand for low-skilled labour in specific industries. Although the effect of international outsourcing was found to be only negligible for manufacturing as a whole, in namely the electrical engineering, chemical, office machinery/computer as well as the paper and pulp industries, international outsourcing is of higher importance

Table 6.3 Employment share of high-skilled labour in %

Industry	**1978**	**1993**
Petroleum	0.50	0.56
Stone and earth products	0.25	0.29
Iron	0.23	0.27
Non-ferrous metals	0.27	0.30
Foundries	0.19	0.23
Cold rolling mills	0.22	0.23
Structural metal products, railroad	0.26	0.30
Mechanical engineering	0,35	0.40
Road vehicles	0.22	0.26
Shipbuilding	0.22	0.28
Air- and spacecraft	0.52	0.57
Electrical Engineering	0.36	0.43
Instruments	0.31	0.38
Finished metal products	0.26	0.29
Toys, musical instruments	0.25	0.30
Chemicals	0.45	0.52
Office machinery, computer	0.51	0.72
Ceramic goods	0.19	0.23
Glass	0.21	0.25
Wood working	0.22	0.23
Wood products	0.22	0.24
Pulp, paper	0.22	0.26
Paper products	0.25	0.27
Printing	0.25	0.32
Plastic products	0.25	0.27
Rubber products	0.25	0.28
Leather, shoes	0.18	0.28
Textiles	0.23	0.29
Clothing	0.18	0.27
Food, beverages	0.34	0.35
Tobacco	0.32	0.39

and explains between 14 per cent and 47 per cent of the observed decrease in the cost share of low-skilled labour. Together, these industries account for about a quarter of averaged total employment between 1978 and 1993. This indicates that international outsourcing can indeed play a major role in determining the relative demand for different skill groups. In the light of further integration in world markets, for instance due to the eastern enlargement of the EU, international outsourcing is even more likely to lead to further negative demand shifts away from less skilled workers in the future.

Acknowledgements

The author would like to thank: J. Bitzer (DIW Berlin, WLT), H. Brücker (DIW Berlin, WLT), P.R. Gregory (University of Houston), J. Haisken De New (DIW Berlin, SOEP), M. Pannenberg (DIW Berlin, SOEP).

Appendix A: data

The empirical analysis is based on aggregated manufacturing industry data for the period 1978–93, following the German SYPRO, which roughly corresponds to the three digit ISIC classification. Unfortunately, systematical changes in the industry classification after 1993 prevent the usage of more recent data together with older time series. Data is available for 30 manufacturing industries with eight observations over time, yielding a total number of observations of 240. Shipbuilding was excluded from the analysis due to the typically erratic and unreliable character of the input data.

Data on the average wage, as well as on the total wage payments at a sectoral level are available only for the broad groups of production and non-production workers. High-skilled workers are assumed to be non-production workers. This can be justified by the fact that the share of higher skill levels in non-production labour is higher than that in production labour. As unsatisfactory as this approximation may seem, there are however no better data available. Data can be obtained from the online time series service of the German Federal Statistical Office (www.statistik-bund.de). Investment data in prices of 1991 and nominal production values can also be obtained from this source. Nominal production values are adjusted to prices of 1991 using the aggregate price index for manufacturing (Federal Statistical Office, Fachserie 17, Reihe 21).

The values of domestic and imported intermediate inputs are derived from the biannual German input–output tables (Federal Statistical Office, Fachserie 18, Reihe 2). Input–output tables with a common industry classification are available for the years 1978, 1980, 1982, 1984, 1986, 1988, 1990, 1991, 1993. However input–output tables from 1991 onwards include data for the former East Germany. The time dummies for the years 1991 and 1993 in the regression aim to control for this structural break. The value of domestic and imported intermediate inputs is adjusted to the prices of 1991 using the aggregate producer price index for manufacturing goods (Federal Statistical Office, Fachserie 17, Reihe 21) and the price index for imported manufacturing goods (Federal Statistical Office, Fachserie 17, Reihe 8).

Notes

1. Compare Geishecker (2002) for an analysis of the labour market impact of international outsourcing during the 1990s.
2. The shift–share analysis decomposes the overall skill upgrading into skill-upgrading within and between single industries according to: $\Delta S^{HS} = \sum_{i=1}^{n} \Delta S_i^{HS} P_i + \sum_{i=1}^{n} \Delta P_i S_i^{HS}$ where S^{HS} denotes the share of high-skilled workers in total workers, the subscript i industry and P_i the industries share of

overall employment. The first term denotes skill upgrading within industries and the second term between industries.

3. Schimmelpfennig uses data from the German Socio-Economic Panel with highly aggregated industry classifications.
4. Low-skill activities are typically outsourced to low-wage countries.
5. As foreign inputs become relatively cheaper, a substitution towards these inputs should occur, increasing the share of the respective foreign inputs in total inputs and thus pushing down the average relative input price. However holding the weights constant, underestimates the actual impact of the initial decline in the relative input price.
6. Explained proportion in $i = \chi_{\text{ILS}i} \times \sum_t \mathrm{dln}I_{it} \Big/ \sum_t \mathrm{d}S_{it}^{\text{LS}}$.

References

Anderton, Bob and Brenton, Paul (1999) 'Outsourcing and Low-Skilled Workers in the UK', *Bulletin of Economic Research*, 51(4), pp. 267–85.

Berman, Eli, Bound, John and Machin, Stephen (1998) 'Implications of Skill-Biased Technological Change: International Evidence', *Quarterly Journal of Economics*, 113(4), pp. 1245–80.

Berman, Eli and Griliches, Zvi (1994) 'Changes in the Demand for Skilled Labor Within U.S. Manufacturing: Evidence from the Annual Survey of Manufacturing', *Quarterly Journal of Economics*, 109(2), pp. 367–97.

Blau, H., Hofman, H. and Meyerle, W. (1997) 'Labour Market Studies Germany', Report, European Commission.

Brown, Randall S. and Christensen, Lauritis R. (1981) 'Estimating Elasticities of Substitution in a Model of Partial Static Equilibrium: An Apllication to U.S. Agriculture, 1947–1974', in Berndt, E. R. and Field, B. C. (eds) *Modeling and Measuring Natural Resource Substitution*, Cambridge, MA: MIT Press, pp. 209–29.

Campa, Jose and Goldberg, Linda S. (1997) 'The Evolving External Orientation of Manufacturing Industries: Evidence from Four Countries', Working Paper 5919, National Bureau of Economic Research.

Christensen, Björn and Schimmelpfennig, Axel (1998) 'Arbeitslosigkeit, Qualifikation und Lohnstruktur in Westdeutschland', *Die Weltwirtschaft*, 2, pp. 177–86.

Diehl, Markus (1999) 'The Impact of International Outsourcing on the Skill Structure of Employment: Empirical Evidence from German Manufacturing Industries', Kiel Working Paper 946, Institut für Weltwirtschaft.

Falk, Martin and Koebel, Bertrand (2002) 'Outsourcing, Imports and Labour Demand', *Scandinavian Journal of Economics*, 104(4), pp. 567–86.

Feenstra, Robert C. and Hanson, Gordon H. (1996) 'Foreign Direct Investment, Outsourcing and Relative Wages', in Feenstra, Robert C., Grossman, Gene M. and Irwin, D. A. (eds) *The Political Economy of Trade* Policy: *Papers in Honor of Jagdish Bhagwati*, Cambridge, MA: MIT Press, pp. 89–127.

Feenstra, Robert C. and Hanson, Gordon H. (1999). 'The Impact of Outsourcing and High-technology Capital on Wages: Estimates for the United States, 1979–1990', *Quarterly Journal of Economics*, 114(3), pp. 907–40.

Fitzenberger, Bernd (1999) 'International Trade and the Skill Structure of Wages and Employment in West Germany', *Jahrbücher für Nationalökonomie und Statistik*, 219(1 + 2), pp. 67–89.

Freeman, Richard B. (1995) 'Are Your Wages Set in Beijing?', *Journal of Economic Perspectives*, 9(3), pp. 15–32.

Geishecker, Ingo (2002) 'Outsourcing and the Demand for Low-skilled Labour in German Manufacturing: New Evidence', Discussion Paper 313, DIW Berlin, 2002.

Griliches, Zvi (1969) 'Capital Skill Complementarity', *The Review of Economics and Statistics*, 51, pp. 465–8.

Hummels, David, Ishii, Jun and Yi, Kei-Mu (2001) 'The Nature and Growth of Vertical Specialization in World Trade', *Journal of International Economics*, 54, pp. 75–96.

Lawrence, Robert Z. (1994) 'Trade, Multinationals and Labour', Working Paper 4836, National Bureau of Economic Research, Working Paper.

Neven, Damien J. and Charles Wyplosz (1996) 'Relative Prices, Trade and Restructuring in European Industry', Working Paper 1451, Centre for Economic Policy Research, Discussion Paper.

OECD (1994) *Job Study, Part 1*, Paris: OECD.

Reinberg, Alexander (2001) 'Arbeitsmarktrelevante Aspekte der Bildungspolitik', Beiträge zur Arbeitsmarkt- und Berufsforschung 245, Institut für Arbeitsmarkt und Berufsforschung.

Schimmelpfennig, Axel (1998) 'Skill-Biased Technical Change vs. Structural Change', Working Paper, 868, Institut für Weltwirtschaft, Kiel Working Paper.

Slaughter, Matthew J. (1998) 'What are the Results of Product-Price Studies and What Can We Learn From Their Differences?', Working Paper 6591, National Bureau of Economic Research, Working Paper.

7

Monopsony and Employment Inflows. A Microeconometric Analysis Based on a Panel of Belgian Firms

Benoît Mahy and Isabelle Paindavoine

1 Introduction

About deregulation effectiveness. The monopsonistic case

It is often asserted among economists that regulation prevents wage adjustment process towards equilibrium by pushing wages above their equilibrium level. Therefore, a way to get rid of unemployment is to deregulate the market, leading to a perfect competition state with no unvoluntary unemployment and each worker being paid a wage equal to his marginal productivity. The basic reason for some economists to consider that deregulation could succeed often comes from the idea that a main cause to unemployment, from an unperfect competition point of view, is related to union bargaining power (Lindbeck and Snower, 1989). Deregulation could reduce this power through reforming the social security or the employment protection systems, abandoning or reducing minimum wages.

But the problem is that empirical analysis does not necessarily verify the assertion that higher union power has to be associated with higher unemployment (Blanchflower and Freeman, 1994; Cahuc and Zylberberg, 2001).

Gregg and Manning (1997) analyse the way regulating the labour market influences unemployment level in a different way. They consider that regulation merely relates to four institutional elements, that is, the social security system, the minimum wage, the employment protection and union activity. They show that deregulation would be totally inefficient if we assume that labour market power is in fact merely concentrated at the employers level. This concentrated power, which can be at most associated with monopsony if only one firm hires (a certain kind of) workers, then determines labour market disequilibrium. In such a case, the wage paid by the firm can be lower than the equilibrium wage, leading to labour supply shortage and high 'voluntary' unemployment, voluntary in the sense that few labour suppliers exist at this low wage. In such a situation, deregulation leading to lower workers power would make the situation even worse.

From a theoretical point of view and in terms of labour market policy, it is therefore important to estimate whether this other monopsonistic behaviour assumption actually applies to the Belgian situation in our case.

Empirical facts. Is there a place for monopsony in Belgium?

Robinson (1969) first introduced monopsony to study labour market behaviour. He assumed a market with only one buyer. Nowadays, 'monopsony on the labour market' merely applies to models where the firm faces a labour supply which positively relates to wages.

From the last 20 years, many researchers consider that using this monopsonistic assumption could be relevant to study labour market behaviour. This is due to the fact that recent empirical studies tend to show some results that are not consistent with competitive approaches, like a positive effect which is often estimated between minimum wages and employment level (Boadway and Cuff, 2001). These results suit to the monopsonistic behaviour, which implies that both wages and employment should be positively related to higher minimum wages (Manning, 1995; Cahuc and Zylberberg, 2001).

From a Belgian institutional point of view, it is a fact that many labour conditions and wages are determined during the bargaining process between workers and employers unions. The bargain merely takes place at a sectoral level. For instance, wages are actually determined in each of 168 so-called equal, based on a 50–50 per cent representation power between employers and employees representatives, sectoral commissions. Another important related fact is that when guidelines have to be bargained over at the national level, sectoral representatives possess two-third of the total number of votes at the union level. As a result of the bargain, wages are related to skill levels of the workers and to workplaces in the firm. They are also closely linked to inflation, that is, at a 100 per cent indexation rate. At some periods, proportional wage premia are bargained over. They apply to all the workers of the sectoral commission. That is also to say that union coverage, which determines union power, is high in Belgium.

Close to the bargaining process, it is also worth to mention that Belgian government plays a role in wage determination, especially when employers and employees disagree. More important is probably the 'law to maintain competitiveness', which was first decided in 1989 and amended in 1996. Under this regime, Belgian wage bargaining is supposed to be preventively ruled by the observed and expected evolution of the labour costs among the three biggest Belgian trade partners (France, Germany and The Netherlands). For example, wage growth was supposed not to exceed a level of 6.4 per cent during the period 2001–02.

These institutional facts show some rigidity in wage behaviour: wages are bargained and apply to (nearly) all workers. It is therefore hard to believe that monopsonistic behaviour should be dominant in all the wage process, that trade unions could accept either low wages and low employment level. But it is possible to assume that monopsony could apply to some firms or little groups of firms, for the following reasons:

- at a wage level, wages are bargained over to compensate for different labour force skills or workplaces, not labour force productivity as such. It can therefore be possible for a firm to classify a worker at a level which does not necessarily correspond to his actual productivity. And this process could especially be favoured when reasons related to unperfect competition on the labour market prevent workers to move easily from one job to another, for example when they possess specific skills. It is also important to notice that some of the commissions do not fix specific minimum wages for low-skilled workers. These workers then receive the overall minimum wage, which can be lower than their productivity;
- at a bargaining power level, commissions include firms that belong to different (sub)sectors and possess different levels of market power. This heterogeneity could allow some higher productivity firms to pay same wages as the others. Second, bargaining can take place at the firm level when sectors only contain few big firms. There could then probably exist a larger place for monopsonistic behaviour;
- also at a bargaining power level, union power can be low even if union coverage is high, because of the economic situation in the firm or in the economy. And this weakened power situation could finally favour monopsonistic behaviour in some firms;
- finally, government regulation in the bargaining process can also weaken unions ability to negotiate wages related to productivity, especially when regulation takes the form of guidelines to moderate wages.

So either international and Belgian institutional facts do not necessarily seem to reject the assumption of potential monopsony, at least in some firms. Our applied analysis, focused on labour demand behaviour, will try to shed some additional light on that.

In a second, theoretical, part, we will present the basic framework and the tests to be performed in order to approach monopsonistic behaviour. In a third part, we will detail our dataset and the estimation technique we use to estimate to what extent Belgian firms actually act as monopsonists. In the fourth part, we will detail and comment our results. We will also try to apprehend the relation between monopsonistic behaviour by skills and age of labour supply. The final part will conclude.

2 Monopsony on the labour market. A theoretical approach

Theoretical background

Profit maximising firms are supposed to determine their labour demand in the traditional way, at a level where marginal productivity equals marginal cost of labour. On the labour market, they can hire utility maximising individuals that determine their labour supply at a level where marginal disutility of labour equals wages.

Depending on substitution and income effects, labour supply can positively or negatively relate to increasing wages. Remember that a first effect of increasing wages makes labour supply always increase, as the opportunity cost of leisure then increases, while a second often makes labour supply decrease, as wealthier people often want to work less, leisure being often a normal good. Though the net effect of wages on labour supply is not that robust, especially when we consider labour supply segmented by gender (Blundell, 1993; Blundell and McCurdy, 1999), we will assume a net positive effect of wages, costs of labour from a firm point of view, on labour supply.

Under these labour supply and demand behaviours, labour market equilibrium will crucially depend on the level of competition on the labour market. We will consider perfect and monopsonistic competitions.

In a perfect competition situation (see Graph 7.1), firms are wage-takers. At the branch level, perfect competition guarantees cleaning market wages (w^*_{cp}), where aggregate labour demand (L^D) matches labour supply (L^S).

At the firm level, equilibrium wage, which is then also in this case the marginal cost of an additional worker, leads each firm to fix its optimal

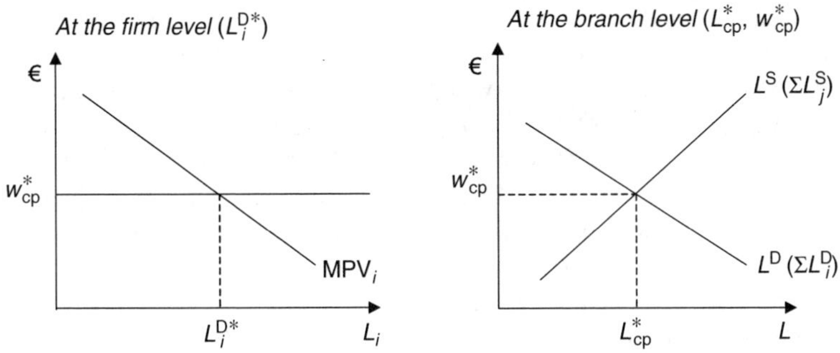

Graph 7.1 Labour market equilibrium under perfect competition

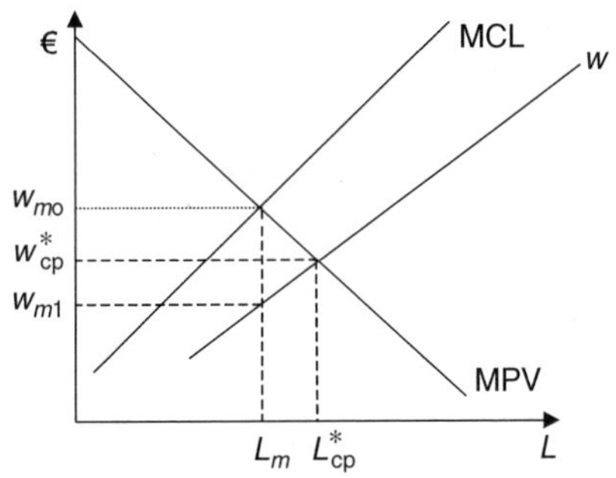

Graph 7.2 Monopsonistic equilibrium at the firm (and the branch) levels

labour demand (L_i^{D*}) at the level of equilibrium between this marginal cost and the value of marginal productivity (MPV_i).

In a monopsonistic competition situation (see Graph 7.2), the firm is wage-maker. It faces a (positive) labour supply function, where the marginal cost of labour is higher than the new higher wage to be paid by the firm to hire a new worker, given that this higher wage has also to be paid to already hired other workers, assuming that the firm cannot discriminate among labour suppliers.

So the marginal cost of labour (MCL) covers either the new wage of the additional worker and the wage-premium to be paid to other workers. The marginal cost function is higher than the wage (w), which is the inverse of the labour supply function, the relation between the wage to be paid for a given level of suppliers to be hired.

The equality between marginal cost and productivity then determines the labour demand chosen by the monopsonistic firm (L_m) and the corresponding wage level she will pay the workers (w_{m1}). At that profit maximising level, marginal productivity, corresponding to marginal cost w_{m0}, is higher than the wage (w_{m1}). The difference represents the monopsonistic power of the firm, the fact that the firm can, unlike in the competitive case, pay its last worker a wage which is lower than his productivity. And this wage–productivity gap will be higher, the lower the labour supply elasticity with respect to wages.

Note that this positive relationship between the marginal cost of labour and the labour supply to be hired can also be observed in other situations than monopsony. From a labour demand point of view, Manning (2001) suggests another explanation to this positive relationship, referred as 'Generalised monopsony' and related to adjustment costs behaviour. He suggests that hiring or firing a new worker should not necessarily represent constant adjustment costs, which should be necessarily independent of the level of adjustment. And if diseconomies of scale exist in either hiring or firing, than additional labour force to be employed should be associated with different marginal labour costs to be paid, increasing with the level of employment. That is also to say that a positive relationship between labour costs and employment could then be observed in either perfect competition or monopsonistic situations. Note that Burdett and Mortensen (1998) or Masters (1999) also stress on the fact that, in the case of mobile labour force and information costs, the firm has to choose a wage level which is consistent with a given number of workers to be hired and which is such that it minimises total costs, including adjustment costs. On the other hand, Rebitzer and Taylor (1995) have proposed variants of monopsonistic behaviour, assuming efficiency wages to be paid when higher wages in turn provoke higher productivity.

Coming back to our positive relationship between wages and labour to be employed in our monopsonistic model, and considering the fact that the firm equilibrium is also the branch equilibrium in this case, monopsonistic competition leads to lower wages ($w^*_{cp} - w_{m1}$) and employment ($L^*_{cp} - L_m$) than in the perfect competition case. From this schedule, we can also understand why imposing a minimum wage at the perfect competition level leads the monopsonistic firm to hire more workers. Facing a minimum wage, which then also represents its marginal cost, the firm will then precisely employ the perfect competition level of employment at the equal marginal cost–marginal productivity optimising condition.

The basic model. Testing for productivity–wage gap, a first test for monopsonistic behaviour

Following Boal and Ranson (1997), we can model the decision process of the monopsonistic firm we just described before. To determine the profit maximising process, we first consider that firms revenues (R) depend on the number of workers to be employed (L) and that their production costs are only labour costs. Workers (L) can be hired at a wage (w) that corresponds to the inverse of the labour supply function.

The maximising process can therefore be modelled as

$$\underset{L}{\mathrm{Max}} R(L) - w(L) \cdot L \tag{1}$$

First order condition implies that monopsonistic labour demand (L_m) is such that:

$$\frac{\mathrm{d}R}{\mathrm{d}L_m} = w_m(L_m) + \frac{\mathrm{d}w_m}{\mathrm{d}L_m} \cdot L_m \tag{2}$$

The first term refers to marginal productivity and the second to marginal cost, composed by the new wage to be paid to the additional worker and the wage premium ($\mathrm{d}w_m/\mathrm{d}L_m$) to be paid to the L_m others. Note that monopsonistic outcome is the same as the perfect competition one if the wage premium is zero, that is also to say if the labour supply is perfectly elastic.

Developing equation (2), we obtain

$$\frac{\mathrm{d}R}{\mathrm{d}L_m} \cdot \frac{1}{w_m(L_m)} - \left(\frac{w_m(L_m)}{w_m(L_m)} + \frac{\mathrm{d}w_m(L_m)}{\mathrm{d}L_m} \cdot \frac{L_m}{w_m(L_m)} \right) = 0 \Rightarrow$$

$$\frac{\mathrm{d}R}{\mathrm{d}L_m} \cdot \frac{1}{w_m(L_m)} - 1 = \frac{\mathrm{d}w_m(L_m)}{\mathrm{d}L_m} \cdot \frac{L_m}{w_m(L_m)} = \eta_{(w/L^s)} \Rightarrow$$

$$\frac{\mathrm{dR/dL}_m - w_m(L_m)}{w_m(L_m)} = \eta_{(w/L^s)} \Rightarrow$$

$$E(L_m) = \frac{\mathrm{MPV}(L_m) - w_m(L_m)}{w_m(L_m)} = \eta_{(w/L^s)}, \tag{3}$$

where $\eta_{(w/L^s)}$ is the elasticity of the inverse of the labour supply function, or the wage function.

Relation (3) shows that, in the case of monopsonistic equilibrium, a positive mark-up (E) exists between marginal productivity and wage, given by the wage elasticity at the maximising profit level of labour demand (L_m). This mark-up is also referred as the exploitation rate. If it is zero, perfect competition applies.

Boal and Ransom (1997) therefore suggest to estimate this mark-up in order to test for monopsonistic behaviour: if the mark-up is positive, there could be monopsonistic behaviour.

Controlling for other reasons of positive mark-ups

A positive mark-up is not a sufficient condition to conclude for monopsonistic behaviour, for at least three reasons. First, union power in the bargain determines union capabilities to achieve some goals, like higher wages. It is therefore also likely to observe different mark-ups between different (groups of) firms, when union power is relatively different among these (groups of) firms. Second, if we assume that gross wages are not flexible and that the marginal tax is different among firms because of heterogeneity in the structure of the labour force, we could then also observe differences between marginal productivity and cost of labour that do not necessarily relate to monopsonistic behaviour (Cahuc and Zylberberg, 2001). Finally, the firm that works under unperfect competition on the product market can fix a higher price than the one that would have prevailed in a perfect competition context. She thereby creates a wage–productivity gap which cannot be explained by labour market monopsony but rather by product market power.

We would like to control for these three other explanations to positive exploitation rates, in order to better identify the true existence of monopsony. For empirical reasons related to data availability, we can finally control for product market power.

A second test for monopsonistic behaviour

Given that positive exploitation rates are a necessary but non-sufficient condition for monopsonistic behaviour, we propose to apply another test, also non-decisive. If firms have a monopsonistic behaviour, this should also be the case that when these firms occupy more people, then they have to pay higher wages than other firms. This other test of monopsony has been proposed by Dolado *et al.* (1996). They suggest to estimate the following relation:

$$w_{it} = \alpha + \beta_0 w_t + \beta_1 n_{it} + \nu_{it}, \tag{4}$$

where
w_{it} is the logarithm of the average wage in firm i at time t;
w_t is the logarithm of the average wage in the branch of firm i at time t;
n_{it} is the logarithm of the level of employment in firm i at time t.

The basic test is therefore that, other things equal, additional employment to be hired should not influence the wage paid by firm $i(\beta_1 = 0)$ if the firm is in a competitive labour market. While additional hires should increase the wage to be paid by the firm if the firm has monopsonistic power, given that it then faces a wage which is positively related to labour supply ($\beta_1 > 0$).

We can therefore suggest monopsonistic behaviour if β_1 is significantly positive. Though we can control for unobserved heterogeneity characteristics of firms, it is worth to mention that other elements can still explain this positive relationship between wages and employment (Allaart, 2002). That could, for example, be the case if higher efficiency wages have to be paid in bigger firms, when shirking is harder to control in these firms.

Summarising previous arguments, we therefore want to observe whether (1) positive exploitation rates and (2) positive wage–employment relationship exist for some firms, in order to approach monopsonistic power. And we want to control for potential positive product market power in the first case, which can also lead to positive exploitation rates, with or without monopsony on the labour market.

3 Estimating monopsonistic behaviour among Belgian firms

Building a dataset and estimating the exploitation rates

Estimating exploitation rates

Different approaches have been considered to estimate exploitation rates. They were often conducted on the labour supply side. For example, Scully (1974) or Zimbalist (1992) compare wages and marginal productivities among baseball players. Marginal productivity is proxied by different performance indicators. Brown (1993) estimates monopsonistic power of the National Collegiate Athletic Association, which establishes the rules to be followed by American football players in colleges. One of them is that wages cannot exceed a certain amount. He proxies players productivity by team revenues and players performance indicators.

To test for monopsonistic power in schools, Luizer and Thornton (1986) regress teacher wages on control variables (number of students, students average incomes,...) and on the Herfindhal index, which represents the ratio of teachers in a district occupied by the four biggest employers that could form an oligopsony. Exploitation is therefore indirectly estimated.

Boal (1995) tests for monopsony in the coal mining industry from Virginia, during the end of the nineteenth and the beginning of the twentieth century. In this isolated region, monopsonistic power is reinforced by the fact that workers have to change from home when they want to change from jobs. Boal estimates potential, non actual productivity–wage gap by the elasticity of the expected inverse labour supply function of workers in the firm. This source of non-mobility of workers as a cause for monopsonistic behaviour is also stressed by Ransom (1993). In the case of American universities, older teachers that dislike to move from jobs are estimated to receive lower wages often controlling for characteristics like gender, research field or experience. Exploitation is therefore also indirectly estimated.

Our approach analyses monopsony from a labour demand point of view. To estimate exploitation rates, we consider firms annual accounts for the period 1995–99. To be included in the dataset, firms have to publish complete accounts on the overall period, which is a necessary condition to obtain their value added in order to estimate this productivity. They have to be constituted under a so-called 'anonymous society' status, to be sure that they function under a profit-maximising goal. For estimation reasons, they have to present positive value added on the overall period.

Under this set of assumptions, we consider a balanced sample of 6585 firms, classified in 53 activity sectors. Due to our assumptions, very small firms are relatively less represented in our sample.

To calculate exploitation rates for each firm during the period 1995–99, we first estimate marginal productivities assuming a Cobb–Douglass technology:

$$\mathrm{MPV}_{i(95\text{–}99)} = \left(\frac{\mathrm{VA}_{i(95\text{–}99)}}{L_{i(95\text{–}99)}}\right) \times \beta_1, \tag{5}$$

where VA_i is the value added during the period 1995–99, L_i is the labour force in firm i and β_1 is labour productivity, estimated at a two-digit sector level.

Exploitation rates, $E_{i(95\text{–}99)}$, are then estimated as the mark-ups between estimated marginal productivities and the mean wages paid by different firms (w_i):

$$E_{i(95\text{–}99)} = \frac{\text{MPV}_{i(95\text{–}99)} - w_{i(95\text{–}99)}}{w_{i(95\text{–}99)}} = \eta_{(w/L_s)i(95\text{–}99)} \tag{6}$$

Considering average wages: monopsonistic behaviour by skills

Besides testing for monopsonistic power, we also want to qualify monopsonistic behaviour by distinguishing firms paying lower or higher than mean wages of the sector, in order to apprehend whether monopsonistic behaviour merely appears among skilled or unskilled (lower paid) workers.

Low-skilled workers could be more hired by monopsonistic firms, as they are probably less mobile than the others or because the relative demand for unskilled workers has gradually declined during the last decades. But on the other hand, if higher skilled workers have more specific skills that cannot easily be valued in other firms, then (some) firms with higher skilled workers (and higher relative wages) could then also act as monopsonists. So a lower level of skills has not necessarily to be associated as such with higher monopsonistic power of firms.

Estimating product market power

To control for the fact that positive exploitation rates are not necessarily related to monopsonistic behaviour, we estimate product market power indicators by firm at each year. For each firm, we then compare the mean of these indicators during the period and relate it to the product power of the median firm.

We use the price–marginal cost ratio proposed by Siotis (2000) to estimate the market power:

$$\left(\frac{P}{c}\right)_i = \frac{1}{\left(1 - ((P-c)/P)_i\right)}, \tag{7}$$

where $((P-c)/P)_i$ is the ratio of the difference between the value added and the wage bill on the one hand, and the value added augmented by the costs of firms intermediate consumption on the other hand.

Grouping the firms in eight categories

For each two-digit sector, we classify each firm on the basis of these three previous criteria, that is, the exploitation rate (potential monopsonistic behaviour), the relative firm-sector wage (monopsonistic behaviour by skills) and the relative price–marginal cost ratio (product market power).

For each sector, we therefore classify our firms in eight groups. We then face estimation problems due to missing data in some groups of some two-digit sectors. To tackle this problem and improve the level of significance in our results, we aggregate our first 53 sectors in 24 activity branches, following the classification proposed by the Belgian National Bank. We therefore finally consider eight groups of firms in 24 activity branches. Note that data are still missing for three branches: no firm in the sample belonged to branch 22, while the number of firms belonging to branches 15 and 23 is too small to make possible the classification in eight groups.

Estimating wage–employment relations

To estimate the wage equation in order to test for a positive relationship between wages and employment and a possible monopsonistic behaviour in our panel of firms, we apply the Generalised Least Squares estimation technique with a correction for random individual fixed effects. We introduce a random effect to control for firms unobserved characteristics (union rate, productivity, ...) that may also influence wages. Given that the observation period is quite short, we assume that this random effect only influences the constant of the regression and not the regressors associated to explaining variables. We therefore estimate the following relation:

$$w_{it} = a + b_0 w_t + b_1 n_{it} + (u_{it} + \varepsilon_i), \qquad (8)$$

where ε_i are the individual fixed random effects and u_{it} the error terms.

We want to estimate this wage equation for each of the eight groups of firms from each of the 24 branches. Because of a lack of firms data, we finally estimate these relations for 119 out of the 192 potential groups.

4 Results

Exploitation rates

The results related to the decomposition of firms in the eight different groups and the 24 activity branches are presented in Table 7.1. If we consider the number of firms which present positive exploitation rates (groups 1 to 4), we observe that they concern 60.6 per cent of the

Table 7.1 Number of firms by activity branch and by group

Activity branch	Positive exploitation rates				Negative exploitation rates			
	Lower (than branch average) wage		Higher (than branch average) wage		Lower (than branch average) wage		Higher (than branch average) wage	
	Lower market power	Higher market power	Lower market power	Higher market power	Lower market power	Higher market power	Lower market power	Higher market power
	G1	G2	G3	G4	G5	G6	G7	G8
1	6	10	0	4	1	5	2	1
2	0	16	0	8	2	2	1	1
3	70	151	25	40	41	22	16	3
4	18	64	14	68	31	10	7	0
5	10	18	4	17	9	0	6	1
6	4	107	2	45	27	23	18	9
7	1	7	1	1	2	0	1	0
8	21	114	6	37	13	2	4	1
9	2	47	3	24	10	24	9	8
10	10	112	9	26	25	6	5	3
11	14	104	15	35	54	39	32	10
12	43	116	19	60	43	3	22	1
13	16	29	4	7	18	6	1	1
14	14	29	9	39	23	14	10	8
15								
16	0	1	18	98	84	19	201	104
17	644	392	235	268	500	41	340	68
18	0	23	0	4	15	24	2	0
19	8	86	23	102	48	29	44	37
20	5	16	2	19	3	1	6	2
21	6	66	36	165	66	35	117	104
22								
23								
24	1	42	1	22	6	20	7	11
All	893	1550	426	1089	1021	325	851	373

overall number. And 61.7 per cent of these firms pay lower than average wages in the branch. This empirical fact suggests that lower skilled workers could be more concerned by monopsonistic behaviour.

Moreover positive exploitation rates, they are often associated with firms that possess higher than product market-power, roughly in two out of three firms (66.2 per cent). That is to say that this high product market could actually also explain these positive rates, rather than monopsony on the labour market. This assertion is strengthened when we look at groups 5 to 8, where negative exploitation rates appear in roughly three cases out of four (72.8 per cent) among lower than average product market firms.

Finally, this first test leaves roughly one firm out of five (20.2 per cent) in groups 1 or 3, where monopsonistic behaviour alone explains positive exploitation rates.

Wage–employment relations

Estimations

Estimating our wage equations to test whether wages are positively related to the level of employment in the firms ($\beta_1 > 0$), we can expect monopsony among ten groups, belonging to eight different branches. We do not reproduce all the (available on request) 119 estimations of the wage equations but focus on those suggesting monopsony. They concern the following branches:

- Branch 3, group 4: Food, Beverage and Tobacco;
- Branch 5, group 1: Wood Products and Furnitures;
- Branch 7, group 2: Coal, Refineries and Nuclear Industry;
- Branch 8, group 2: Chemical Products;
- Branch 13, groups 2 and 5: Transport Equipment;
- Branch 14, groups 1 and 6: Salvage and Other Manufacturing Industries;
- Branch 16, group 6: Building Industry;
- Branch 18, group 5: Restaurants and Hotels.

A first remark relates to the relatively small number of groups of firms that are estimated to potentially adopt monopsonistic behaviour. They represent a total of 280 firms, occupying 8.32 per cent of the labour force (see Table 7.2). This result is not that surprising if we remember Belgian institutional facts. They made us think that monopsony should not be a general practice among Belgian firms. But this proportion could be underestimated. In fact, monopsonistic behaviour could have been estimated to be higher among individual firms or smaller groups of firms than the ones we had to consider to make our estimations. Remember that these estimations are based on groups of firms that are defined by branch and following three criteria. And these criteria are not necessarily sufficient to distinguish for sure between monopsonistic and non-monopsonistic firms. So the groups supposed to include only monopsonistic firms can in fact also contain other firms. That situation could lead to an aggregation bias and to a reduction of the actual number of firms for which a positive wage–employment relation should be estimated.

A second remark is that some groups of firms are now estimated to present monopsonistic behaviour, while these firms have negative